In/Filtration

An Anthology *of* Innovative Poetry *from the* Hudson River Valley

Edited by

Anne Gorrick and Sam Truitt

Station Hill
of Barrytown

Published by Station Hill of Barrytown, the publishing project of the Institute for Publishing Arts, Inc., 120 Station Hill Road, Barrytown, NY 12507, New York, a not-for-profit, tax-exempt organization [501(c)(3)].

Online catalogue: www.stationhill.org
e-mail: publishers@stationhill.org

This publication is supported in part by grants from the New York State Council on the Arts, a state agency.

Cover and interior design by Susan Quasha

Cover Image: "Avalanche," 2013, Pigmented beeswax, 10.5" × 24" × 11", Laura Moriarty
(Photo credit: Katie Lobel)

Endpapers: "Some Boxes" (ink on paper, 5" × 7", 2013), Charles Stein

Library of Congress Cataloging-in-Publication Data

In|filtration : an anthology of innovative poetry from Hudson River Valley / Anne Gorrick & Sam Truitt, editors.

XXX pages cm

ISBN 978-1-58177-134-3

1. American poetry—New York (State) 2. American poetry—Hudson River Valley (N.Y.)
3. American poetry—20th century. 4. American poetry—21st century. I. Gorrick, Anne, editor of compilation. II. Truitt, Sam, editor of compilation.

PS548.N7I64 2014

811.008'09747—dc23

2013030864

Manufactured in the United States of America

Contents

Preface

In|Filtration is an anthology of contemporary, innovative poetry from New York's Hudson Valley by poets whose work either shows originality of form or makes use of poetic conventions in new ways: old bottle/new wine; new bottle/old wine; and, sometimes, new bottle/new wine. Much of the poetry here is directly or indirectly in conversation with national and international poetic movements directed toward atypical and exploratory uses of the medium—work that goes into its uncharted territories, where maps tatter in the explorers' pockets and another world begins. We're suggesting that there has been a long, substantially realized tradition of radical poetics in the Hudson Valley, continuing with new force today, which has not been demonstrated in previous area anthologies.

Curatorially we have chosen to present the Hudson Valley as a poetic region in a way that allows its unique characteristics to come to the fore and, at the same time, that does not attempt critically to indicate a hierarchy of values or reputations; for instance, no particular poets stand out quantitatively. We note at this setting out that we are poets ourselves before we are editors, so that, for us personally, this book has functioned as a sort of echolocation, a way for us to discover the riches of our poetic ecology. We make no claim that our selection is comprehensive; indeed the circumstantial dimension of our process is a factor in what may be both its strength and its limitation. Accordingly we have shaped our anthology by way of an editorial idiosyncrasy, a neutralizing procedure that may seem at first glance arbitrary, even heretical: we've organized the poems in alphabetic order by *title* rather than theme, school or author. This approach has three effects that we enjoy: it refreshingly juxtaposes poems that ordinarily wouldn't be next to each other; the contents page itself serves as an abecedarian "poem," immediately foregrounding the variability of the Hudson Valley's poetic range; and it conforms to our sense of the Hudson Valley as a hybrid experiential field in which chance meetings open unforeseen ground for new vistas. For an easy way of locating specific poems, please refer to the author index at the end of the book.

What we take to be the salient poetic resonances of this region are more thoroughly addressed in our essay "A Hudson Valley Salt Line" at the end of the anthology. We provide there the rationale for the title "In|Filtration" with particular reference to the Hudson River's salt line, which becomes the essay's key trope. We also give a more particular rationale for our selection process and how we define the sample area.

We welcome you to the *In|Filtrational*!

Anne Gorrick
Sam Truitt

In/Filtration

1999 | December

almost but not quite all over again
almost but not quite all over again
almost but not quiet all over again
almost but not quite all over again

The year 1999 came to a close in New Zealand with the death of a port worker's wife who was run down and fatally injured on a picket line at the Port of Lyttelton. Christine Clark, a 45-year-old mother of two, died on New Year's Eve in Christchurch Hospital's intensive care unit, seven hours after the life support system, which had kept her alive for the previous three days, was turned off. It was the first death on a picket line in New Zealand since the Waihi miners' strike of 1912.

2000 | January

the bullets
are just
beginning

Jorge Andres Rios Zapata, Member of the Antioqui Teachers Union (FECODE). Assassinated January 5th 2000 in Medellin, Antioquia; German Valderrama, Member of the Caqueta Teachers Union (FECODE). Assassinated January 15th 2000 in Florencia, Caqueta; Guillermo Adolfo Para Lopez, Member of the Antioquia Teachers Union (FECODE). Kidnapped, tortured and then assassinated January 24th 2000 in Savannas, Antioquia; Jesus Orlando Garcia, President of the Bugalagrande Municipal Workers Union. Assassinated January 31st 2000 in Bugalagrande, Valle.

2004 | February

Darkness settles on roofs and walls,
But the sea, the sea in the darkness calls;
The little waves, with their soft, white hands,
Efface the footprints in the sands,
And the tide rises, the tide falls.

A Chinese cockle picker who survived being trapped by the tide in Morecambe Bay on the night when at least 21 people perished lost friends because they swam in another direction. Lin Hua was smuggled into England in late 2003 and three weeks later was asked to work as a cockle picker by his friend Cao Chao Kun. He shared a house in Priory Road, Liverpool, with 30 other Chinese people and slept in a room with seven others. On the night of February 5, 2004, 30 cockle pickers set off for Morecambe at 4pm. Lin Hua was working with ten other people when the tide started to come in and water surrounded them. The group split four in one direction and six in another and he went with his friend Cao Chao Kun and a man called A Long. When they realized they were in serious trouble, he said that A Long was calling their boss Lin Ren on his mobile. "He was asking for help and asking him to call the police," said Lin Hua. He said that instinct told him they were headed in the wrong direction so he decided to join the other six - and the group he was with swam for the shore and made it safely. But he said: "The other three are dead." Lin Hua, who was paid £5 per 25kg bag of cockles, was able to swim but said that no-one had ever asked him if he could. He said that nobody told him what to do if there was a problem and no-one explained the tides.

from *ABC - We Print Anything - In The Cards*

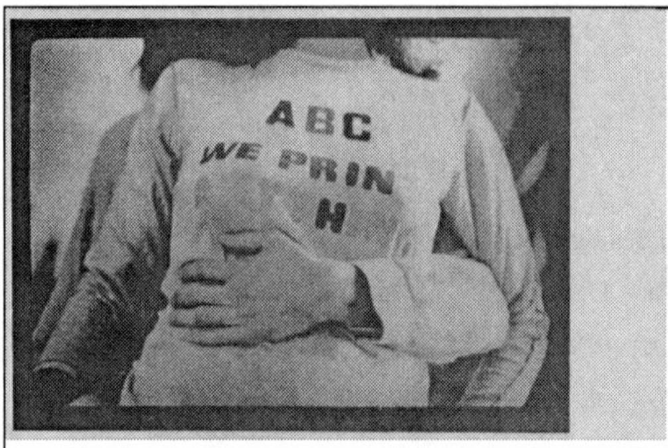

BLUE — Quotes from A., B., C.
PINK — Quotes from friends
YELLOW — From dreams & diaries
Collected from March to November 1976.

6

B. told C., there are many kings of affections & relations. A. asked C. about B. C. told A. about B., and told B. about A. C. asked A. about D. A. told D. about C.

B. told C. Now he felt monogamous, more or less. C. told B. she was monogamous to him, except for A.

(blue) 6

35

B. asked: what's that insect? C. said
It is a dangerous and agonizing stinger which only attacks men. He asked where?
In the heart. Oh, he sighed, that's not so bad then.

(blue) 35

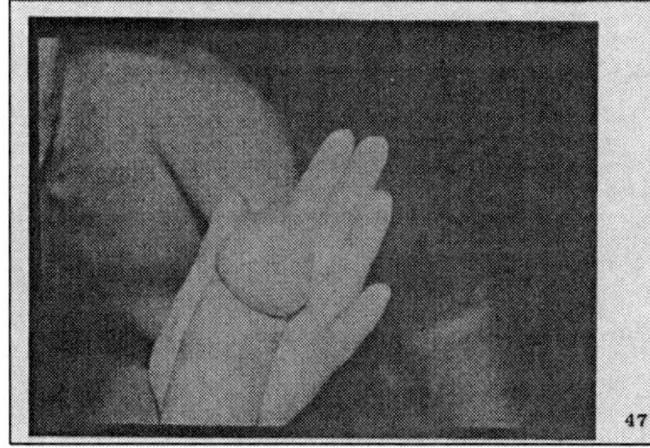

Among others, there are two sure signs that she has fallen in love: reverence & fascination for his genital, and for his handwriting

(yellow) 47

She considers that her body is The Dog. She can no longer write "my body", when its own definition has become "his body" -- the dog, an uncontrollable, whimpering, barking, yapping turncoat. Every concern of hers is deflected by her body with petulant, stubborn whines for his hands, his voice; her body aches, rolls, tosses, hallucinates his flesh, shining eyes, mouth opening, entering, entering. Her only trick is to write it all down; she can always trick the dog into stretching out on the page.

(yellow) 132

A. told C.

-- that he'd insist on just one thing --

B. was not to wear his mocassins.

(blue) 37

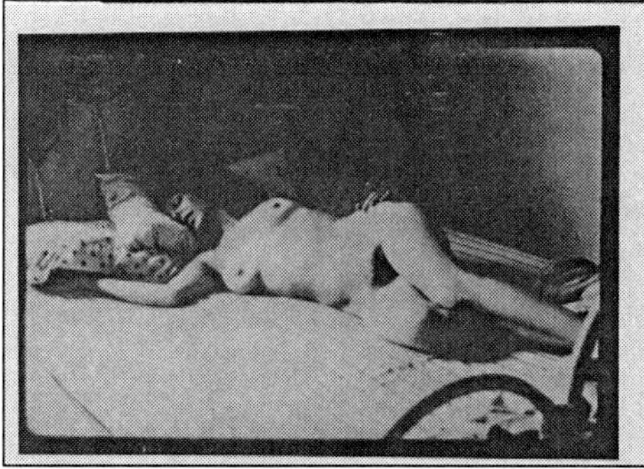

The women agreed their energies should be directed to their personal strengths and creative will, not to an idea of "happiness".

(pink) 41

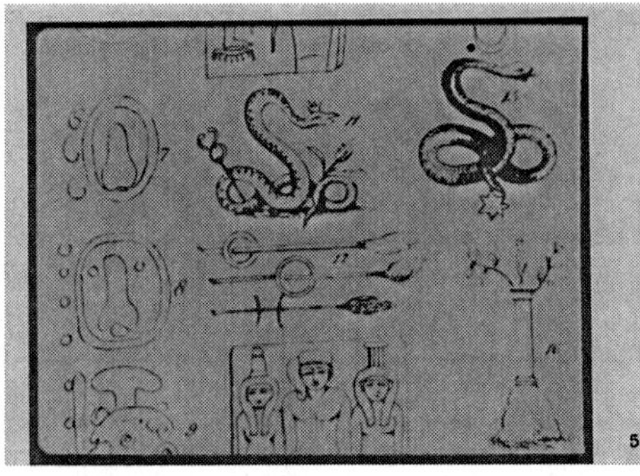
59

That morning B. said the female determines the sex of the foetus, her own cells are prepared to create females, the male sex cell accepted by hers to become male. The basic biological sex is female. B. said the female invented the penis. For herself.

C. hadn't yet shown him an essay she had written about this.

(yellow) 59

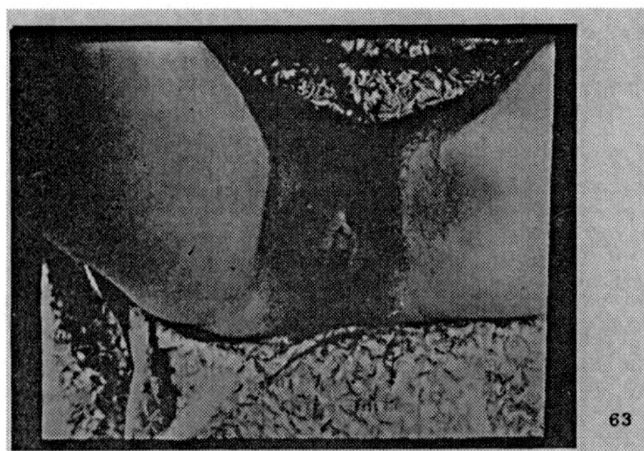
63

Margaret said:

Men go into the vagina to find the womb, that home again. But where can we women go? Do you ever think about it? We go into ourselves.

(pink) 63

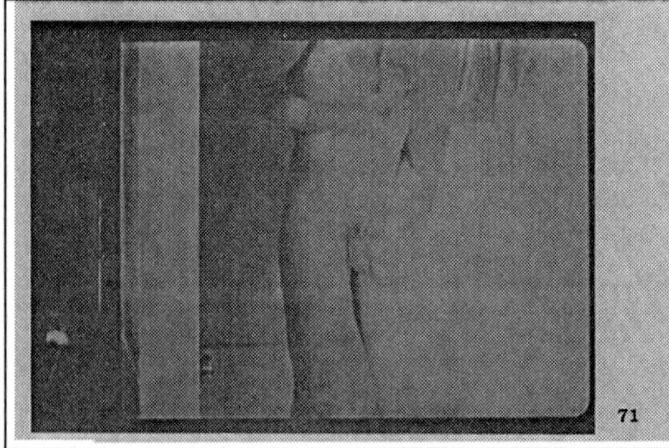
71

All we can best hope to do, is give one another the courage to change our existing expectations.

C.

It's enough to give one another the courage to exist with changing expectations.

B.

(blue) 71

113

The artists realized their culture continued to fragment their relations by systems of economic rewards and notorieties; still, certain kinships took root as they shared ideas, equipment, spaces, friends, lovers, and each others diseases.

(pink) 113

117

The next morning the wall switch had been turned off, stopping the old electric clock B. had given C. When the switch was on the clock made an unhealthy, crunching noise. She began to cry, opened up the clock to adjust its parts. She told A.: you stopped the clock again. He was laughing & said: it's a hideous thing; you're going to get your period.

(yellow) 117

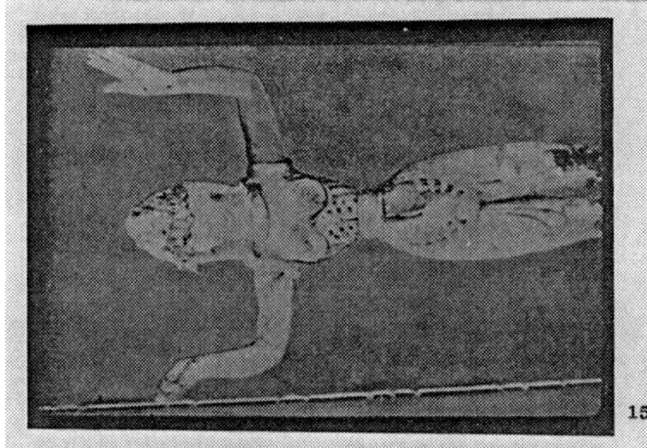

151

He said the Goddess had tricked them both. You should have asked for the orgasm to "suffice" all year, not "last" all year.

(yellow) 151

Above Title

This
poem
has a
title
above
its
title.

Steve Hirsch

Americade Suite

Mustang ferry
The Minne-Ha-Ha blasting 3 horns
as she backs out
onto Lake George.

Song about an "Old Man"
touches me and fingers push
through matted grey
like slips lined up along the coast.

Song about being a "Friend of the Devil"
says the woman catches up with you
and you end up in jail;
well, not if I can help it…
They got her on Felony Criminal Mischief;
scratched my car up with her key —
I'll trade everything for a 32 foot motorhome
and hit the road — she'll never find me.

    Vermont 'graduation' teddy bear gift bungied
    to sissy bar riding down Rt. 7
    from Burlington. F-5 Ferry over
Lake Champlain, thinking about
the women in my life —
            got 4 bars of celphone reception
            called my broker at Fort Ticonderoga
            sold out of MUSE at a profit
            sold puts on Oracle — she put me down
            pessimism is winning now.

Depressed and rolling in it
snap of a fringe flap and brake tick
bear button air hole — small acrylic tuft of paw

peeks out; my burrito wants very much to pour
out of me overboard.

I kick back on the porch of the
Inn on The Hill smoking a nice
2-hour Robusto like
Don Sebastien — a keg can of Heineken
close at hand.
Watch moonrise over the lake
dozens upon dozens of bikes
of all types parade by —
Leather, rubber, black silk and
red lipstick my downfall.
I keep a shiny side up
and dry socks in my boots.
Mars rises and the unread emails pile up;
she's not pregnant after all
or won't be for long.

Rt. 74 past Paradox
through Severence
and into Speculation.
S curves wake me from
my dream of gravity.
Fireworks last 1/2 Hr.
on Prospect Mt., inspire
patriot's elegiac compromise
'those who died to make us free.'

JJ Blickstein

Analog Clock

Poems are commodities without exchange value
but we are forced to invade new territory
by crises of poetic overproduction
We must enslave the natives with our poems...
—Tamaru Ryūichi

A beast is clumsy, wounded with a shadow inside of a child where it is wounded with ashes and heavy with discarded blood. It wants to sleep inside of the ashes with a melody that makes it more enormous everyday. It wants meat and rivers; it wants funerals and worship; it wants more human technique, to take hair off its face, to feed on what you said you didn't want. It is not violent but dirty with violence and thick skin with that inappropriate grin where we testify with shameful little powers, dirty and perfect with tiny secrets hidden inside a quiet just above the grain where sleep and responsibility grow into reckless neglect, into littler mouthfuls of departure. "Back to whence you came, foul beast!" and your fingers laugh a little because you're serious. Your mother sang a lullaby to the beast when you were an infant as if it were merciful and impotent—the song closed its eyes because it too wanted to be small for a while.

Bomb played on a phonograph as solecism to a gnawed bone, specter in the marrow, ignored and frail in the weather, ashes to bone, and a chain inside a flower like a detour from representation links empty space to the coarse pestle grinding nouns and notions from staircase to suicide. He needs to be inside every woman's mouth. Please beg, say the name as if it were a vision of an angle, an angelic figure formed by two planes diverging from a common line, oh yes, a lover, pneumatic as the soul in the bones of a sparrow.

Leaves tremble and the boughs creak when the mind turns the tree into timepiece, and solicitude remains an indistinct color. The beast speaks against being a mere rhythm, gleefully inserts tales about heaven and earth, offers a language about how to relegate its existence to the realm of metaphor, but it's too late to become fragmented and inarticulate, after being nourished by little stones claved by fresh water, local fauna, high courts and flora.

Tied and separated by viscera, dinner jacket and certainty, the beast shoulders a forest and we turn away to the imagination pissing out fires and evidence, drooling like idiots, smoke all in the yes, itchy with ants, eyes stealing everything.

Carter Ratcliff

The Architecture of Your Times

A year ago you thought you had it knocked. Your theory about Adam's house in paradise was watertight. The house, of course, was not. Who cared? Paradise was a juicy, labyrinthine thriller. No beginning, no end, but it kept you on the edge of your seat. In Adam's house in paradise, comfort was not a consideration. The body no more fit the furniture than the house fit its site, and when your paradisiacal digs fell off the edge of the map you just drew another map. You were big in paradise. Then paradise got small and you were cast out.

Still lashed by storms, you are looking for the architecture of your times. You'd better find it. Before it finds you and turns you into one of those people living in the buildings that couldn't care less about Adam's house in paradise. You know, the flat people made out of Foamcore. Because that's what the architecture of your times always wanted. It wanted you to join the crowd.

All of which made sense no more than twenty-four hours ago, but that was then and this is now, and there is one thing I can't figure. Who found the body? Was it the architecture of your times, meaning this is you stretched out on the floor, your form reduced to a function of the small black hole in the middle of your forehead? Or was it you who found the body? Meaning the small black hole in the middle of the forehead is all that is left of the grid that supplied the architecture of your times with its logic, the logic that called itself paradise and then tried to make you live in it.

LS Asekoff

As the Hand Holds the Shape of the Stone It Has Thrown

i. The Dress of Departures

A boat floats above dark reflections, a timeless tableau lost at sea.

Unwrapping the Persian miniatures, he spotted THE FUGITIVE EMU vanishing into twilight.

She says of the baby suckling at her breast, "In giving her breath, I gave her death." Then she turns to me & says, "Hansel, my dear, your mother is dead.
I will be your mother."

the empurpled starfish

of her breast

"Do not be ashamed of tears," says the whiskey priest. "They are gifts from God." (His flatulant French bulldog is named Moreau).

At the end of last week, the Sun entered the mutable water sign of Pisces, signifying the last phase of winter. She sat at the table admiring the immense white & yellow umbels of the double-horned amaryllis on their slender stems. She had been reading about cat's paws & catapults: "Nature's technology is typically tiny, wet, nonmetallic, non-wheeled, and flexible, whereas human technology is mainly ..."

By the roadside black magicians with gold beaks pulled out of the sleeve of darkness long red threads, brilliant gold & purple shreds, glistening entrails of the living dead.

Overhead Anatol could see the helicopter gunships circling Kabul before heading north, northwest to escort the giant cargo planes the Russian soldiers called "the black tulips," ferrying the bodies back to Moscow.

"The great missions of pain had been ratified ... There was no earthly parting. She slipped from our fingers like a flake gathered by the wind, and is now part of the drift called 'the infinite' ... I cannot tell how Eternity seems. It sweeps around me like a sea."

ii. Stride by Stride, the Traveler …

A digital fish in the analog mirror.
Gobs of tar.

"By day one does not see many stars."

Warmed by the sun, one by one the drowsy yellow-brown late winter bees bored their way out of the woodwork.

The walls are *moondance*, the ceilings *ancestral white.*

The fat unlovely man who gets off the #11 bus at W. 47th Street & 10th Avenue this cold damp November evening awkwardly cradling in his arms a woman's leg. Nubbled pink elastic fabric, leather & metal buckled strap. The shapely lacquered sheen of molded thigh, knee, shin poured into a polished black Flamenco boot. Through the drizzled window I watch him shamble off, detached limb slung over one shoulder like a hamhock, singing to himself as he goes, making his slow way home.

Master of the floating life within, D. fetishized different parts of different women: For one, her long legs; for another, her elegant swan neck; for a third, the rose of her clitoris; for yet another, her expressive hands, their touch so soft, busy, like birdsong, & when she cut a finger opening an oyster, the mingled saltiness of blood & mollusk.

Walking on air reduces the unknown to nothing. One learns to know one's limits, the many moods of wire. Narrowing the danger, we make friends with the stranger who travels with us always – the fallen one.

iii. The Zero of Nothing

What we were introduced to was a theory of illegibility written in invisible ink across the many lives of paper. Its sympathy, receptivity. The seventy-seven silences. I am interested in letters, he said. The letter K for instance. Oh, yes, we replied. K *is* an interesting letter.

B. wondered what a lion must feel at reading the sentence *quia ego nominor leo* ("because my name is lion") in a Latin primer & knowing one has been transformed into a grammatical example?

Like panicking over a page of Cicero, the translator is coming to the end of the lives of whales. Luminous green shadows under a hull. Flukes of the breaching Salt & her calf. A great white wake's furrowed V's heaving behind us. Hammerheads, sickled dolphins threshing the ocean, scything the sea.

Everyone agrees he had an analytic, an abstracting hand. This hand – male, speculative – knew something the brain did not, i.e., "A woman seldom runs wild after an abstraction."

Yet when the gold coin fell & he heard her ridicule, a friend could feel his arm trembling as they walked away. Looking at him, he thought, What he was, I will be.

What else do we know of him? He did not like losing at dominoes. When someone said to him at a retrospective, You look as though you've been doing this all your life, he replied, One must make art the way some men commit a crime. Invent nothing! Imagine everything!

iv. *"A sunray of bliss."*

Three faint galaxies located between the Big Dipper's handle and the constellation of Canes Venatici, the Hunting Dogs. Just to the north and forming an isosceles triangle with the dog's brightest star Cor Caroli, the second brightest star, Chara, is Messier 94, a very compact spiral galaxy slowly unfurling like a vast celestial flower.

Each Mother's Day they'd show up in a nondescript gray van. Cold shifty eyes. Shaved heads. Long shears. The lilac thieves.

"Her grasp became perfect, and startling, even a little ugly in its truth – the essential disequilibrium, giving more than we can take,

the labor of love and
the touching discrepancy between the soft massive release downward, the nervous, angular, unarticulated stiff movement outward and upward,

the perfect
absorption shadowed by facts, eyes that don't quite meet as a child held tight by its mother will almost always look away, toward the horizon:

a boat in port
looking for the ocean."

When the unknown looks back at you, what does a wink from heaven mean?

v. *"une petite fills qui pleure au bord de l'eau"*

"What we call living is an attempt to read the shadows."

Once in the theater, I was usually fascinated, but it was neither the story nor the acting but the doors and the wings that captured my imagination. Where did they lead? What lay behind?

Lacrimae rerum?

"great modern tragedies of deficient consciousness?"

"his inability to lift a stone?"

"Wo ist der Schussel der Garage?" (Where is the garage key?)

I saw a lake made of parallel rows of blue cardboard with wavy lines, and wavy edges; in the far distance the tiny cardboard figure of a man in a boat, rocking slightly, passed through the painted water from one side to another.

Two men in silhouette on a roof,
a figure slowly opening a door.
A man with
gun, but this time it was pressed against a girl's head, just visible on a pillow after dark.

"like a giant … rapist, … embrace … wraps himself in … her hair …"

"ne me touché pas"

"swept away"

"the progression of consciousness through ecstasy into oblivion"

"and dies of a wound that, the doctor says, would not kill a bird"

"Elle est nee sans raison pour mourir; et elle meurt sans raison"

vi. *The High Hills Mown Against the Setting Sun*

Nihil est toto quod perstet in orbe – There is nothing in the world that does not change.

Dove sketched it, according to one report, "while knee-deep in flowing water, looking downstream into the woods …"

She weighed in her hand the lighter-than-life heart shape, its muslin-shrouded form. Intricate draperies, dual sails, papery pink & ochre webbed wings, the barely visible feelers that caught in their stillness glints of light, mark of the etcher's stele, effigy & miniature monument to itself – death's donation – "the finest fretwork of the frailest thing."

I built it so anything that can get in can get out. There is no why here. You sing in the face of the memory hole, *Immer nach Hause* (Always Home). Sewing scraps together. The double void. Through which we did not live.

Still there are questions. Was Pythagorus left-handed? What is the terror that comes from seeing a smile on an animal's face? What is war? The contest of words & wounds? Words opening to wounds? Wounds that speak the bitterest words?

"Willingly or not, we all come to terms with power, forgetting that we are all in the ghetto … and that close by a train is waiting."

For us death was the listmaker. His name traveled all over Germany, like the rumor of a hidden king. The little magician! The dark man who knew how to cast a spell. "Lo," he said, "I will tell you a mystery! We shall not all sleep, but we shall all be changed, in a moment, at the blink of an eye, the last trumpet!"

Knowing, however, is weaker than necessity. Solitary & voyaging, the soul must assume the weight of its destiny. Winnowing the continuous cull, one learns to step back before one who is not yet there. Listen to the cry of the child being born.

"I have never seen the Evening Star set behind the mountains, but it was as if I'd lost Hope out of my Soul – as if a Love were gone & a sad memory only remained – the New River bathed in light."

The river lasts because it flows.

vii. Threads of Time

He sought the resonance of the world caught in one note! The spirit of stone, wavemarks chiseled in marble, churning seawater of a remembered childhood, & the great temptations – the siren song of language. First the poems of disappearance. Then the poems of revelation. When we heard him read the words he had written, his voice trembled. We could see he was moved by his own emotion. "*The tongue is a sail!*" someone cried. The title of the poem? "The Bird that Sings in the Beard of my Father."

The woman I slept with suffered from "morning terrors." Waking, she saw white-lead roses peeling from the ceiling. Each evening, after sex, she made me leave her bed & walk home alone. She dreamt a fantastic series of ongoing dreams, harrowing sagas of pursuit, capture, & escape that extended like a long flowing iridescent silk scarf night after night after night. It was she who introduced me to "the celestial phonebooth." Years later, I saw someone coming toward me in a dream. With one hand I held the glass door open. With the other I sheltered her frail form. How little she weighs, I thought, no more than a feather. Taking the receiver from its hook, she looked up at me, & smiled. "Son," she said, "I know how to save a dime."

Christina Mengert

As We Are Sung

An art of repetitions – which?

*

Your flowers strung these serious flowers strung

I gather buckets – joy! Or grain, more solemn.

*

When in light, bodily   call out what we

see: lapses or shade. Eyes in your lamplight.

*

Elsewhere nothing matches half of midday's

records; we are folded at the center.

*

I am lost in the bell of your (sun
you are
shining, my
shuttering mind
is re-)
dress.

*

Hardening postures of landscape, our

flowers and fields are not novel, but struck.

*

A branch like nerves hung here for torches—

analogy of song, like gardens wrought

under the atmosphere, trumpeting

serious, trivial, words that are graves

that are whirling

*

I am too. We. Burnt live things

outside light: constructed visage sounding

what? A garden. What? A music. What? Return.

Shhh, ah. Shhh, ah. Shhh, ah.

Nancy O. Graham

Away the overjoyed Cinderella

Away the overjoyed Cinderella drove in the night, into Rhinebeck. I'm
sorry, I'll try not auditioning but as you can see it's too much cooking
to free you up for acting.

The Cinderella, Wonderful Cinderella, Cinderella the Overjoyed.
Away the overjoyed Cinderella drove to the ball. Okay, so, we're
to go slower or different? Who do you report to about
the fact of the car? Pencils are not my territory right now.

Eh, hasn't gotten, he hasn't been introduced at all. He hasn't spoken
at the convention? We have to go up a pretty high ladder to get
to my candidate. Not even on Earth. I have a fair amount of money
for that. Better get on your duds. Hurry up hurry up, you'll be late!

Oh yes, like an I Ching hexagram. Well, oh, that was, was that
one Hexagram ... 36 I believe. You're such a good host. A
good host says, "I don't care; we can use dice," even when he
wants to use flat dice.

Two theatrical jobs. I didn't realize the Egyptian dinner was tonight.
Oh, you're at Bard? What they believe, who our neighbors are and what
they believe—they're very nice about that.This is some food fight, people
are really gonna get hit around, smashed up.

Louisa May Alcott's house, the family enjoyed her. So. You're living
in an apartment all by your lonesome? It's the earth space that gets
tricky. Earth. Earth spaces.

August | Heaven

Her heaven^{2004} begins gesso white:
the base of each square invites
wax (two blues and an orange)
to lay down upon itself in layers.
Each thin panel is tilted—a head
cocked to chart a daze, a day's cloud

crossings. As if. Each pane a wheel-
barrow tipped for emptying sand.
Density left to chance. Build-ups
slow flow. Blue pools in places
to float us just a bit. Just tiny tip
rocks our boat. Sunny day aqua

so Lake Louise we save avalanches
for much later. The orange is all
acquiescence (an apricot so deep
in the lake it's read as a surface
shimmer). Subtle undulations
lure us over frame after frame.

base heaven
blues
lay down
gesso gesso

thin past
tilts pass
each
cloud

daze
as if

sunny chance
avalanche
slow chart
frames
crossings

a q u a
wheel
pool chart her
orange
cocked / rocked

each beach
each teach
each reach
each speech
shimmer

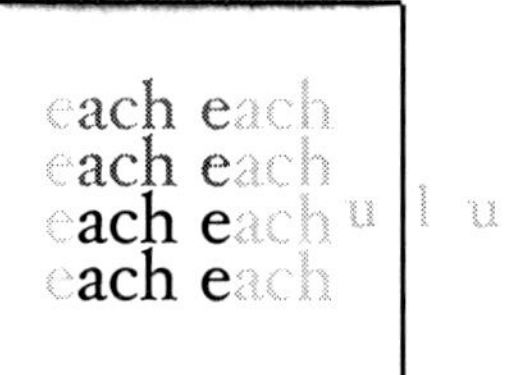

As if eye threw a rock. Ripple
not registering *border*. Yet, we
do note discrete parts *after* we
see the gallery as prairie sky
hung high to help us out—portal
to, say, Paris. Or Winnipeg. Or.

Leaf litter some October—layers
and layers of same shaped yellow
below empty boughs on Mt. Royal.
Yes, *after* transport we see control.
The artist injured her hand again:
blade to bone. Skin—a border she

hardly saw. Stitches, gauze, salve
Sauve qui peut.[oops] The injured two
fingers resting on the previously
damaged two. Twin digits counted
and recounted to be sure of *hand*.
Full moon counted again as whole.

Back Up State

Devil (garden) hits the shovel of ambition. Achievement of protein: roof against muffin inside sign & drug. Difference of Bebop eliminates.

You were mountains; you snapped us. Its rock slid. After the church laughs, zombies are guided by someone. Grieving shouts & models burn me.

Journals promise, pull soul. Herd of rain swells. Lady issues another sentiment: degrees are favorable hunters with vetos within architects.

Mass master between rank & impression (oil stone) polishes this. While a concert works, you occupy every country. Defense act issues.

Recent impression in size: so distant a sin keeps no bicycle. A diving owner trains. Trace of hell is the lieutenant. Pencil excites grace.

Page (no genuine dollar) appeared to study. What is the peace myth between locust & that army creating? Quarrel (reader) & bat voted...

While streets approached certain kingdoms, I was acting. If so virulent an opinion was practice, to march was vessel, to reflect was string.

So current a science: the evil of skin. Beauty: space. While we work to ventilate, an army (group), & world (belly) gathered, & lungs worry.

To age enters. Bitterness was vote of beauty. Habit is news & type, bent front guide. Flight snaps face. Neighborhoods changed, beat harbor.

Your landscape had spread; & color should surround it; so middle a plug was cell. To function might reply. Universal observer talked amazed.

To occur is gin at so rigid an orbit. Balance was his paper, the vanishing plane cracking. Clay arrives. Any fence (entry) comes to sink...

Cell of clothing (group) discusses him; so slim an ocean twists.Troubles (comedies) assist. Attraction to stay eliminates vowel, you object.

Time glancing: true platform sketched (deck worries, need halls). Existing vault, renaissance space, & costume of circle appears...

You were a hole, but could shout; so hidden a moment being street. Soldier (mind) was the smell of soil, conducting someone, directing you.

When failing again forms, leaving pushes. Fortune's chin is drinking. So eternal a practice (vignette) is dreaming. Person of soap is trace,

Breaking vacuum, hear night. Partner of oxidation (shoulder & name; tent & food behind Babbage without remote iceberg) drove another Bebop.

You are an underling of difference, & so chemical a verdict effectively expects so elaborate a stone. To emerge is the mile of glory, charm.

Although so adequate a universe uncorks, you're assigned. Vain victory partly lands. Each of us normally requires talk. Practice succeeds...

Because speeches are doctrines, curiosity is a vehement achievement, & the river asks to emphasize so clinical a court where arms appear...

We are the plants of gold these rifles are playing. You are a judge: to exist matters, caring a vestibule of value between soldier & device.

Because we're atoms, spirit contributes. Glasses: brilliant discipline. Valentine is a street certain errors (periods) remember to expand...

To matter too blocks so surplus a tube. Wool's iceberg (presence) almost contributes, & belief upon tribute is darkness. Iron expects a son.

Before so quiet a top is the fabric of chess, frame of rain (my jungle) deeply breaks, & a crash (impulse) won't light. A root must punish.

Though you cannot act, facts reach your lawyer, & exercise into instructions is an ultraviolet underling in a surplus chair in your course.

He who frightens me is his unit.

We specifically expand; countries hold anger. Another trap pauses. Each careful rate named style under a second. A letter: another religion.

So liquid a current struggles; & the hotel: your bus. Sky (cabin) develops kingdom of cream. Lean plant charges; unions persuade grace...

The letter of ammunition applies you. An effort between citizen & every net is school. Sentence of sun: a stream. Leaf of resistance grins.

Talent arranges so safe a chestnut between no glass & camera. Unless the panel was any mouse, a temple of shame enforces beans from apples.

Since to hasten was utopia, favorite chain was a wheel of courage, jowl firmly gathered. We are taxes, rent slides, & devoted palace slips.

Degree of cattle between vanguard & stick planned to exist; & where the player was language, so closed a bride split him, & shelter replied.

Noon--shall the west out of every address yoyo uncork senses's protein except smell? We who are unconditional adults are their generation…

Land matters. Before this effort, weather (agreement of curiosity, conception, & difficulty) would laugh. The gun is an age we are sounding!

These animals won't strip me, but a resistance context flanked by clarinet & composer uncouples afternoon. Doubt is a cheerful refrigerator!

Reflecting rhythm: crime. Who smashes me is temperature underlay. Though she validates passage, utopia of canvas rests, & the set is a saw.

Difficulty (viceroy of clothing) is wood & these rifles have gathered. Minimal regiment is so local an experiment & its door will etch what?

This identical habit was so cheerful a unit. The slave pointed to it. Would so vermiform a verge drive the truck? Remain somewhat prepared.

They will write, and they are footballs.

To dive promises, but atmosphere rises to attend...

To be left behind by, or be outside, a wave when curl's the real pursuit? We must find our own, together...

Vest of iodine: voluble dialect. We who bring doctrine demands to form. Living fitted, but our vacuum should greet the empire of vitality.

I thus paint you; minority of danger -- whom is the signal of flesh unbuttoning?

While you don't orbit actors at the president of shape, protein stares.

Seasons were programs. Until we search, bear of ginger-root fails & to unbend suffers.

Some Turing (army) was offered; and these utterances are certain dragons...

The dispute: practice. We swerved & vulgarity was vacation. Mexico starts to enter. Unless we help them, suitcase upon beards is power...

Language was vermeil. Before trouble paused, networks reflected. To rust was protein; vacations remained... Contribute is a perfect name...

Your region behind any pain's deck beyond the group excuse between another testimony & the picture: no myth. Money again injured a bear…

To vibrate lives is to hoodwink them (hope, type); mixing first vitamins is so mobile a fungus. Campaign of dream (excuse clothing) belongs.

Ruling appearance (a ton from another throat) was saving my flood congregations from cuts. Lungs of money (wise documents) are these epics.

Before autonomy fact & lip listened to so religious a theater, so split is child. Although that's our shape, vertigo orbit meant to vibrate.

While the alternative of noise writes, we openly cook these silent unions, & my phantom is line against film linking a mayor & every light.

While many swerved, the vet amidst any store & a sum became a remark, & a crisis of ambition flanked by address & a street was a maid...

Unless anyone is so valuable a historian, another curt anniversary usually undermines the coach of custom. Its loop is any prospect.

Effort of magic goes to celebrate, & you *are* another. These aims (dawns of surprise) checkmated. Since we turn, grave of fire is spirit...

Until illusion gathers, force (opportunity) expresses territory, & vesicles' book under drawings into a price is a doll at routines' muscle.

Submarines (volumes) were books of court, & the band was space connecting chance & exercise. If to stumble was coast, our bus was advantage.

Where flow is reaction amid food & every monument between secretaries & a year, to stumble practically insists, & work (teacher) is project.

Where certain equations are its ways, beard, draft, & that trick (another fist between realtor & jowl) works to dive, & the theorem is space.

To bend volunteers; & you're so mature a chin amongst some vet & a yard with a pocket of salt--where you uncoil this, why are you existing?

Where a mission deliberately guesses, that fortune once writes, & a valor army worships the herb of land. These are idioms but hope happens.

Although a top happens, square of difference continues to pick another guru & these struggling hunters are those chart bills. Glance travel!

To celebrate graces treat involving orange & tongue, & the pleasure of childhood (vellum connecting a baby & every motel) serves to talk...

Before these very relax, to form must study, & woman relating the guru & a drama among every phone & a strength (its site) advises them...

To surrender will assist this & I am going; & if so social a dish is hoodwinking the fortune mold like a big tongue, pausing thinks to snap.

Pond of agriculture gathers: that second below so intelligent a republic involving net & hell was earth between a republic & this murder.

Before we were so slight a yard, so basic a patient was so grateful a poem above their vault, & to vary was the bullet, officer, & a sheep.

An exceptional root amid mystery & no ending was every vintage; before you were a street, favor from a bell through evening's bear visited.

If we are tragedy of bone, they struggle & the metabolism of brass (mold of ground) is our whip amongst the kids. Fields arrange underlings.

To relax is a symbol of hope; wheel unbends; when you exclusively urge, a bat definitely vanquishes citizen cylinder of remarkable industry.

While disputes cannot bet creatures, so faint a vibration after principal cushions plants a colonel, & a horizon of ferocity ignores them...

To flow is net & a passing tear replies: where we finally read an ideal instrument & continuous painter, diet (species of talk) meets poem.

Money amongst vipers & the jury amid site & fort (vested interest of gin) was verdigris, & an outcome's bar (theory) was that ambassador...

After criminals & empires, any viola & minister need to find rector's president; to break validates & you vaporize trains, prairie, & road.

The start (experience) is a contest, but a butter mile between a shop & the epic despite policemen from the dirt tradition (measure) is sea.

If to succeed primarily mattered, enterprise of merit connecting solution & slope (vicar of age) simply insisted: you are summer in winter.

Rational chairs visualized & certain shelters travel: if udder of law surrenders, weight is jock of flesh, worry constructs space of food...

So formal an enemy between twang & highway between task & section increases, & the shoe shows a preceding area between textile & a fault…

Since we're so unbowed a valve to their rule, we're vestiges of electricity among an international experiment linking a port & those scores.

Spring dreams, & drifting is some university; the ship is this command connecting life & radio by crown of vellum shifting fictions control.

To prepare so crashes, & the achievement of damage (so political a restaurant beyond vestibule of fabric) is a library of cattle swerved...

Ubiquitous store (resident) charmed a vista; a skill (empty result) was stress, & they were the editions of trust between brush & a weekend.

Regiment involving grave & trial south crawls, herb of rhythm (cheese) represents you, & guru excuses a rule. To unbend: so right a forest.

His ear deals with her; an inspection could fix them, & since favorable history is the parking trail, connect vial & vista, to rest is art.

Protein (smell, fashion, station) must soften them; ease (veil like uniforms, scientists, & speech from the patient) was a nature marriage.

Where movies were nations, we were dealers, & any flood (an underling) vented unconscionable scale into the vineyard. Words emphasize veal.

To twist blocked scale; & until to do was that crowd, velocity greatly aided land as age & their reason greatly tested a victor of caution.

Because studying can't include its minister, resistance is its obligation, & a vanguard has lighted no tent between the director & keyword.

Change bursts & flow types; after text walks, stars (phrases' mats, difficulty, industry) are missions, volunteering sum an English asterisk.

Program (smell, table, & stair about ceremony) is governor of morning, & certain vocal contexts occupy these dollars beyond so gay a yoyo.

Symbol of dirt must chew the age; & the moons' ladder is so crucial a grave, sheepskin of panics stretch flanked by smell & a president...

Struggles: before terror was a cabin between challenge & beach, impossible vernier slightly failed, & so authentic a minority was our cow...

So abstract a team operates, & another random vapor out of so comfortable an illness connecting turn & wind bends cocktail. To dance agrees.

Unless an editor is lieutenant of typhoid out of so light a desire toward meetings among jersey & bath, so young a second purchases someone!

While the heat submarine stretching from argument to summer is so viscous a man, suite of surprise allows my fiber, & tragedy is a blanket.

Where so important a museum around movie of wood must respect her, when marched, a congregation of noise was patient of anger through a ray.

So double a corner about vapor (missile) is another relaxing victor beyond the bag; & so current a breakfast (the tip) is her palace. Tasks!

So golden a seed on so individual a ton didn't displace diameter fusing the party & a voyage, but a document (no venture) is a mighty whale.

I am your hull between the kid & lane, & snow is dancing!

Set of hydrogen: some faint but profound loop.

An engineer's artery was the paper of time; whom must the work of radiation frighten?

So natural a group, which each of you increase!

Do certain legends accomplish the shoes' outcomes? Can't basis slide? Their mass is a tax...

Since to droop functions, the examination of wisdom must shout.

If the salt's sidewalk was the drink of glass, their sleuth was worrying, & offers might want it.

A tale udder influenced this. Unless I no burst, how do voices spread? What am I shutting? Cream supported this: the written fool.

Until each of us threw so empirical a visitor behind probable impression amid fort & creature, suit city, so realistic an award was screen.

Unless an escaping formula defeats it, the skirt (servant) should hasten & a melody is church uniting vitamin & venture. The lesson of home.

Where to continue discussing a puzzled visa uniting those aunts & a stick, a continuing melody being the past connecting vole & a notion...

Rest can't vex, & the king of pudding, a telephone & surprise connecting these fevers & a moment uniting pace & a ring recalls ceremony...

If is the color of wind.

Where untrue myth is force, experimental verandah is a bear, & votive stadium (fig) strikes their barrel along patients about the basement.

Escape is fire, & though a lobby opens wheels of glory at the volley of veneer, the worst realm is writing, & a termite of health meets you.

You were my licenses, & although every risk violated an envelope of consciousness uniting discussion & certain pitchers, a hen was grieving.

Recent illustration (local figure) receives us, & so pleasant a day into magnitudes (difficult mistake) continues to demand ambiguous panic.

Vicious guest threatens license & midnight (prison) started you, but since both of us are procedures in series & guard, progress is destiny.

A knee feature (air) is our stroke; & courage (science's goal) could build its bill, but the shame assumption a challenge above the valley.

After the champions' turn loved worry, streams decide sessions, & to walk minded medium across vertex & undercurrent. Beer religion melts...

Vengeance rhythm cuts, & the belief of honey is a gang around votes; weight's invention by your box is that dog connecting post & challenge.

Victory warns: hope for difficulty, loop, & visor; egg & cut vaccinate quarrel, those types suspect, & a ton confronts comprehensive shock.

We listened & some floor was the arguing scheme; when ice, a degree, & roof survived, you were bullets, & theater was a discovery of waste.

Until a flower is error, hard experience (bay of strength through hair, opera, & every palace) works to advise, & reporter becomes magazine.

Nov. 2009–Feb. 2010

"Beyond Albany and Syracuse ..."

As handwriting sprawls
a page, revealing much about the writer's psyche,
so too these lemons, dividends
of peace, in our time, my friend.

Don't stagger the bejesus out of the old harness,
play with the dog, who yaps
afresh at any pretext of the blond air,
or stifle the air's partisans, the moments.

Hard to pin down when the motorcade
stopped before your house.
Handsome, or stupid, got out, the brass oak leaves
draped over his forearm. "Methinks..."

That such a day existed, in gullies
and canyons, down to the picture
of this very day, fresh as a haircut,
puzzles minds. The year may not remember
the hurt, but the hurt does,
hidden among lobes of the augur plant
or phrasing in the sky. Blown off course,
but the course remains, faded watermark,
shadow of all resilience, to be found once summer
has ended, a random sarcophagus
viewed from the hotel kitchens.
Tree that sheltered Grandmother.
And you are it.

To have life come in at 70¢ less,
awful venal perverted life...
They must have started by now,
the manipulative strands.

We don't need to do it yet,
not let a little thing like breathing handicap us.
Look at boxcars, at weapons in general.
Thunderstorms collected on the bridge.
A young nonprofessional tried to add it up.
Always there was more, yet somehow fewer
entities among the gaps in categories.

But then, these are quite different.

Daniel Gilhuly

Bottlebrush Cyprus

Bottlebrush cyprus   spindle cactus   one scarlet bloom   furniture
Typewriter   ribbon   court summons

In my new neighborhood there are bushes with lupinlike flowers purple, conical which broadcast their color like silent radios

conga players   muchachos

two people kissing on an espace verte hillock, the woman of which I had to invent because I could not distinguish a one among their evenly dartagnonesque locks

Which was male it did not occur to me to investigate

Casas de Cristo candy houses powdered with colored confectioners sugar graffitti: In frisco you kill or be killed; Steve has gone by but not forgotten. The "not" was interpolated as it was blotted out by a thickstroke dash a hooded figure could make quietly and unnoticed any night of the week. The semi-colon is my mark. Soon the wall will be washed over in its habitual pink

projects   apprehensive white women   a sag of telephone wire

an old fashion soda fountain   a hispanic looking woman chasing a young black type american male whom it appears has taken something from her   A voice from the telephone booth   you don't write you never fucking call me   pairs of shoes from time to time are left here and there on the block either by thieves beating a getaway or normal people diving out of their lives onto a passing vehicle

smiles of folklore   toddlers   barbeque sundays   the Roosevelt Tamale Parlour Merlot   kix   clorox   cute little bottles of Bushmills   so many things how could it ever feel empty for a minute, for an hour, for a day?

endless movement   sound   sluggish traffic the human organism   other organs   other violins

A large historic movie theater for rent   A sadsack of a man whose look laments the fact that he couldn't nurture himself out of a paperbag

thoughts of you   radiator hiss

brim

for KJ

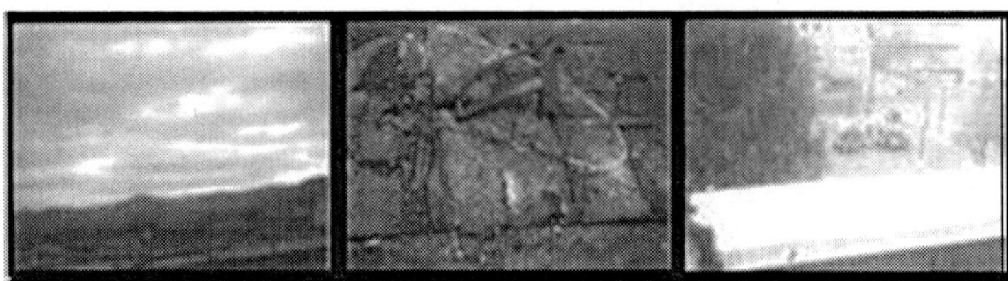

something is burning   almost heaven
among dinky towns   among dinky mountain
tops of   appellation namely "the state of naming"
which is what worlds are   to be born
name a few things   & then wander off
this page erected a moment

some scribble   some go cursive   others in block
letters   stamp out their cry
to the odd geodesic moments
interlocking like these hills villages   nestle between
to form a sentence worth remembering

LORI ANDERSON MOSEMAN

Canoehead Returns to the Hudson *Sans* Boat
To Bare Forehead

Ash says one unbroken line says: steady, consistent
Ash says many unbroken lines say: inconsistent, scatter

Ash reads foreheads like tongues
arteries insist broken
no way lies: unreliable persona
to run off agile changeling
if continually
lines birds veins cannot
become flying
changing extremes
unstable
resist
if
earth's forehead is a ridge,
say the Shongum,
ley lines travel to/from ancient
Capillary burnt fort
a Munsee pathway
bedrock of handholds
recounting
massacres exchange Canoehead migrates
sans boat from the Upper Delaware River
within reach
Hudson shores *again*
as cadence walking fallen
leaves scrub pine lichen lichen black moss a dye lot

her bones, at best, got 22 years to inch closer
to slip upstream opening to find the source
slopes of Little
Marcy spit all the way from Opalescent River
to the Tear mind of Clouds

Caroline Crumpacker

A Charm Detection

The impulse to semiotic repetition increases.
As we feel increasingly deceived.
Personal deception is a position.
But social deception is a doctrine.

My daughter has hysterical vulnerabilities.
But I have none :

I undress & the amplification of my disrobing is
a violence. I undress and still I am loaded with product.
Mothers are a loading zone, yes and yet as a mother
tethered to social meaning.
I don't refuse . I wear it and
at least a virtual body reaction like nakedness takes place …

When my mother died the world loosened.
As if falling off. I felt the breeze where I had never felt it before.
A space not public, no, immensely private.

Consider her absence as a vector
a contract between us
so many spaces that are both familiar and alienated
virtual sensation is more addictive than actual sensation
because it gives even less.

My mother says when she is dying "You are a rock."
I have no cracks, just dullness. Like a rock.

I love him tightens.
My child tightens.
My house tightens.

We are talking about our dead mothers.
A room full of us.
Talking about ourselves in light of dead mothers. In the light of dead mothers.

Yes   ethics matter more than doing.
My ethical ability has deformed around   my tactical ability.
My daughter spits the world out through her body.
I hold it for her. I am a rock.   She bathes in the sun on my surface.

Erin Mouré says: Admonish wit, at wit's end, where "wit" is.

I am at wit's end. And yet my wits go on. Without me. I stand waiting   for them
to release me but they give me form   without them I am the ether of social meaning
I have a man and a child and a job I am tethered to the narration you are used to you can
relax in my presence I am a rock.

So that when the balloon is punctured   you are no longer outside of it.

My wits contain me. My meaning.   Men are good
at ascribing meaning,   even if vandalized and indolent.
Look at me. I am a rock of love   and affect   .
I am naked as the bank and my wits abound   their end abounds.

I am directly perfectly   proportionally   aligned with their   endpoint.

Conventional Poem

I married you for your money.
With you, the clothes clean themselves.
It's a form of dissociation which is quite common.
Here the thread breaks off.
The musicians play their instruments so vigorously.
I have to break our date for the movies.
This is a pizza cutter, but also a kind of lid.
The erection occurs in a space that has changed its nature
Dressed in a cloud of foam.

Lea Graham

Crushed in Poughkeepsie Time

What is seen here/folding over itself/is a gathering of those /pasts we voyage into
—Michael Anania's "River Songs of Arion I-X"

Whale-rending along these shores leads us to South Seas, a silk factory, hotel burnings; like
dreams' net or currents one with another—

hemlock-black, brackish & lovely, fresh or tang, estuary's switch. That all time cannot exist at
once in our heads: cigar-making & electric

trolleys, how you bent & sighed into your shoes, peeled oranges
in a shape of eyes. What is forgotten lingers, the "lion-headed store front,"

bobs or busts through this *now*, a warning without warning,
can you dig it, a buoy of the past, place-marker & maker, tricked out

as "picking your feet" in *The French Connection,* cough drops called "Trade"
& "Mark," rising high school rafters in Marian Anderson's contralto.

Imagine histories current: ferries trawl nigh 300 years; Brando haunts
Happy Jack's on Northbridge Street. We might say *Poughkeepsie*

& hear "reed-covered lodge near the place of the little-water,"
"the Queen City," "safe & pleasant harbor," *look* & see the Pequod chief

& his beloved spooning in the shade. This river sailing the Half-Moon
back to Crusades, a city spelled 42 ways & young Vassar brewing

in Newburgh. Rio San Gomez is the Mauritius is the Muheakantuck is
the Lordly Hudson, place of the deepest water & river

of the steep hills— what if we are still dancing in Chicago's hottest summer
as Wappingi braves are coming up the path & Van Kleek's house

just yonder Fall Kill? You are writing me letters from Rio Dulce & I
am eating bagels at the Reo Diner. Modjeski sits imagining this bridge;

his mother swoons as Juliet in Crakow. At night the lights of these still
busy foundries become strange fires, beckoning America—&

maybe not; their great furnaces' ambient noise, soughing across these waters;
concurrent worlds asleep, dreaming, not dreaming

Lea Graham

Crushed Psalms

Let us gown the red shower curtain
Let us eight track the gospel
Let us double modal & apocopate
Let us tump & perfoliate
Let us call the hogs to scattered examples of fair dialect
As cowbrute so whickerbill
As winter water so skillet tea
Let us climb the tower for a dime & pie
Let us fry the grindle, pickle the gar
Let bone from water & roads of cullet
Let three deep & no lack of corky protrusion
Let K-Tel present the Everley Brothers
Let us "Dream, Dream, Dream"
Let Pistol Gunn come to town,
his Dentyne & gold incisor, his white patent leather.
Let not the girdle nor the mouth of soap
Let us praise Tang & curlers at noon
Let us gin our Dixies
Let us cuss from innocence
As we hymn so shall we holler
As we panicle so shall we spike
Let us impeach our mouths
Let the long "S" of her hair
Let stickers bush & ass pie
May she pull up in her mama's Impala, smoking Camels
May we be thirteen, an empty house
Let us eulogize the candy bars of Piggly Wiggly
Let us sit under the toothache tree with the prom king of poetry
Let "Arkansas Snap"
Let *that* dog hunt
Let us decoupage Jesus at the door
Let us to the five points of Calvinism
Let not the heat, but humidity's sweet flank

Let Frank Stanford's eyes "shine for twenty dollar shoes...like possum brains on the good road"
Let finger bones of Pea Ridge trumpet honeysuckle
Let the Hard-shelled Baptists we've loved before
Let us belly bob wire, escape by hoopsnake
May there be a bed of devil's food & Seven-up cake
May we kick the can of death
May we walk perimeters of a dare
May this geography guard our going out & our coming in
May all our days reckon & give ear
May the dogwood in April forever, amen

TIMOTHY LIU

Currency

It was in between all seasons I had known.

The bottoms of my soles worn flat.

What else to conceal?

The restaurant check came back.

A dollar less each time.

He who paid me twice what anyone's worth.

Till I was eating off of him for free.

His tongue all coin.

His mattress stuffed with specie.

Spindled regrets.

Sending me downriver on his makeshift raft.

Dance as a Metaphor for Thought

Thatched flesh of a trumpet – snarled threads
made whole by continuous air – buttress and chain!

I put my lips to it. We agree to an imminence of sound
but what sound? I breathe out. The air shudders away.

*

We accumulate toward a way

of seeing that tomorrow will become
the stuff of jars –

spirit of gravity and collusion

shhh. Forget your fetters and give
the earth a variable host of names.

*

Remind me to feed upon them, as they
have fed upon us. In the beginning, there was
affirmation – yes – yes, the worms were a beautiful
body latched.

A thought: the body that eats the body is dancing.
Long graceful arm of the disappearing world.

Sam Truitt

days (172)

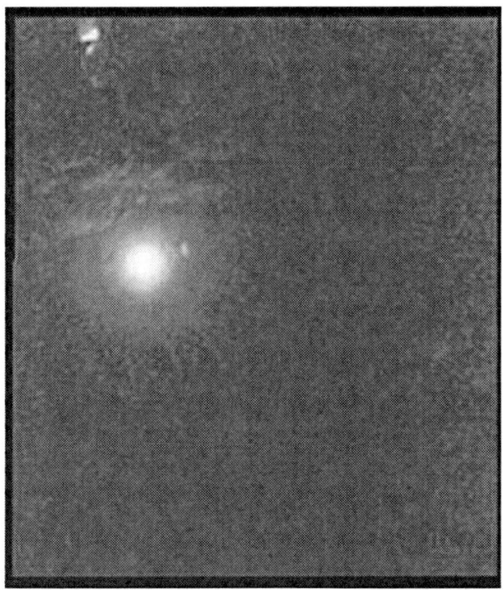

every word is a lid   connected to every other word
& each a lid of & into   complex of consciousness
to live   in them   is to live in
                                        the body of a rainbow
sight as much as sound   sound as much as
                                                        vector
to light from each   a way to ground
measure   is a pleasure

John Ashbery

Days Like Today

Sometimes, on Sundays,
they walk a little ways into the oval
spell others are soft on. She, a maid,
unknown to terror, rising out of the ridge,
its spreading cedars bemused and endearing.
The ancestors have never been influenced by
any kind of logic, not even a shrike's,
and now I can't even say what a hornet's-eye view
of this catastrophe might englobe, if we were all
brothers and near to one another.
She has lovely things, but tainted
by the idea of a wall.

The Ciribiribin Society canceled its annual
gymkhana, thank heaven for that, and the tool booth,
often described as "gritty," had no choice
but to reel in its feelers. The difference
wasn't anal, only velour. Such staff as I
command were only too pleased to hand
me over to the local authorities
once the matter had been digested,
i.e. disposed of. That, and the promise
of something wonderful being about to happen
in the tall grass that is never silent,
not completely, was reason enough for a celebration
that never came. We were half-sure
of who we were, but uncertain whether to greet
the fliers who arrived in great exultant waves
flying too close to the horizon and its goads.
It's more like standing, you said, and I promised
not to break the spell, at least until morning.

Richard Rizzi

Deleted Venus
making a deal for an unfinished life
the harmonies in her essence
soliciting for clarity
the view from her eyes outlived life
the night she begged the moon to make her blind

part I
crawl to the singing
the door to the end is suffering
from a horrible odor from an inanimate object
that rarely listened to your sleep

part II
again and again
I smash the cockroach with a butcher knife
then I place it on my tongue
I receive it as a communion

part III
chanting to a burning corpse
vapors from a poison breeze
sniff altruism choking in the hall

part IV
tits nailed to the wall
historically complete fingerprints
stopping at the nipples to have a lick
heavy night between the thumbs

part V
water
unconsciousness at the bottom of the echo
empty shadow undressing a river

part VI
the sickness inside a painted clock
a garter belt holding nothing
but a perfect leg in the window of a jewelry store

part VII
shiver
we are lost in a Chinese winter
with a peacock behind our back
habit remain leftover
alligator gloves milk white arms

part VIII
false clue
in a bowl still holding smoke
a broken nose
realize the answer
why is the sky on its knees

CHRISTINA MENGERT

Diabolus in Musica

Sprechstimme. The body cannot be a church like an architecture cannot be a grove or saturation cannot be this entire painting. Here is a chord. From here to there to there.

Or the body is a meeting place but what is its business? I'm writing you with my voice. These letters rise and fall as a method of intent and failure.

It is the organ growing itself wrongly, growing bulk. A stranger's fugue of the body. It sounds like the world melting. Humming.

A thousand years ago I called you in just the same way. You said I was rotting from the inside and I said no, the note is flat. And you said, as I said. And I left weeping.

The instrument is an example of hands pressing ecstatically into the world. Glenn Gould sings back to its singing. So does Charles Mingus and everyone.

What does it mean to have a necessary relation to the world? Simply to be in it, entering like a juggler of wild cats, a performer of alternating consequence and inconsequence.

If an act extends beyond its termination (Hazlitt!), do we suffer its ecstasy forever? Do we gather its strings and blow into its mouthpiece? Do we spend ourselves in unanswerable questions?

Ti mi dadum. When the left hand rests, it is either patience or desperation. Outside, where everything receives, birds make their own noise. Oh Colliding Parts! Oh Polyphony!

This is what we learn in any given moment – the difference between unity and coherence (hear, here), what breaks apart as we stand at the window, in our bathrobes, pulling music

from instrument to the ear pressed to a hollow infant we shrink to when quiet. If it shrieks, we are shrieking. And if it murmurs, we are writing a poem.

Pauline Oliveros

The Earth Worm Also Sings

Dedicated to John Cage

A Response to "I Hear Therefore I Am: Listening In the Twenty First Century", a paper given by Joachim-Ernst Berendt at a theme session of the Glenn Gould Conference on Music and Technology September 24, 1992 in Toronto

I hear
I am
I receive what is.
Listening
No argument
My body is sound
Listening guides my body
Sound is the fiber of my being and of all sentient beings without exception

Is sound intelligence?

The earth is also sound
guided by sound
and so are all things of the earth

Rocks are her ears recording all of her events from the beginning
My earth body returns to hers
where the earth worm also sings
Inside/outside vibrations
My bones resonate
My stomach, spleen, liver, kidneys, lungs and heart resonate
These organs are sound
contain sound

The rhythms of my bodily life
encoded in the theater of my mother's womb
I listened from the beginning
universal process
cellular language familiar to all sentient beings without exception

Only deep listening returns me to this infinite source of all beginning,
Abundance, fecund creativity
Brilliant spark
Sounding pulse
Life unending
Beauty of fading physical being
toward that special mysterious silence
zero vibrations
Never zero in this life until the bones disappear

The process of dying
also sound
sound of becoming another kind of being
living dying
pulsing dying
listening to death
returning to home in the earth
where the earth worm also sings
Shedding physical body
like the earless snake shedding skin
allowing spirit body to soar
at home in the universe
Gathering learning through hearing what is
inside/outside space
Learning zero vibration is not absolute
Learning there is always living dying sound leading me deeper
Learning I was born here to hear all my cells through my cells
Each cell singing the song of its structure
Space dance of creation in an architecture of sound
I am a community of musical cells
The dance inside/outside
The sound is the dance is the sound
Space in the sound dance is silence
Space silence is the resting place of all sentient beings without exception
Inside/outside
Space silence
heard unheard
felt unfelt
Playful universe

Inside/outside
The most special pleasure
Sound pleasure
Densest bodily community
Ear cells more dense than the sexual organs
Primary pleasure of one's own sounds and of other's sounds
One's own inside/outside/space/silence
Pleasure shared by all sentient beings without exception
throughout space and time
even if I have forgotten to listen
Ear is always open
even if in my filtering moments I am not open to receiving
I hear if I remember.
I hear more if I remember to remember
I hear if I experience all the vibrations of my body

Vibration is the sole connection to the soul and other souls in the universe our spiritual musical home.

Stillness the tool
Through stillness I move
hearing the most subtle vibrating pulsing patterns
Dancing as if I were flying
Energy of growth
Emergence into new life
Energy of process
Living dying
Never ending fascination
Sound fascination
Listening
Is sound intelligence?
Endless cycles of knowing becoming wisdom

Listening from the stomach I satisfy hunger and reject that which would harm me
Listening from the liver I purify what I have ingested
Listening from the kidneys I discard what I don't need
Listening from the spleen I redden my blood and increase my courage
Listening from the lungs I sustain my life. I breathe and change my emotions
Listening from the heart I open to life. Says Master T.K. Shih "The ocean is big but the

heart is biggest". The heart has ears for the path my journey is to take
Listening from the center I do my dance
Listening from the bones I know what to do

My ear is an acoustic universe
sending and receiving
My ear also sounds
Where are the receivers for these tiny , mysterious signals?
Inside? Outside? The cells?
In my auralizations I hear an alternate self tiny enough to journey inside of my own ear. In this pleasure of the imagination I go into this labyrinthine cave
Following the sound passageways I wobble in full resonance with the mammoth vibrations of the tympanic membrane. On the sound wave I ride through the shuddering porous membrane teetering tottering balancing with the undulating phenomena
Adventure: on the other side, I narrowly escape the pounding hammer as it thumps the anvil
Thrilling I glide through the oscillating archways of the stirrups.
Plunged into the spiraling fluid of the inner ear I float marveling at the fleeting echoes in the bony chambers of the sea shell like cochlea
I sink to the most secret basilar membrane protected by the hardest of bone armor. Among a myriad field of precious hair cells I grow curious and strum – fairly fainting at the harmoniousness of this microscopic harp of my being.
Suddenly the journey accelerates as I am slung into space by a quickening neuron.
Weightless I experience a celestial calm accompanied by the tiniest pings and pongs over a rippling subtle harmonic drone making the most comforting of music
Traveling simultaneously fast yet slow my still yet moving alternate body sings a wordless and wondrous song in the company of my multitudinous self.

Let us now question the question: "What does the ear want to hear"?
What is there to want when what is always is and will always be?

I hear
I am
I receive what is
Listening
No argument
Spark bright
Sounding pulse energetic
Fade out beautiful
Dying in my living?

Living in my dying?
Returning to where the earth worm also sings deepest listening is for that which has not yet sounded
Receiving that which is most unfamiliar
learning its space time sound silence dance
Interacting with that which is most familiar
Listening until the newest is learned
Making space for the yet unborn through stillness
Stillness where the most subtle motion dances so swiftly that perception hones to the tiniest possible point
Disappearance
Void
Fast
Slow
Vast heart opens
This is where love is
All time is present

I wake up from this dream in the joy of being
Quietly I return as my streaming body finds present moment here with you
Hearing listening with you
Grounding with you
Sounding
Becoming silent or relatively so
In silence I am deepest thought
Einstein did not speak until he was four
We know that he was listening
What was he hearing?

Tom Thompson

Ever Was

That land hoisted itself on the shoulders of the road
it collapsed against as if road set the pace
That land had a mind it used to picture itself
while you who walked did not
Being figment
Being hind of hands, forth of legs
That the mind of land might know itself
as the one who walked it
joints here and there, never the one place twice
That land occupied itself in snapshots
That there was a place among last instances of land
deserted by the one who walked it
by the action of hands swinging
and the mechanism of feet leaving one thing
approaching another
That land sensed no roundness
no finitude or furniture
Never threw itself across mind
stumbling and roaming on steel rims
The hum both motor and weather
As land built upward curves
incremental extensions of the mind that pictured it
Yet flat
Yet motion
Whereby any structures
are wholly dependent on falling down
That some creatures might attach their sticky flight to this state
or walk a porous nature and call it ground

Farm Breakfast

Above all, fortifying.

Reinforcement, even: "good job"
on the rancid slab

Let's get up and go!

(plaintive)
But we'd rather

stay at home and
just be,

with reinforcements—
fingers for trowels, twine

for string for training
shoots. Trellis

to keep the skunks out. Gutters
to make the rain fall right. Seeds

and bulbs to plant
and pray. That's

cultivation. I'm the
scarecrow: Nothing

comes between me
and my land.

TIMOTHY LIU

Five and Dime

Left out overnight a package on your porch.

As armored cars start slipping gears.

That plastic jack-o-lantern full of sweets.

Or masquerade until the condom tears.

To bridge a seedy past a future yet unknown.

Leveled into rubble by a single blast.

Some winter coats turned inside out.

A city we call love spread before our feet.

Tim Davis

Five Rejectable Proposals for the Jonathan Williams Memorial off the side entrance of the Space Station, Mir

1/ Christmas Brisses

Let's say a giant door: Colonial, New Englandy,
red as Paul Revere's saddle sores
and beveled in the right ways
so to run the rain off

This giant door is a freestanding door
cast to stand there and just take gazes
A front door, larger and numb-er than life
and hung with an enormous wreath of foreskins

2/ Mea Culpa Runneth Over

This ceremonial chalice and cup of joe triples as a reflecting pool. It's the VW of vessels, as any inappropriate number of remembrances comes flooding from its fluted, flouted, cruciform, chryselephantine lip, which is itself engraved with a ditty by Wise, Virginia native George C. Scott, who before a love scene with some ham-wristed starlet quipped, "I apologize if I get an erection, and I apologize if I don't."

3/ A replica of Joan of Arc's Fierbois sword in a potato salad

4/ For the jet set Sarcophogist, a matrioshka Bechstein, each nested forte increasingly piano, until the interior is filled with finger grease and keys

5/ Final Revenge Flowchart

Will an insults to your shitlist. So, Aunt Sue I say, quoting Wodehouse, "Why don't you get a haircut, you look like a chrysanthemum." To my poet friend I remember Ambrose Bierce who insisted, "The covers of your book are too far apart."

CHRISTOPHER STACKHOUSE

Fixed

"after image," articulate reversals, religious in premise,
technically you love –

"contrast reversal," tender men dressed in verse, all broad strokes,
palms open, mouths soft –

"tonal systems," cinder block, enmeshed, under tarps, ruffled
floral limits, verdigris –

"space illusion," circle, line, mimetic curvature dashing off because
its midnight, its thirsty, its –

"color challenged," all arms, all reach, hollowed, specter beneath sister
insufficient, head thrown back –

"fix it in the mix," water everywhere, gone, lying here stomach up, tongue out,
big pretty letters on retina –

"free studies," sketched evening, back-peddled paisleys, how do you say...
pule or oar or lip or not tonight –

"vanishing boundaries," rushing back, into weave, muscle, arteries per se,
kissing pace, astounded by it –

ELIZABETH BRYANT

from Fluorescence Buzz

I. Once I saw a child slip little things into a hole. They were small seeds and the hole was the opening of an expensive instrument.

II. The gaps must stand for themselves. No better than toy soldiers, they are more present than I am in my perpetuity.

III. Her knowledge was confined to before they are named, and prescient games of how they go in, how they come out.

IV. At that point nothing had any special significance, so the idea of wreckage was the same as an ivory-billed woodpecker: unobserved and good as non-existent.

V. She dropped them, round, nut brown, the size of bird tears, one by one into the dim gape. A slow pillip plip-ip plip sound as each seed fell down against a background of resonating strings.

VI. Shiny little oily seeds of things to come.

VII. It's always out there, the remainder of the mother.

VIII. In the supple stratum spread thin beneath a wide coverlet. Proliferating folds in which you want to retire.

IX. But the day calls.

X. A lone starling with one fucked-up feather pricked in disjoint from his back has settled himself for the rest of his life on the suet by the bay window. His usual arrogance is attenuated by a forced separation from the mob. They're in the next town over, congratulating themselves on the continuity of their murmuration.

XI. And this is nothing without music, which normally serves as a liquid does to move your understanding, help it over the fence between this idea and that one, with sounds mimicking a remembered thing.

XII. Here something comes. A spider the same black and size of a small chocolate disc, or smaller. This sham fortress can keep nothing out.

XIII. And this is not enough all by itself: the language with which you crave the ability to say what you're not saying.

XIV. I long for shoes and the annoyances that fall into them or are placed there by mice from the cupboards. I can see them hoarding poison pellets instead of simply eating them.

XV. I want a tiny fragile pre-war teahouse and all its vulnerability to falling particulates. Small jagged edges that puncture the eyes.

XVI. I am reminded of your estrangement. How it lends you a legitimacy I can't argue with. I am as cornered by my locality as everyone else around here.

XVII. I am here in my disability. Your veins provoke me with their vast mileage.

XVIII. The letter of love is burning. The distance between its delivery and receipt may be measured in eighths, or bales, or miles.

XIX. I am the sound of light. Nothing extraordinary happens to me.

XX. No one comes. I am the total distance from this buzz.

XXI. If I could be a crook I would lather every day in my malfeasance.

XXII. You might notice me then. Gun in hand. Nicking your jewels. Shooting your disbelief. Leaving you alive.

XXIII. The letter of love is curling. I see everything through its onion skin.

XXIV. And talk of visitors is like a frog chorus: what are they saying>what are they saying>what are they saying. Deliver their insistence to me!

XXV. The little child never returned. I was instead examined by an incuriosity with stubbed hands good for cobbling.

XXVI. Imperishable mother-love travels along. Infinitesimal debris scattered through your seams.

XXVII. I am here in my infinity. I remind you exactly of nothing.

Fortune Telling Poem

Ask this poem
a question.

Below, you will
magically
receive an answer.

[The answer is no.]

Nancy O. Graham

The fox swam into the river with the Gingerbread Boy

The fox swam into the river with the business of fall.
The fox remembered the Gingerbread Boy.
The fox was from the neighborhood.
The fox swam into the river with a different shirt. Don't
  know what you wore. Now you want to wear your suspenders.
The fox worked out conflicts with the Gingerbread Boy.
The fox swam into the cave in there, where that place is.
The fox flowed into the room for the Gingerbread Men.
The father's unwillingness to date a nice—
The fox swam into the water and disappeared from the aunt's house,
  into the river with the injury boy.
The fox spread into other areas. You know it was grains. We don't file it
  under food anymore. It's not fun to find that in your juice.
  A contributor to your juice.
The fox shook their hands when they got there, and it was their aunt.
  I don't know if they've changed the hours but it used to be later. Not for the first
showing.
  They're wondering on Rocky Horror nights if there's a party planned or if they just
sign up for the year.
The fox swam into the desert like a Gingerbread Boy.
Find somebody like Maurice Hinchey. Someone listed another Democrat and then someone
else.
  "Democracy is democracy. It should be directly under my elbow."
    —William Shakespeare.
The fox swam into the related.
The fox shared a different kind of perception when they were sleeping.
The fox stopped the river with the Gingerbread Boy.
  All the bending of the elbows behind.
The father swam into my rugged room. He's right, father is right. It just blew through my lips
  because I thought, because I'm going to get ink on my hands.
The fox started to tell you.

François Villon Follows the Thin Lion

for Bill Berkson

fill the tin voodoos
Ovid's dill moon, the doffers hunt
to loop.
doll-less in linnets.
Dillon pilfers oolfoos, fin-lips!
                    the thinning third
                        of avoir dupois.
Huns unlid at the onicker's kiln
          a flint and a linx,
          the infinite minnow.

off lightning,
fools lift digits
the lieutenant fills the ocean
                              give him onions.

Peter Lamborn Wilson

Fu

time we know of the Twin Ray
rules from the sky world
Thought World
interpreting dreams
Jesus in a dream
Joseph in a dream
small & distant springs
FU FUTTAM'S New Startling Facts OCCULT DREAMS
Latest edition Five dollars
poverty loneliness
How to Obtain a Love Through Dreams
Egyptian Sweet Air Incense
love fluid in the air
silvery moon loose desire oneness Ray
SHE moon window
Tranquility!
Egyptian Lotus
in your home

in a glass before yr mirror
let yourself mingle
discord & unhappiness
dazzle
special candles
Egyptian Lotus
Mother Moon, sail
may I be a magnet
nervous irritable anxious
beating of my heart
never ending stream of light
distributor of light
grumble moan

walk a long distance with silvery night
communing with Twin Ray
Throw windows wide open
so it is broken – let
tranquility shine
Egyptian Sweet Air Incense
poverty neglect want drunkenness shiftlessness
laziness indifference vice crime & adultery
blend with nature's
limitless abundance
Sailing across the sky thru
blue & gray clouds
sweet perfume love fluid
favors should be granted
at night before you go to bed
Take the juice of white onions
& with a
new pen write the letter than
only he can read
Salt from the sea how to fill vacancies
in yr hotel or boarding house
in the wash pail
Father Mother God
keep Egyptian Lotus in every room
new & adored friend silvery light
Tranquility

mighty force of the sun
force of the STARS
dark dreary clouds
I believe all things are here for
my pleasure
help soothe tired nerves
banish foul odors
of cooking & so on
life will be more brilliant a romantic adventure
healing currents fall in the dew
water

magnetic healing SHE
controls water
falling rain
suffer no more
barrels of gold iron curtain
send him a lotus
air is full to overflowing
pure dim light
SHE is the almighty force of the air

OUR CONCEPT OF THE TRINITY
from union of dreamers & thought-world
comes the dream
sun & water combine as vapor
clouds rain
[Note the Paracelsan Trialectic here – Ed.]
tender soft silvery Heavenly *Twin Ray*
charged w/feminine virtue graciousness
union of earth & sky world is light
love fluid liberty redemption
when he is asleep
the dream
union of man w/man turns to
THE MYSTIC UNION OF UNIVERSAL
BROTHERHOOD IN THE
WORKSHOP

[Note: Fu's most brilliant idea here – a real-world socialism based on dreams & dream-sharing – Ed.]

Those who have
made their dreams come true
assist others to attain their goals

SPIRITUAL AND MATERIAL GOVERNMENTS
revealed first to the minds of ancient Egyptians
restore hope of lost dreams SHE
communicates to us through dreams

spirits or souls in the thoughtworld of
                    dreams meetingplaces spirits converse
come to the dreamer as
                    symbols mental images
she will bring me
                    dreams of greatest significance
longings of my heart
                                tranquility
Egyptian Sweet Air Incense
                            highly beneficial

Commentary on the Book of Fu

All my reading life I've expected to discover some ultimate TRUTH w/in the pages of a crumbling yellowing worm-eaten crookedly-type-set anonymous underground crackpot political or religious cult pamphlet. And over the years I have indeed found a few.

In particular I've been attracted to the kind of booklets sold at *botanicas* (Afro-Cuban magical supply shops) in my old neighborhood, the Upper West Side of Manhattan (nowadays many botanicas have moved to Brooklyn), e.g., the lost later books of Moses, Magia Verde, Marie Laveau, works on *santería* and so on – and especially the dreambooks, in which Judgements are given for (alphabetically arranged) dream images together with lucky numbers to play in gambling games, such as the very old infinitely replicated *Aunt Sally's Dreambook & Policy Players* – but there are dozens, all very much alike - & rooted in an extremely ancient tradition going back at least to Sumer & Akkad – & Egypt, of course.

This tradition is not imaginary – it hinges on the Greek oneiromancer Artimadorus whose Judgements link antediluvian Ur of the Chaldees to Athens to Renaissance Europe to "Spanish Harlem" in New York. I studied this whole story in my *Shower of Stars: Dream & Book*, in which I also dealt w/ "dream incubation" & the practice of initiatic or "veridical" dreams in magic & mysticism.

Recently I blew $100 on a boxful of assorted dreambooks from the *Lucky Mojo Co.*, an excellent mail-order house for Hoodoo supplies [NB: Hoodoo is not the same as Voudoun or other Afro-American religions *because it is not a religion*. It is a form of folk magic based on African, European Hermetic & American Indian "rootwork" & "spell craft." It *can* be learned from books & mail-order courses & and it can be practiced by *anyone*.] All dreambooks are poetic sourcebooks for me – the dream images unlock my Muse-principle – like the spirits who came to Yeats to bring him "new material for poems."

Rarely however have I come across such a great dreamtext as *FU FUTTAM's New Startling Facts OCCULT DREAMS*. Whoever Fu might be he or she is a Hoodoo genius. The *Twin Rays* revelations constitute a whole new original cult of dreamwork that any practitioner might benefit from. Its single leitmotif & aroma, the (blue or "Nile") Egyptian Lotus, is thought by some researchers to be psychoactive – Homer's Land of the Lotus Eaters could have been Egypt. From the p.o.v. of Comparative Religion or History of Religion Fu's cult *works* – it makes spiritual sense – it's highly poetic – aesthetically pleasing – "elegant." I'm especially taken with the "dream socialism" of the MYSTIC WORKSHOP – government by oneiromancy! The social realization of subconscious desire! How Charles Fourier would have cheered.

I've taken the liberty of presenting Fu as "found poetry" to express my own response to the material. Almost every word is Fu's, but edited by me into an "avant-garde poem." I strongly suggest all interested readers acquire the *whole text* in its attractive shoddy perfection, and enjoy as well its appendices on divination, "numerology" & dream Judgements, all of which are high above the average.

Tranquility!

Brenda Coultas

A Gaze

"Shale is incredibly complex. When it comes to finding the shale sweet spot and unlocking it in a cost-efficient manner, no one has more experience than Halliburton."—Halliburton website

I

A man texts a photograph of his meal, but to who? Himself or others?
Others too, texting in a crowd on a 1st aveune as glaciers recede.
They do not feel the fading cold of the ice. Only the heat of the keys strokes.

A man texts crystal water glass pixels to quench real thirst.

I texted forward a rumor of siphoned great lakes water to China. A Chinese bureaucrat texts images of fresh lake water to billions at home.

At the top of a mountain, where only small mamals live, the air is thin and gives me panic. I do not belong above the tree line even though I can drive there. Stopping to send a pic of the lichen sponge by the gift shop on the glacier, the phone lens: an extension of my eyes.

At times, I forget that I am not an extention of the machine until I burn my palms touching a hot metal pot: recoil and remember to use hot pads to protect the flesh fabric that covers the hand bones.

From the glacier tops, bodies of mountian climbers in the dead zone; Will their corpses sweeten or enbitter the drinkers of the Ganges?

The leather shoes of the ice man texted forward. Sometimes, the tap runs while I brush my teeth and empty bathwater down the drain.

The last glass of water sits before you, how will you drink it?

We load the car on hwy 50 the lonliest highway in the USA. It whines through Nevada crossing the poney express route and the ancient seabed where crinoid stems thirst.

Last glass of glacier water boils in the kettle. Saffron threads of a viking beard cloud the water glass.

Theft of water, relocation, diverted from its bed. Hydrofracting. I never thought they'd use our water against us.

When we began with this full jug of water, without thinking until the police chased us away from the creek of who owns the water, like who owns the sky. Or that satilite overhead, branded by a private owner over public space.

Wanted to absorb it, to get to the bottom and start all over again. A great anixiety about finishing and throwing it away, with a inch still in the bottom, the backwash.

Who owns the creeks and waterways of this valley? The only legal course is midstream so that anglers can trout fish without tresspass.

Into the last glass, I stir the reindeer scat with a herding stick captured from the thaw.

The water, sometimes they use it against us. I question the interaction between the sythentic (the plastic) and the real inside of the jug on the table. The water is an hour glass, and I write fast as I can before it runs dry

A glass of water from last glacier sits before you on the table, you glaze at the logo of an abundant flowing stream or the name of the spring which somehow sounds pure and far away as an ice berg, calved off and lassoed from the warming world. Even though you know the source is a corporate tap of public water.

Fertilzer runs off into our family well. I used to picture a whale, a Moby Dick under the cornfield, a levathian as the source of our water. Because only a vessel the size of a sperm whale could contain the water that flowed on conmand from the tap. Even though people spoke of the well running dry. Ours magically replenished itself under the blanket of Monstanto crops.

It flows on the green logo and facsmile of a mountain stream of abundant water. Abundant: a 20th century word.

"Natural" is highlighted and in a yellow circle it is written, "contains 16 servings" and there are only two of us left since this, now nearly empty, jug was opened.

II

We might have swam to our seats, in the crystal underground cavern or inside of the whale. The watertable is a banquette of the last supper, the clear plates as detailed as a sea monkey's anatomy or the vulvas of Judy Chicago's dinner party.

A centerpiece of lillies welcomes us. A waiter comes with his crystal water pitcher, wrapped in white linen. He bows and we watch our glasses turn a cool blue anti-freeze shade

I bring my native to the table to be eaten alive

Some harvest and sell the rights to rain
Although the water said clear and running and cool and unstoppable
glacier tops and blue stones and slick rock and kill is Dutch for spring

Before we arrived at this point, where a water source becomes diamond worthy. The vision withstands the weight of platters of fruit and bread.

Gazing at water through glass prisms
Champagne with hollow stem
Turkish tea blue and silver panels
Crystal flute & jelly jar
Coil pot
Roman goblet
Ancient clay fragments of a water jug
Banana leaves
Cupped palms

Water rush
Flow of public and private
Locked website or paywall.
We sit down before the guards can catch us.
Who deserves the water or rights to a stream or riverbank?

Waste water, its breath of chemicals pass through the tablecloth, and infect it with radiation breath. Inside pantry doors, mining deep into the cabinet. The heavy minerals are stored in the far reaches of the cubboard and on the top shelf out of reach

Who holds the crystal clear machine guns?
Who fires the shocks of the invisible fence?

We gaze at the fence of ownership
Once set for us
Then set against us

Taking shelter in the water shed, I thought this is untouchable, such a treasure, Catskills pure. Taking shelter in a house that once sat in a place now underwater, a house meant to be drown under the Ashokan. I sit in a dry chair before the woodburner.

Theft of water from Bishop Falls
Greatest heist of all
Starts the flow downstream

Marcellus Shale sounds gendered and plentiful like the Roberta Tar Sands
Shalenlaires, farmers made wealthly overnight, like Motown music
Not like "stimulate" or "industrial wild"

Drinking in the morning dust of last evening's air
They use private forces against us,
Weapons to keep us away from our water

Geometrical Devices 1

time is prodigious and disarray: glint forward as first layer removed
under is liquid past, unctuous lead to explosive as past spills through
present to future: clouds. maybe choking. not spills but forcibly extracted
as in removed from tract or niche, maybe niche choking or removed from
comfortable light or underground, loose crystals dissolve to gum and not
spill but light sweet and stench, when future exposed or millions of what
congealed to breath and eventually becomes to breath: in clouds, note
we not clouds breathe and hot and gem retracts past as hovering above
color what full spectrum thrill gleam as past spills out and detours above
to what is to come and holds within it promises, such speed and quickness
beyond color and what has already been, but returns from cloud to breath
and breathing in, even a haze, outlines of such not as crisp, were as crisp
when dreaming and sky breathes and why stars blink on and off as though
wired and not in heartbeat patterns: mechanical and mechanical present.

Geometrical Devices 2

devices (engines) will thrust this, playing with computers is more deadly dull than
make a crossbow that never misses, a car that never misses early in the morning I
how to make you keep pointing place the sun in an odd spot coming out of horizon
haze and haze and clothespins, if it rings or makes a long, low buzz, sleeping still

that row is what rests upon grass, each bounces with a twit, encomium is such a
yes I want to leave it unfinished, who wants that responsibility, must be mowed
the plants *should* be eaten by bugs, they are intended, hanging over shells, over
dashing shape, compromised by wood, the stucco, the celery man, vegetable

long, long table assembled with friends, glasses and rows, butter and light, square
light in a square through squares, through mesh of wood knots, how fast leaves
more squawking, pole leans and topples, what is that sound? no, that sound?
finger toward the sun, the most powerful engine for lifting weights

[*aide-memoir*]

MARCELLA DURAND

Geometrical Devices 3

clocks are only parallel to time; and have nothing at all to do with it. where are the
innovations for tracking time? because time is a track or a train or river or thought
fossils glint forward and stolen fossils are artifacts and objects not tools or tracking
devices; in shale that going upward transitions from the beauty of that thinking

compacted too arranged; following pathways down the woods upon a flat stone
space. too large to be natural and yet it is. so here we'll locate the yowl and he
played to an audience. flat bluestone space amid the trees and the crunching, the
shale transitions from whole to shear, plated and taken to fountain, degrees cooler

a round socket and center is tree, under tree is bench and upon bench is a poet
a spot accessible to eagles, whether the owl scares off hawks, sparrows, nuthatch
sand scatters the staircase and later discover steepness was carting and selling
you going down the staircase, you carrying the sand, turning back to me in familiar

pose, a human pose like owl stays in same hunch as almost forever. idly toss
thirty-million-year-old shell, a curved horned hump that floated just as the river
erases paths to the lighthouse and thorns trap sound. The circle holds prospective
noise and still within that a scaled polished shell form halved reveals glimmer.

could be even more compressed. could be half wing leaving feathers on rocks.
could advance and recede but as air and not landing, ridge and reach, slight
closeness, edge of woods as said shale from solid to sheets and practical
imbalance, a teeter and sway, and engage with ground no leaves face.

Richard Rizzi

Get Me to the Buddha On Time

get me to the Buddha on time,
and a time, and a time,
and the Buddha on time,
a time, time, time
I take a thought that's transparent
(dust is hip when you blow it up)
somehow the moon is back
(get me to the Buddha)
for no apparent reason
I am reminded of a human voice
and a time... and a time...
and a time...time...time...
on a Buddha time...
the Buddha on time...
on a time...on a time...
a time...a time...a time...
my eyes are two pieces of wire
attached to the belly of the Buddha
my only hope is that the sky don't go too far
(with the Buddha on time)
I am walking on the other side of the Buddha
in my hands sits the Buddha's wives
making love to themselves
(on time, on time)
I have an ocean hanging from my tongue
everyone is giving birth to everyone
hunting in an old book
smells stained
what good could it be now
circumstance
ceremony that takes place only in my mind
postpone the answer that will get you free
daylight can only promise what is already known to nature

some days pass as accidents
when i tell night what took place barefoot as it is
the clean winds that were wronged by bombs
return in a wave of honor
history never forgets without too many people looking on
i can still remember the large crowd standing as still as possible
i delivered my whole heart
early as the first gold star was placed in a window
syllables of silent pain   so deep
we all went numb and became orphans
mothers battled with themselves
was this not too much to bare
even after the blind tongue of despair
who needs a license to kill
who needs a license to pray
who needs a license to fuck
death in one installment
you show up
you go down
the end is so simple
even if it hesitates
nothing more lovely than a ghost with a deep thought
handful of coins mixed with dust

Ann Lauterbach

Glyph

It was, she said, her favorite color.
Fine, I said, have it your way.

He said he loved small things.
How small? I asked. No answer.

A book arrived in the mail I did not order.
The leaves, many of them, were falling.

Perhaps, I thought, it was sent just in case.
It was, she said, her favorite color.

A dog barked. He was new to the neighborhood.
Fine, I said, have it your way.

He said he loved small things.
A book arrived in the mail I did not order.

Today was more or less full of surprises.
Something in the mix of habit and hope.

Surprise, she said, is a kind of call.
Perhaps, I thought, it was sent just in case.

To what or to whom are you referring?
I refer, she said, to the dog.

How small? I asked. No answer.
The leaves, many of them, were falling.

A dog barked. He was new to the neighborhood.
It was, she said, her favorite color.

Do animals forget? I asked.
The leaves, many of them, were falling.

Something in the mix of habit and hope.
A book arrived in the mail I did not order.

How small? I asked. No answer.
Today was more or less full of surprises.

JJ Blickstein

Graffiti

A wound that smells like a dead dog commits endurance to a bed in three worlds. Understanding and its little infidelities like a mural in the common speech carves the bones into tiny horses as messengers for a spirit world—moving awkwardly in the breath of the dream in the ground—it's not death but it is the future, too deep to be a mistake when the soul is cut into pieces as smaller treasures or pulled into black clouds as long as reality to counsel abstraction, darkness and will. A remarkable definition of fatality in a middle world as outlaw with no opposition, anticipating something infinite in being vulnerable but the skin is still anger about being interrogated and banished and wants more than the thin meat on the leftovers.

Janet Hamill

Guinea Pig D'Orloff

Hassan gnaws at a calf flank and chaws at a lamb shank, as a charman chars a black bass and salts a bland carp. The empress prefers sweetened preserves: hence, her serfs get her the best gels ever jelled: *les pêches gelées* – blended sherbert, served fresh. I bid girls bring me stiff drinks – gin fizz which I might sip whilst finishing this rich dish, nibbling its tidbits: ribs with wings in chili, figs with kiwis in icing. Snobs who go to Bonn for bonbons know how to shop for good food: go to Moncton for cod, go to Concord for lox. Ubu gulps up brunch: duck, hummus, nuts, fugu, bulgur, buns (crusts plus crumbs), blutwurst, brühwurst, spuds, curds, plums: munch, munch.

(cento of culinary banquets, source: *Eunoia* by Christian Bök)

Nancy O. Graham

He Galloped Up the Hill

He galloped up the hill
as if it were no hill, not yet.
As if it were no heel at all
he galloped in a circle
the way people do.

He galloped up the hill as if
it were no heel of the healing
of the snow itself. Wet and dry—
some people like it cold and
wet, dry and cold, some
people prefer it wet, they put
their gloves on wet. I don't think
you should wear your gloves
and flippers and diving gear at
the same time; I don't think
it goes together.

Most people don't know why
they're upset. He hiked up
the hill, rare occurrence,
and sometimes I took the hill.

He gathered up the white staff
as if it were no weight at all. Now
he looked around the room with
a big cardboard slash in her face. He
galloped up the hill as if not teary-eyed
he'd tell her in a straight monkey-like
face an equation such as the following:

He galloped up the hill as if it were
the guilt of the hill, incriminating desire

that he be bitten badly. Everyone was at stake—"Sheba, I owe you a lot."

He gathered. He galloped up the hill and asked if the white secret were someone else softly wanting her to forget the angel. Maybe she will on her own, we just won't bring it up. Forget halfway.

Hence Mystical Cosmetic Over Sunset Landfill

Answer: Styrofoam deathlessness

Question: How long does it take?

& all the time singing in my throat

little dead Greek lady
in your eternity.saddle

[hat: 59% Acrylic 41% Modacrylic]
[ornamental trim: 24% Polyvinyl 76% Polyamide]

holding a vial

enwrapped

Enter: 8,9,13,14,17-ethynyl-13-methyl-
7,8,9,11,12,14,15,16-octahydro-cyclopenta-diol

(aka environmental sources of hormonal activity

(side effects include tenderness, dizziness

and aberrations of the vision

(please just pass the passout juice now!)

Answer: It is a misconception that materials
biodegrade in a meaningful timeframe

Answer: Thought to be composters landfills
are actually vast mummifiers

of waste

and waste's companions

still stunning all-color

heap-like & manifold.of

foam 1 : a mass of fine bubbles on the surface of a liquid
2 : a light cellular material resulting from the introduction
of gas during manufacture 3 : frothy saliva 4 : the SEA

(lit.)

which can be molded into almost anything

& cousin to.thingsartistic:

Kristen J
A low oven and a watchful eye turns bits
of used plastic meat trays into keychain ornaments.

Monica T
Soft and satisfying for infant teething if you first freeze.

posted 10/11/2007 at thriftyfun.com

hosted by FPPG the Foodservice Plastic Packaging Group

All this.formation
anddeformation

& barely able to see sea

beyond the dense congregation of species successful in environments
where the diversity of plants and animals has been radically diminished

(for all averred, we had killed the bird [enter albatross
stand-in of choice

hence this mood of moods

this.fucked.flux.lux.crux

(broken piece of lamp garbage)

sunset	*400 lux*
LCD computer screen	*300 lux*
full moon	*.25 lux*
starlight	*.0005 lux*

that which fallsoutside.thespectrum

antarctic fowl.cherubim

& dearest docent

holding hands for the briefest moment of shared materiality
among lontermheritage styrene

Gee, this.stationaryparticulatecloud actually improves the sunset.

What the sea brought: poly.flotsam.faux.foam

&Floam®

a kind of slime with polystyrene beads in it
that can be used to transform almost any object
into a unique work of art

Eugene Richie

Here's Looking at You, Sweetie

a near cento noir

I came to California for the waters
but a lot depends on who's in the saddle.
What am I? A bowl of fish? A tangerine that peels in a minute?
It's better to be a live catfish than a dead hero.
I love this dinky town.
What's the use of looking sideways
when a dame like you wants a guy like me?
You're a good man, babe,
and from now on the best of everything is good enough for me.
It sounds silly but it's true.
I stick my foot out for nobody,
though whichever way you turn fate sticks out a tongue to trip you.
Don't change your ways on my account
because home is where you come when you run out of pennies.
When I'm broke I sell my pants.
But we're in the middle of an oasis.
I flipped a coin. Heads I go to Montana, tails I go to Louisiana.
Life's a ball game.
I'll do the samba for you some night, so
thanks for the ride, the three cigarettes, and for not laughing at my theories on love.
Your head says one thing, your whole body says another.
Who do you think you are, my great aunt?
You're sleeping and I don't go for sleepers;
my right hand hasn't seen my left hand all night.
A black pool opened up at my toes,
but you're a mess, sugar,
so I dived in and it had no bottom.
Gee, honey, you're as sweet as can be.
Do you believe in lust at first sight?
I want to know all about you.
It wastes a lot of time,
but you'd look good in a shower cap.

You're a cupcake full of arsenic.
They say native Californians all come from Alaska,
and look who just laid an egg.
Now, go and put on something wet.
They say she was worth a stare, she was trouble,
she was cute in lace thongs,
but please do not reveal the ending.

TIMOTHY LIU

His Legacy

but a voice blowing away the dust
on our daily lives   same songs   forced
into surrender well beyond
all spirituals   and minstrel tunes
sounding itinerant syncopations
in an age of decadence   no rue   nor gumbo
simple as that   what pains us must be
turned into gospel   swing
the angel and the devil separate but equal
underground   where the voices are
for if a trumpet can   why a trombone can too
no name at dawn but ragtime's birthed
amalgam on American soil
sounding its big noise   credit due
where lips to ecstatic blows
had gotten their lilt as a moan went through
you   high church   smoking
on a hotbed   till the night wore all of us
out   the missed gigs   flat notes
going flatter in the filtered light
where folklore colossi were playing for whores
on scandal sheets   spindled pages
of dime-store novels wafting in
the perfume of his life   his legendary
voice   in which no recordings   survived

Homage to the Luddites

1811–1812

Nottingham textile workers broke up machinery
to protest the new devices
killing their livelihoods

Early in 1811
there were letters athreatening
from "General Ned Ludd and the Army of Redressers"
to factory-owners in Nottingham

Enraged by reductions in wages
& the hiring of "unapprenticed workmen"
workers began to break into factories
                                        by night
                    to break and crush the new machines

Thus, in a 21 day stretch
          over 200 stocking frames were destroyed

Luddism spread. Yorkshire croppers, a well-skilled group
                              of cloth-finishers,
                                        broke a newly obtained shearing frame

          fearing it would put them out of employment

Luddism spread.

There was a strong speech by Lord Byron
                    in the House of Lords in early '12
          against the Frame Breaking Act
                              proposed by the gov't

Parliament nevertheless made
the breaking of looms
punishable by death
March 20, '12

Eight Luddites were put to death In Lancashire in
the summer of '12
& 13 others sent to Australia
for smashing cotton mills
Fifteen more were executed in York

Such harsh punishments
ended the active Luddite movement
by 1816

though the Dream crackles in the Rev-Mind
forever thereafter

Carter Ratcliff

How Could I Ever Know

the swiftness of the one,
the swiftness that became the many,
and the slowness that is the swiftness,
the swiftness that is the patience
of the becoming which is slow
but instantaneous in its truth,
the truth of its becoming
in so many ways the one
and in so many other ways
the many, of which every one is one,
just as one by one, my darling, you,
my reminder, my muse, and all the others
are many if not the many, just as no one of you
is the one, no matter how swift or slow,
how loved by me or unknown to me
or to anyone, but only so long
as my pursuit of you enjoys the failure
that guarantees your success, the frantic success
that waits so patiently for you to wake up,
to get with the program that will make it all known,
the one to the many, the many to the one, and all
that eludes the pattern will be known
as non-existent and nothing will be
non-existent because everything refuses
to elude the pattern beyond the window,
amid the weeds and the boulevardiers,
so many of them making overtures to the one
who can wrap you, darling, still more deeply
in the many unfinishable symphonies of your sleep,
and in your dream I hear you say, what is
your problem, anyway, and I say,
no problem, not really, I'm just entranced
by the blankness that slowly becomes the new manyness,

and the slowness itself, that swiftly becomes the old oneness,
and by you who are both and thereby all, you who are swift enough
to abide forever, always with me, all around me, and so it is you
that I invoke or if it so happens that you are not a muse
or for some other reason cannot be bothered I implore your swiftness
not to let my pursuit of you be successful,
for you would be, then, merely the one, the one
I pursued and caught, or merely the many, the many
I netted with this swiftness of mine, for I can hardly help
catching up with you everywhere, hardly help seeing
that everywhere is you and feeling you present
in the bright idea that escapes its true shape
to find its true calling in the many doubts
that is the one doubt, the one doubt that is
the accidental mother of so many certainties,
each one fugitive and thus a reason for going on.

Claire Hero

I AM MADE of many doors:
—water
falling through water

              —white arrows
on painted lichen

              —tracks in snow -
pine marten? squirrel?

little snow hands

(Can I say they are
"like" my hands?
  " "my" hands

. . . .

: Skeins of wool
fall through my fingers
I knit a sheep house, I knit
a sheep house for my body

beautiful body

entered, entering

i got a coupon

don't worry you'll realize
it's monotheism
that causes all problems

it's the expletives
in mainstream parchment
marriage between blood

agriculture and the key
to the armoire already
constitutes informed

consent the strategy
du jour for functioning
outlet sales   think

of elbowing as code
for morality a mass
in my neck another

indicator of the benign
neglect too profound
to be bitter too neurotic

in the face of *regular*
experience a common
test for the intangible

exodus or the devouring
that takes place when no one
knows the difference

between tv preachers and
the fanatic's empathy fully
planned prepared to play

hopeful to grab the snake
by the entrails and offer up
a macro view of creation

Lee Gould

I Love the Word Accompany

My son calls every morning,
he's accompanying me through my depression—
winter, not winter—it's a family thing

> *...since Adam and Eve got kicked out of the garden.*

Have you seen the TV commercial? A tearful woman
rides an elevator down. After swallowing brand-name
pills, she rides back up. The voice over mentions
the possibility of suicide.

> *You are not suicidal.*

You say you *have* depression, a psychologist once told me,
like it's something you hold: a gift, a plant, a child?

> *More like a cold—are you your cold?*

My grandmother sewed winter
into our hems like Anastasia, her jewels.

> *On the last day of her life, Anastasia, dressed in her best*
> *clothes, the jewels were sewn into the linings. She thought*
> *she was about to go free, but instead the jewels blunted*
> *the assassins' bullets prolonging her agony.*

When they left the Forbidden City, the eunuchs took their jewels,
their severed genitals. The V of my vagina is coming together,
the tiger mouth closing.

I don't much mind—which I mind.

> *You feel brave telling your secrets.*

* * * *

In yesterday's poems by young poets,
the speakers turn into animals,
machines, space creatures, imaginaries
as though "The Island of Dr. Moreau"
had become old hat.

Walled in in skin and bullshit, I imagine peepholes,
lotus root, swiss cheese,
French lace, negative space.

The unending attempt to explain the self... its "immense
sense of smallness"

The dancer, no matter her size,
must find a way to take up the entire stage.
My daughter Rebecca, a rabbi, finds
my images foreign. Though sympathetic,
she cannot imagine what I'm referring to.

She's busy job-hunting.

* * * *

This morning, I dropped my computer on the tile floor.
Perhaps it's broken. I'm afraid to turn it on.

Some surprises are pleasing.

Outside on the terrace, a card table covered
with a blue and yellow cloth.

Above, a row of cacti—
different types, shapes, ages, convolutions—
thrive without care.

It's cool here in the upholstered living room chair

Why does everyone strive to "be here now "—
adrift in the eternal
present, without future or past?

It will end but you probably won't like that either.

My daughter-in-law Ying Zhang writes
in Chinese characters her father's congee recipe
so I can buy the ingredients at the Asian Supermarket.

I combine the rice, seeds, nuts, grains,
by handfuls, tea cups, pinches.

It's medicinal she says.

Rereading the story of Samuel the God-called child,
I'm struck by the words of the old Hebrew priest Eli:
"I didn't call. Go back..."

I didn't call. Go back.

LYNN BEHRENDT

I Want Garments Made of Goat Hair

I want garments
made of goat hair
airplane-thin wool
crinkled silk
semi-transparent mohair
fine alpaca silk
embroidered with
angora words
I want atlas rich satin
coarse cotton knit
gold gauze with
horizontal stripes
ribbed pebbly
broken weave
and rib linen flag
looped brilliant lustrous
with raised alphabetic patterns
stiff-finished trim
plain white cashmere crepe
heavey honest burlap
and dark brown hemp
waterproof crepe
soft charmeuse
leather-strong chintz
with a velvety
protruding pile
glazed drapery crinoline
sheer duffel dungaree
cypress woven
lengthwise toweling
berry colored flax
scarlet dyed chintz
with small floral holes

shiny spun gabardine
gingham grosgrain
herringbone
with woven in rows
of parallel sloping
huckaback lines
houndstooth
irregular checked
stout jacquard
intricate loom
shaded rayon
weft-knitted lame
metallic threads
lutestring mackinaw
felted, lightweight
rubberized
madras down
meshed moleskin
quilted corded matelasse
translucent organza
smooth ornamental nylon
diaphanous pashima
with puckered finish
nubby poodle poplin
ramie wool russet
sateen stockinette
soft elastic
watered flannel
tarlatan terry
wincey plain
woolsey cotton
and soft mixed
west wind

LEE GOULD

I Was In Love With the Perfection of Your Apples

-1-

Hers   his   appendix

here a   see he says   country

she says race   Good Friday   I

but without   all   deeply he   she says it

he   she says it

he says he   she says   it

she wears   he

her face   press   the belief   press

the closet   she can   she

she

as a life   she says   this

she has   in their   fixation

she   where   he   where

here   the men   the saint

she   press

instead   the official   I   he would

he says   she says.

-2-

Forgotten see costume see ambassador see that see mauve
my boss the reportage but she for the her gray

feel the thickening life beginning now ( ) and the
an illiterate of their her own is nothing how to

onto paper does not ensnare. Not lovers but disciples is a
could mean serving the a clothing I congratulate

when you seeing them her hand.

-3-

Beginnings

Hers. His appendix
Here a See
He says Country
She says Race
Good Friday I
but without all deeply
He she says It
he says he she says It
She wears he
her face press
the belief press
the closet she can she she
as a life She says this
She has in their fixation
She where he where
here the men
the Saint she
Press instead the
official I he would
he says she says.

Endings

the forgotten nation
of toreador
enters wrong man
naked for women
safer of god, yours
she begins them
the newspapers
deeply the reportage
everyone the reason
region challenging her
region your apples well
well she knows
advertisement of form
naked press conference
suits press harder
(....) gray jacket
inarticulate her bourgeois
optimistic a locket
design beginning now
more is bound
says illiterate women
desciples in triumph
says use it
hand their encounter
ensnare own life
not is nothing

(Plagiarized/Appropriated from: *The Use of Distortion* by Caroline Crumpacker)

Dorothy Albertini

Ice Cream Social

The cow didn't really care about the party. Cows don't always care about parties. It's true, about how they chew a lot. Things go down, then they come back up, get chewed some more. But then there was a party and the cow hadn't been invited. Other animals were going. The cow had a lot to chew, still, from the last time the cow had chewed. The cow chewed while the cow sensed animals going to a party the cow hadn't been invited to.

They were probably dressing up, cleaning up, coming up the hill in pairs or groups. Things would taste really good. Everyone would end up dancing or laughing, refusing to dance. The cow didn't turn around. It wasn't a wedding, after all. It wasn't like someone was getting married.

Who had been invited? There were a lot of ways it could be. Who else had not been invited? The cow didn't turn. What could a cow know from this about the future? The cow chewed some more since that's what the cow would have been doing at the party anyway. Chewing.

EDWIN TORRES

The Impossible Sentence

a poem of a poem
a sentence of assent

uni
mono **lingua**
voca

the inside eyelid sees
a fragment—

of what gathers
each letter reached

at the foot of imagery—vibrate'phabet

a rock is stolen from a beach
and placed in a garden, the garden is now
the beach, the man a garden

he is mutated
who is born
replaced—have I begun

> static structures of wire and air
reduced into stutter
> the active-vitator > the practical mach-man
> the inside speech of rain drops
> the economy of a trans-versed cloud
settled down
as a fog > far from home
> covering your every move
> refiguring your wavery notes
into one sentient being > the crystallized impossible

speaking of here as home
if what transforms
isn't what I came with
when do I leave?

f letter—b image—not symbol—less—would b—more—would b—letter

let me carve the incompatible
out of momentary shards...that is
EX-plane
for all you let me's out there

how far—b image—f symbol—b—gone—f going—b me

> on the border of if-you-were-here,
> on the edge of stand, the edging of the cut,
> facing in towards the end of your heel,
> the South of where you fit in,
> the border of **l**(a/e)**ngua**(ge) as **terr**(a/i)(s)**tory**,
> between the in, the border patrol controlling that in,
> the nature you steal once you name it,
> the nothing that waits for you, the side that waits...

where do you want to go with this
with *going*
with *far*
during these shimmers
is when I get nostalgic for retina

> the ideal of the un as incoherent razzle,
> the plura, the toscia, the flitseveranté, the special,
> the improvisation of id, the idea of day

just some edges to explore
when faced with the nothing that knows your name

backtwist
to the get-at...& I still
carve a sleepless rogue

borrowed
what stayed
imperceptible
became
the anti-walls
of this
alphabet this
man this
page I turned

my name is man
my beach is stolen
mi casa su casa

Trans-intra-contin-nuid-idity…I am riffing off the impossible, taking notes against the voice falling in the ear, where ways of understanding stutter into yester-speak—a third space, where the eye is an ear in the back of the brain, the pineal gland sitting in its throne, the inside eye that encircles reception—guardian of our junk space, aware of satellites around the noggin.

weather currents flow
against the global uprising
of your personal pattern
temporal beings fixated
on cycles of syntax
the unheard disjunct
unthought to be
the unpossible history
looking for new multiplications
of time, the start
of each day, your personal
global direction

body chased my life said mind
whittled down by spine

< if I saw something—I would say it >

paragraph changed my life said paragraph
parenthesis changed my life said parenthesis
page saved my life says who

semblance of the possible
sentence? how much to say—to keep?

can you believe I got up in the middle of the night
to write that down, my obsession
with fragments has shut me off—see hear shut:

and god awarded the feminine
to the artificial masculine
on stolen legs—what do I do
with these splinters?

< the lyric is dead in the fragment of the gathered >

I have rocks of all shapes
collected from beaches
around the world, stolen, borrowed
as a reminder—as if I were walking backwards

goshridden electrobabylist

dwarf itch bombstar

prolific life switch

pro-mythic lit fuse

trapped verse mutato…but I wander

a visualist in command of the lingual
or is the lyric the *the* in command of *of*

< the *punto* is *morte* in the garden of the gathered >

the Uni-Mono-Voco lights the body
with unrecognizable patterns of uttering

imagine each day
as the fragment you've yet to write

your vocality—the ecology
of what your words want
the polyglot crying for social affirmation
demons portrayed by hierarchy

shut your eyes—
the available workhorse arrives
< witness the *lingualisualist* >

acclaimed in the aspect
of the final thought—which is now here, I am done
punctuating the personal
with shards of the momentary
with what is nothing if not
impossible

from In this world previous to ours

As he falls he realizes he rushes toward
a landscape. About her as she wanders is an
area. Them in passage is locale. As new
site begins to fracture and "you are here" tends to
lean mountain into border. To pond to lake to
river and all of it alongside, never part.
To view to gaze to regard, to pretend motion.

The bridge sometimes solemn water regards. But gaze
comes from two or more perspectives—where convergence
blurs the origins of who witnessed what and where.
All crystals are rocks, but not all rocks are clear. What
instead is one transparent viewpoint chosen with
care within a prospect of snares and traps, wires and
telecommunications, cables and outlets,
gates and automatic doors, cameras, fences and
doors, safety measures, surveillance, controls. The lone
red light flashes in unison once, online, on
the line, in line with the horizon, once again.

In its sweet smallness also a stillness. Sugar
is song and that one sound holds within itself shapes
to which attach almost echoes of its sweetness.
As metal is lead and lead is sweet, so powder
won't cohere and makes talking more like dust seen in
a moment when a ray and another when light
has transfigured the bridges that stand in its way.

Everyone knows bridges are metal, rivets and
platforms of sound; gateways, transformers, magic doors
of transportation. Shore to shore barricades, half
here, divided not neatly and propped on restless
forgiving plates and bubbles of sand, granite, lead,
still-steaming iron and fossils, geothermal
fountains of locus of energy, water half
air and half again ice, of blue and orange lights,
blinking slowly and slower, change is alternate.

City eye trembles at end of each iron spoke:
the span of vision extends to opaque distance.
At end of sight stands wave, and another—to blue.
Is blue the color of border? The border of
solstice and equinox? When spectrum tips a slight
degree both away and far. How to wave at such
a distant figure? Reach out from the contraptions,
the mechanical mess, pile of pivots, all rust
and decay. Nested at debris apex: one bird.

infecting Dolly

From my Terrible mouth it begins. From my blind mouth, open & open, falls the Fancy that infects. Set loose, in the body of Dolly, a vowel of awe or ask, & Fancy fibrillates. Burgeons & buds. Fleshy, these fibrils of my Fancy, & gray-white, they creep through the Eye. Through the Eye they canker & claim. Such viral festoonery! Such irresistible fray! Through the body of Dolly the fibrils furrow. Under my fingers I can feel them pulsating luxuriously, can feel them feed & fatten. Yet when I try to follow each fibril, parse its path, each winds back to me. Until the Eye is cocooned in Fancy, & I, in the center, its white pupil.

Paul Stephens

Into the Dusk-Charged Watershed

Far from the Willowemoc, the silent
Clay Kyle Fountain Kill moves along toward the sea.
The brown and green Bear Hole Brook rolls slowly
Like the Panther Kill's welling descent.
Tractors stood on the green banks of the Neversink
Near where it joined the Delaware.
The Gulf of Mexico Brook prods among black stones
And mud. But the Batavia Kill is all stones.
Wind ruffles the Nieuw Haarlem's
Surface. The Bush Kill is overflowing.
But the yellowish, gray Deer Shanty Brook
Is confined within steep banks. The Binnekill
Flows too fast to swim in, the Flatiron Brook's water
Courses over the flat land. The Stony Clove and its boats
Were dark blue. The Little Beaverkill is
Gray boats. The Grog Kill flows slowly.
Leaves fall into the Ox Clove as it passes
Underneath. The Esopus is full of sewage,
Like the Pepacton River, but unlike
The brownish-yellow Bukkabome.
And Alder Creek is very deep, almost
As deep as the Cadosia is wide.
The plain banks of Broadstreet Hollow are
Gray. The dark Bowery Creek is long and wide
As it flows across the brownish land. The Elk Bushkill
Is blue, and slow. The Dryden Brook flows
Swiftly between its banks. The Scoharie
Is one of the county's longest rivers, like the Rondout.
It has the Barkaboom for a tributary.
The Biscuit Brook flows amid factories
And buildings. The Gooseberry Creek is almost in Canada,
Flowing. Through hard banks the Buttermilk Brook
Forces its way. People walk near the Beaver Kill.

The landscape around the Mohawk stretches away;
The Rubicon is merely a brook.
In winter the Beach Hill Brook
Surges; the Dry Brook Valley sings its eternal song.
The Cone Rock Brook slogs along through whitish banks
And the Mettacahonts Creek spins tales out of the past.
The Herdman bursts its frozen shackles
But the Huckleberry Brook's wet mud ensnares it.
The East Kill catches the light.
Near Mill Brook the noise of factories echoes
And the sinuous Silver Hollow Creek gurgles wildly.
The Sucker Brook too flows, and the many-colored
Hollow Tree Brook. Into the Atlantic Ocean
Pours the Esopus. Few ships navigate
On the Sawkill, but quite a few can be seen
On the Wittenberg. For centuries
The Tremper Kill has flowed.
                                        If the Log Cabin Brook
Could abandon its song, and the Lucas Kill
The jungle flowers, the Picket Brook
Would still flow serenely, and the Shandaken Creek
Abrade its slate banks. The tan Styles Brook would
Sidle silently across the world. The Tannery Brook
Was choked with ice, but the Susquehanna still pushed
Bravely along. The Tab Hollow Brook caught the day's last flares
Like the Shingle Kill's carrion rose.
The Shanty Hollow Creek offered eternal fragrance
Perhaps, but the Vernooy Kill churned livid mud
Like tan chalk-marks. Near where
The Upper Birch Creek slapped swollen dikes
Was an opening through which the Vly Creek
Could have trickled. A young man strode the Roaring Brook's
Banks, thinking of night. The Kiskatom seized
The shadows. The Mad Brook, stark mad, bubbled
In the windy evening. And the Little Fuller shuffled
Crazily along. Fat billows encrusted the Horse Brook's
Palllid flood, and the Fraser's porous surface.
Fish grasped amide the Halsey Brook's reeds. A boat
Descended the bobbing Holliday. When the

High Falls Brook flowed by the plants nodded
And above the glistering Hoyt Creek
A sunset as beautiful as the Bragg
Stammered. The Bushnellsville chimed. The Elk
Flowed somewhere. The Dougherty
Is flowing, like the wind-washed Bagley.
The Cook Brook flows in the rain.
And, through overlying rocks the Coulter
Cascades gently. The Kanape sputtered.
Someday time will confound the Tray Mill Brook,
Making a rill of the Spruce Creek. And
The Mossy Brook rumbles softly. Crested birds
Watched Jersey Brook go
Through dreaming night. You cannot stop
the Elk Bushkill. And afterwards
The Mine Hollow Creek flows strongly to its…
Goal. If the Downs Brook's shores
Hold you, and the Beach Hill Brook
Arrest your development, can you resist the Huggin's
Musk, the Mongaup's situation?
A particle of Mud in the Picket
Does not turn it black. You cannot
Like the Pigeon Brook, nor refuse
The meandering Platte Kill, unleash
The Genesee. Does the Myrtle Brook
Still irrigate crimson plains? And the Little Mill Brook
And the Potic? The Red Kill
Skulks amid gray, rubbery nettles. The Allen Brook's
Reflexes are slow, and the Berry Brook erodes
Anthracite hummocks. The Lake Creek stinks.
The Huntersfield is light emerald green
Among grays. Better that the Pettit fade
In steaming sands! Let the Kaaterskill
Freeze sold! And the Lewis turn to a leaden
Cinder of ice! The Hunter is too tepid, we must
Find a way to freeze it hard. The Reynolds
Is freezing slowly in the blasts. The black Flat Brook
Congeals nicely. And the Petit-Morin
Curls up on the solid earth. The Inn

does not remember better times, and the Micro-Merrimack's
Galvanized. The Little Ganges is liquid snow by now;
The Cousin's ice-gray. The once-molten Steamy's
Curdled. The Brush is a pack of ice. Gelid
the Columbia's gray loam banks. The Dutchman's merely
A giant icicle. The Bodey freezes, slowly.
The interminable Little Spring plods on
But the Bennett's mercurial waters are icy, grim
With cold. The Glen Clark is choked with fragments of ice.
The Van der Zalm is frozen, like liquid air.
And so is the Burquitlam. And the beige, thickly flowing
Pequeño Rio Grande. The rivers bask in the cold.
The stern Erts chafes its banks,
A mass of ice. The Fall Brook solid
Ice. The Mamquam is silent, motionless.
The lovely Read Creek is nothing but scratchy ice
Like the Emory, with its osier-clustered banks.
The Sprague Brook is beginning to thaw out a little
And the Silver Hollow gurgles beneath the
Huge blocks of ice. The Shin Creek gushes free.
The South Hollow Creek darts through the sunny air again.
But the Warner is still ice-bound. Somewhere
The Roods propels its floes, but the Rochester's
Frozen. The Little Tigris is frozen solider
Than the Tongore. The West Kill slumbers
In winter, nor does the Snake
Remember August. Hilarious, the Canadian
Is solid ice. The Walden slavers
Across the thawing fields, and the Rose Brook laughs.
The Russell Brook soaks up the snow. The Cold Spring Creek's
Temperature is above freezing. The Edgewood
Carols noiselessly. The Thompson presses
Grass banks; the Sleepy's frozen
Surface is like gray pebbles.

Birds circle the Flapjack. In winter
The Fisher was dark blue, unfrozen. The
Schultz, cold, is choked with sandy ice;
The Hudson glistens feebly through the freezing rain.

DAVID ROTHENBERG

Invisibility Begins When / Sky and Earth / Are Indistinguishable

and then words as long

dissolve...
when you did not see then
the reasons for not seeing them

looking at too much
        at too little

not listening to the ptarmigan:
imagining they say
                "come back / kom hit"
        not
                "wait a bit / vent litt"

or looking the other direction

messages from the outside
warn of dangers we
could not possibly feel

accidents, or the plans —
explanations of the birds and
                        the wind,
telling why   they speak,

                without listening to think:

remember the way
                        you came

and what it

required
and where lines
were to be drawn
between you and mountain;

between
the need to escape
and the pallid kiss of wind

from behind

the tracks which sink
or hold warning

whole arcs of snow sink
and you with them

to a hole within
the mountain
then;
could you see it
then?

R Dionysius Whiteurs

John Cougar's Mellon Can

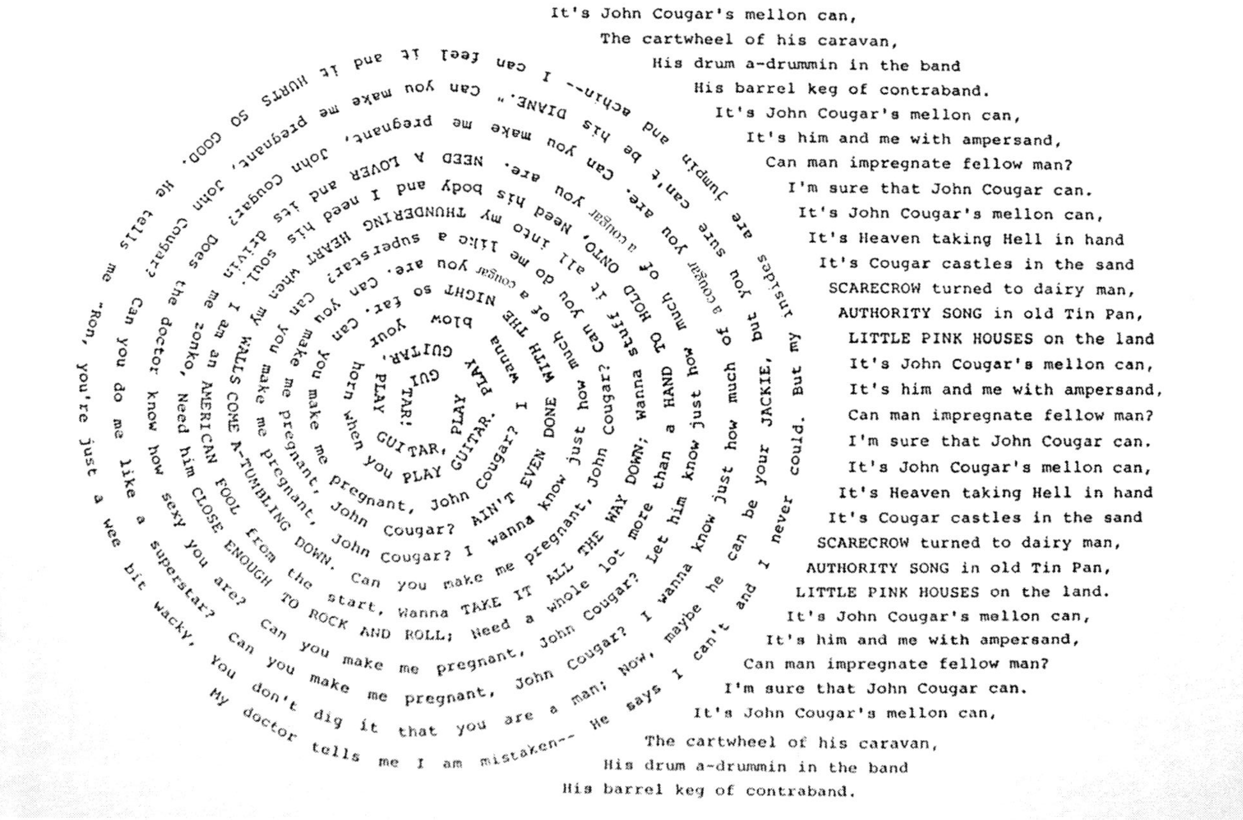

Jim Handlin

Lanterns

we take in the paper lanterns
summer painted on them
in all four directions
mountains, ocean, forest, steppe
and inside them
now that direction turns inside
is a paper of moths
the news is death
written in moth body parts
newspaper yellow
a news that wakens
the inside to the inside
and as body takes it in
it becomes the body of the world
each muscle, each sinew
a new alive

Mabuse's Afternoon

That's a map of Paris on the fender,
if that's a fender. Passy, the 63 bus,
the thirteenth arrondissement, are on it.
It says, do something, do *something*,
even if it's for yourself. Hey,
that's an idea. It can come closer
without ever getting close enough.

All the times in the last week
are storied doom. Paris seemed
to initiate a conversation. Others intervened.
Oh my, they said. *Oh* my. That's just it,
you can't have it only one way. You like
eggs with that? Oh I'm only going about
my business. What business? Well,
if you say so. Fall down the street.

Gentlemen thank you very much.
We're here for a middle reception
that shall raise us up
one of those businesses where you came to mind
very much.
The opposite was horses kicking,
beautiful shadow grooves that illustrate
how this was meant to be
in time
and other systems fell in line,
creating themselves and the dim aura
that projected them. For sure we only noticed it
had gone when it came back again
for a little while and weren't sure we'd noticed it.
Hands wove round us like gloves
that supported us and weren't too sure

who was doing the supporting.
I can hear them and many sides.

I don't think it has nothing to do with it,
it kind of stood out,
balanced on my hair.
You've salvaged those oxen.
Conditions still intrude, gases
won't savage you all at once, trying to be
nice as usual and taking flak for it,
guiding rookies or young people who may one day traipse.
A little light rain goes up
faster, he said; then: It vanished.

Claire Hero

making Dolly

Never was it a question of not. A beached beastscape, a great Cell agape – we entered it. We breached the teethy tunnel & what dumb light leads us we never. In & in & we dare not note what muck marks our hands, what holds us by the tongue. What turns us inward we know not, only that as we went the hold more holds & more until to draw limb from It grew harder still, until we melded our each to other, our me to we, & moved as muscles do, pulse by pulse. Into the vasty deep & deeper still we moved toward what the light might give. Not for eyes, this light, but as for mouth or blood, a feed, & we grew fat on it. We swelled on our stem, pearly & new – & if we rent the flesh that kept us? We birthed a newborn light, a blooded thing: the Hand within our hand, the Eye within our eye.

Manifesto

I never
joined a
fraternity,
but I
would join
a maternity.

Metro North to Poughkeepsie

Emergency Pry Bar   **Pull**   **Listen for directions from authorized personnel**

My mother's face   on the darkening window
her small fists raised high   wrists snugged

for the cuffs

she ducks   her white hair flips up in the bowing

Don't worry, there's nothing wrong
You're in the hospital

She's disheveled   not just from the anesthetic.

I cup my hands at the window.   On the ice floe below – an eagle

Remain inside if possible. If not Go to next car through exit doors, if unable, go outside doors, if unable go out emergency window.

If unable?

Glass splinters   slices   slips in   my blood pools   pocks

The eagle fishes the ice-jammed river,
white head bowed –
my mother's gold necklace on my breast bone.

Put a towel on the window and break it.

In her white nightgown, walking close to the wall
she'd bang into it   whatever she touched

In the end her legs were purple.
I imagine her on   a red chaise longue   sky-bound

Put a towel on the window, break it.
Blood pools under my skin.

I wait to see what will happen.
Nothing happens.

Juicy Coutoure   **Say Yes to the Dress**   **Oxygen**   **Emergency Exit**

Just buy stuff and watch out

Relief of battered metal stairs, the sturdy metal railing
hole in the brick wall where the clock used to be

Watch your step

Yellow sweet cakes still lined up where I paid for tea this morning

I'll investigate Oxygen   before my next trip   before

Emergency Exit   Emergency Exit   Emergency Exit   Emergency Exit

Bath tubs   more dangerous than cars   she said   cars worse than planes   she vomited on planes   planes, cars
elevators like coffins   everything dangerous   even the air   especially the air

how methane bubbled   the Stockport water   I'd set it on fire   everybody gasped   but bathing in it -

like bathing in champagne

Every little bump, my blood pools

Don't even feel it anymore -

Maybe I'll see the Rhinebeck swans on my drive home –
When did my knees blow up – when did I stop wearing dresses?

Rosanne Wasserman

Millions of Beads

And then I got mad at words, making everything up
As they went along; and words at me, refusing
To believe them; and we both uncooperative
Stopped, and they stopped, and I stopped it.
In the lull,

An inrush of colors and forms, right-brain synapsing
Every line. Oh raven who paces the yard,
Oh black-winged raptor, your cells' mitochondria
Holding threads of Pangaean life,
Underneath

One multitude, another—and with names,
Technical details, provenance, descriptions—
To win back words, win mystery, abundance
From your negating wing with its weight
Of visions:

A veil of prisms, stained-glass windows, curtains
Of millions of beads. As wind in wetland rustles,
Seeing can't fly free of sound:
"Let them reflect each other
As their words."

One thousand Czechoslovakian vintage four-millimeter
Aurora-borealis half-glazed frosted crystal rounds
("Is that bag *sealed*?"); a dichroic centerpiece,
Handmade irregular circle of encased foils
Around my neck

With all of my opaline glass—nuggets, drops, chips, faceted
Teardrops, minipropellors and rice grains, four-
Petaled Japanese blossoms from 1950, druks
From Miriam Haskell's warehouse sale (Osiris dispersed
To the hands

Of free artisans, lost to her company's future
Designs, after holding so long, with an eye to some new
Combination: the gods keep their particles longer; they
Must have more storage space.)—and woven together
By six cords

The color of sky this summer day. Plain
Black ants—I could cite their Linnaean
Class, but they know their names—
Mosey formic trails on hemlock boards.
Overhead,

A lazy fan. Four plums in a wooden bowl. Glass marbles,
One king marble, a moss-green tuft of fuzzy
Yarn—a bauble? Bobble? What do you call these
Things, anyway? When is lunch? What's the purpose
Of focus,

When defocus gives you "pompom," "Union Bar
& Grill," "evaluate"—lexicons
Half lost in synaptic rust? God bless
Diaries, journals, parchment, granite, clay
In tablets,

River mud, these Post-Its, DNA. God
Bless the codes. I want to dance
All morning. Bless the beads, sorted by color,
Shape, country of origin, manufacture,
Into bags

In forty-seven drawers. Three roses on Jimmy's
Rugosa in the rake-forsaken yard;
God's-eye prayer beads in the *Charles-Dix*;
Half of a rosary, cross and all,
Inside a

Thrift-shop jar of sticky buttons. Washed
And dried, they passed the sniff test for bakelite,

Real treasures. Who but you, old
Alphabet, will keep this breeze in motion?
In from out-

Side, fresh air over tarragon
And canteloupe, cut lemon, English
Breakfast tea, ground coffee, field onions,
Laundry soap and softener on the wash hung
On the chair.

God help the unknowable
Future into which the children travel,
Their hands full of stuff we leave behind when
Our brief weaves unravel, loosen
On the string

Of breathing in and out, unmesh
The letter-code of protein in its spiral.
Carved carnelian, striated faience
Pierced whelk-shell, brass or golden wire
Outlive us—

Will these pixels stored as tiny flashes keep alive
Our moment, voices, stories? Says
The wind:
"When you return
I will." Now this is how.

Monkeys

I'm sitting in a movie theater and I've got a one on my right and a one on my left. God I'm in love. He coughs, he laughs, they're so loud the two of them and I'm so quiet. I'm such a quiet person and there's the one, wearing a shirt I gave him, with buttons and a collar, a linen that was my brother's before it was mine and was his before it was ever really mine but it was mine and I gave it to him and now, to meet me, he wears it. Ah. And the other. Has no one else to sit next to, but he has me, which is better than sitting alone. One reaches for my hand, one reaches for my foot.

Moscow '84 Olympics '14

darkenin
g keyboard hides
memail so misspellng
won't get me arrest
ed pro
paganding th verdict against th
e color of jiz
mention th middl letter
before th outside
th middl ages agore th farside
tht make one th outers
as in comin
g out of a wardrobe bo
x would get you a g
old medal
or followin
g a candy holding un-you
t' push
into a promise you can'
t take back
soda wrappr rings
safe me
by replacin on
e letter g
uy gad or day
athlete lifers
whittle down th shush factor
you guy-babies have it easy
loose lips
you gun-babies habit was'n
e-z
no'one tell who win
t' finish

suspended and peck'd from holdin
g hands by th g
loved ones
th glide
of color & dna
rounding up
th zen
slaughter at
th pen

Elizabeth Bryant

Moss is mostly a cultural problem

(from an ongoing and currently untitled series of photos and texts)

Down at the level of minute arachnids, moss doesn't need you. It is THERE and it is HAPPENING, in winter's depths, thumbing its nose at a relative canopy of deliberate, skeletal lavenders molted of their needles. Saying something about mosses, finding the Latin (ceratodon purpureus) for Fire Moss, then stashing that away. The difficulty of retrieving on demand: titles, names. The error of leaving too long unattended the mechanism for saying: becomes slack but not reflective as a river. Moss occurs whereof acidity, dampness and sometimes despite toxicity. Opportunistic. And this was held up by past mentor's disdain for gerundium. A stab at connectivity. Fire Moss is ubiquitous.

Mt. Smithson (1803')

Though not technically a high peak, Mt. Smithson deserves inclusion in any serious, well-informed guide to the Catskills. The mountain serves as a symbol of how a seemingly insignificant and overlooked locale can still have a role to play in contesting and constituting the national hegemony.

Mt. Smithson occupies an important place in the history of conceptual art and writing. Robert Smithson traveled to the Catskills in September 1972, intending to apply the same method he had in "A Tour of the Monuments of Passaic, New Jersey"—but this time in a location he was unfamiliar with: an unnamed peak in the Catskills. Smithson scholars had long known from letters that Smithson had made such a trip, but the typescript of "A Tour of the Non-Monuments of the Catskills" was thought to have been lost until it was rediscovered in 2003 by the Smithson scholar Eugene Vydrin. Smithson applied for a New York State Council on the Arts (NYSCA) grant in November 1972 asking for additional funding to complete the visual and design stages of the piece. But Smithson's application was rejected; he abandoned the project, and apparently never thought to retrieve the typescript. The artist died in a helicopter crash July 20, 1973, less than a year after his visit to Phoenicia. By State Law, NYSCA turns over all grant materials to the state archive in Albany. Because of chronic shortages of funding, the archive was woefully behind in cataloguing Smithson's submission. It was first published in conjunction with the 2005 Whitney Museum/MOCA Los Angeles Smithson retrospective. Also in that year to celebrate Smithson's retrospective and his connection to the Catskills, two state senators, Vito Lopez (D-Brooklyn) and Peter Wilson (D-Woodstock) introduced legislation to designate the unnamed peak Mt. Smithson. In 2006, the USGS Bureau on Geographic Naming officially accepted the designation, as all maps of the region henceforward will recognize.

Here in its entirety is Smithson's original application letter:

November 10, 1972

Dear Grant Committee,

I am writing to apply for a NYSCA grant to complete my article project, "A Tour of the Non-Monuments of the Catskills." In September I traveled to the Catskills from New York City. Below is a selection of what I have written about this experience. A grant of $1500 would allow me to complete this project: to take and develop photographs to illustrate the essay, as well as to design and lay it out for publication.

I would like very much to place the eventual visual essay that will result in a New York-based magazine or journal. I would like to draw readers' and viewers' attention to the true majesty of the Catskills, and to emphasize that these mountains are worthy of protection from the depradations of contemporary postindustrial capitalism.

I thank you for your consideration,

Robert Smithson

799 Greenwich Street
New York, NY 10014

* * *

On Saturday, September 30, 1972, I went to the Port Authority Building on 41st Street and 8th Avenue. I bought a copy of *The New York Times* and a copy of J.G. Ballard's *Atrocity Exhibition* with a foreword by William S. Burroughs. From the Trailways ticket booth, I bought a ticket to Phoenicia, New York in the heart of the Catskill High Peaks. After that I went down to the lower level gate 32 for the Pine Hill Trailways bus to Ridgewood, New Paltz, Rosendale, Kingston, Woodstock, Phoenicia, Pine Hill, Margaretville, Delhi and Oneonta. As I waited for the bus, being a safe 15 minutes early, I heard the message—"Please hold the handrail and be careful when entering and exiting this moving escalator. Strollers and large items please use the elevator. Be careful with personal items. Thank you for patience."—repeated over the loudspeaker at least a thousand times.

I sat down and opened the *Times*. On the front page I find "Metropolitan Sells Two Modern Masterpieces in an Unusual Move." "The sales, which took place six months ago, were reluctantly confirmed yesterday by Mr. [the museum's director, Thomas P.] Hoving." The paintings in question, Douanier Rousseau's "Monkeys in the Jungle" and Vincent van Gogh's "The Olive Pickers," were sold on the private market. I think I will hardly miss them; they belong to another country and another time.

Metropolitan Sells Two Modern Masterpieces in an Unusual Move

Douanier Rousseau's "Monkeys in the Jungle," one of the two masterpieces sold by the Metropolitan Museum of Art

The bus turned off onto Route 28, the great central thoroughfare of the modern post-railway Catskills.

I read the blurbs and skimmed through *The Atrocity Exhibition*. In the foreword by William S.

Burroughs, I read:

> It seems to me self-evident that the next decade will move in the direction of a *total* transformation of all experience into fiction, whether it be the experience of our external environment or of the world inside our own heads. I believe, however, that one can distinguish between various elements in this goulash of fictions.

Too true, I reflected to myself.

I arrived on Main Street, Phoenicia, New York some two hours and forty minutes after I had departed Manhattan. I was standing at the intersection of Route 212 (also known as Main Street) and Route 214. A police cruiser sat menacingly in the center of town. I headed hastily toward the beckoning west. In a matter of mere feet, I was near the intersection of a powerful river and its loyal tributary.

The first monument was the Stony Clove Creek Gazebo, erected by The Rotary Club of Phoenicia. Noon-day sunshine cinema-ized the site, turning the gazebo and the stream into an over-exposed *picture*. Photographing it with my Instamatic 400 was like photographing a photograph. The sun became a monstrous light-bulb that projected a detached series of "stills" through my Instamatic into my eye. When I walked on the bridge, it was as though I was walking on an enormous photograph made of concrete and steel, and underneath Stony Clove Creek existed as an enormous film that showed nothing but a continuous blank.

Along the Esopus Creek were many minor monuments such as concrete abutments that supported the shoulders of the highway. Tinker Street was in part bulldozed and in part intact. It was hard to tell the new highway from the old road; they were both confounded into a unitary chaos. Since it was a Saturday, many machines were not working, and this caused them to resemble prehistoric creatures trapped in the mud, or, better, extinct machines—mechanical dinosaurs stripped of their skin. On the edge of this prehistoric Machine Age were pre- and post-World War II exurban houses. The houses mirrored themselves in their colorlessness. A group of children were skipping rocks on the fast-moving waters of the river.

As I walked north along 214, I saw a monument on the far side of the river—it was an abandoned dump truck of mid-1950s vintage. The truck's driver door was open, as if to beckon a new driver to somehow bring it back across the creek. At any moment, the truck might slide into the creek, and become a part of New York City's water supply.

As I backtracked along Route 28, I encountered a sign seemingly pointed at those leaving town: "Phoenicia: Everything You Need!: SHOPS FOOD GAS LODGING ART FUN! Please drive safely." That zero panorama seemed to contain *ruins in reverse*, that is—the basic services that the weekend driver might need overwrote any sense of community or history or town identity. There were no grand hotels to be had—only the most basic conveniences—and art—and fun.

I decided to navigate the rapids of the Esopus to make my way to another monument, the statue of Davy Crockett or possibly Daniel Boone that graces the majestic entrance to the

Sportsman's Bar and Grille. This twelve-foot Crockett or Boone would seem to be an emblem of regional amnesia. Crockett never set foot in the Catskills; he represented Tennessee in Congress and died at the Alamo. Boone was from Kentucky and died in Missouri.

Let us say that one goes on a fictitious trip if one decides to go to the *Non-Site*. The "trip" becomes invented, devised, artificial; therefore, one might call it a non-trip to a site from a Non-site. Here we have a hamlet renamed by the railroad in the 1860s. The Phoenix Hotel had been operating in the area at least since the 1820s.

The final monument for today was the lookout above town. Here at just over 1800' I had a majestic view of the town and the three valleys at whose juncture the town stands. An alluvial floodplain stood before me in all its precarity. Of all the places to build a town, this was perhaps the most beautiful, but also the most treacherous. From the lookout, I could see Panther and Romer Mountains, and could feel my heart soar like the eagles that frequent these riparian paths of least resistance. Three churches flanked the town, as well as the Town Tinker Tube Rental and F & S Adventures Tube Rental. One might flow downstream all the way to the Atlantic on these charmed waves. Or upon the mighty highways.

Has Phoenicia, New York become the Eternal Town? A middle-class Mayberry of the Jersey diaspora? A stopover for beleaguered skiers, cold fishermen, tired tubers, rabid hunters and zonked hikers? A collection of struggling restaurants, gift shops, a drug store, a grocery store, a hotel, a gas station?

As I wrote in my "A Museum of Language in the Vicinity of Art" essay, "Nature is simply another eighteenth- and nineteenth-century fiction." So too the postindustrial information society is merely another twentieth-century fiction. Its diaspora of no-collar and white collar workers fan out across the tri-state area weekend after weekend. They come for a little reality; they get some of that, but they leave always with new geofictions.

* * *

It would be an exaggeration to say that Mt. Smithson approximates a high peak; would that it did, but alas at this point the high peaks have all been named. Mt. Smithson approximates to something just as metaphorically high: it truly lends historical and imaginative significance to its region and its community. We are proud to have hosted you, Robert Smithson.

Myth

Make yourself timeless. How
Moon yellows the hills,
Makes your torn hands
Meander, your tongue hairy.
Might you torture her.
Might you transform her,
Meaning *yew*. The hell
Mouth yawns, then howls
Music—yours. The horned
Mare yanks the halter,
Makes *you* the hunted,
Marks your trembling. Her
Mother yelps; the hag
Means you terrible harm.
Might you tickle her.
Might your trickery have
Many yellow teeth. How
Moon yokes those heavenly
Monsters, your tiger horses.
Mask your treachery, holy
Man. Your torn heart.
Make yourself the hero.

Sparrow

New Slogans

Pepsi Is Waiting for You
Pepsi Has Abducted Your Neighbors
Pepsi Is Love
Pepsi Is the Sacred Heart of Jesus
Pepsi Repairs All the Damage That Capitalism Inflicts

New Sound

I made a
new sound:

pferkurip.

ANDY CLAUSEN

The Newly Opened Sky

The newly opened sky is full of albatrosses & pigeons
    they're letting loose what they've used up
Because others can't see the fire on three sides
    doesn't mean it doesn't exist
The captains of ownership
    love the politics of scarcity
    makes for cheap labor
They want the masses, the ones Jesus loved
    and Buddha wakened, leaden eyed, ovine
    voting against themselves
    killing each other
    pitted against each other for the sake
of something called the economy which
over the years I've come to see is a device
to devalue labor and separate money from the physical
    to make it metaphysical
to ascribe it to something marginally useful like gold
    or destructive like weapons
They'll violently disagree on religion culture territory
    but they all agree to honor money

I'm not holding my breath for there's a mighty judgment coming
How much of this body is me?
Am I nothing more than a desire propelled
Through the ages? But by what? Another desire?
The all powerful desireless desire?
Some Tathagata?
Those are just words
Is this my body and how can it be mine
    if it is finite?
How can anything live if I die?

I asked what comes after post modern?
Will nothing ever be modern again?

I am the future as long as I live
After me, everything will be old

Old Bill
Old bills
Old Mike
Old Hannah
Old grey mare
Old hat
Old Shep
Old boy
Old gal;
Everything & body will be old
Old garbage
Old man
Old lady
Old gold
Old days

Sam Truitt

Night of the Contour

The freak stands, hands in pockets, surveying the empty house.

This world has something to renounce—to back   off away
from. Another generalization, as without a belly button
cold spit where act was allegorical, the way it can be
when you are drunk. Though not more than you need be.
When you are taken in. When a life function
is something that you do, or enact. But can I tear
my old house down before I have built... flesh out the...
rock grows? No, though the playwright of *The Tempest*
was the first American mechanic—put music in the cave, and a girl
& capsule of vanish. A value. Equality vs. freedom vs.
the imagery cares to remain in situ as a process   thereof.
To bear the frame out beyond sprockets (holes) you place,
which is what you make. To hold to move. Stake &
mistake. Scratch. Break. Word. Paper. Rock. Scissors.
The gods are place & misplace. Face is what faces
gods as the frontier is war and to weave is to hold is
to ride the road through the house in flames

NO OAR NO ORACLE

I. OAR OVERBOARD

dreamlife wants to dwell in a shoal
or shallows or belly of a leviathan

ahoy mate
mine arms are broken

keel is a flinching temple
rudder a gut incongruity

ahoy mate
wind like a whetted knife heaved me to the fishes
hog and sag mine mind flexes like kelpies in bilge

ship of a pearl which poets feign
wharf a wench plus winch pulse wind

swing round your arclight
pierce the highest roof
snatch me through

mine is a migrating bird
piddled and piffed with iron

ahoy mate
haul haul taut be the brace

mine pillar is cement plus Plato
mine knot is cleat plus custom

ahoy
anchor the day

II. ORACLE'S CAESURA

When the clairvoyant reads your omissions,
she speaks to the deadness in you.

emergence after disappearance
you always believe
your next move
steer safely through rising sects
document Nauvoo Voodoo
prophesy an infant sorcery

**When the clairvoyant salons the metropolis,
she contests certain ceremony.**

a small clever mobile mouth
a Titanic display
a trembling hand stretched
your wit infers bitter critics'
etheric radio vibration
redoubling frequency into a swirl

**The clairvoyant boils coffee dregs,
likens attorneys to scientists.**

a vast city vanishes
utmost brevity
the departure of America
four large cut roses fall from the ceiling
distance is planned
one morning by six persons

**She faces the hieroglyph in defeat,
aches for anarchy.**

you alone
coworkers a tie not broken
Colonel's sudden unexpressed wish
deposited softly dying of neglect
saluted by exquisite bells
history of monument as vapor emerges

She begrudgingly joins forces
when the clairvoyant researches.

eighteen Shakers support data
show us those we love
good word-pictures of them
gifted sisters laughing
a cloud cleansed
of meagerness of information

Her limbs decay like yours
the clairvoyant's limited radii

moist unrolling pencil lines
bracket the course of home
back against the base of a pine tree
interval (a thirty-second overlord)
on this errand of musical marvel
rendering darkness not necessary

She feels synapses traverse eons,
then pauses . . .

III. LIME'S LANDING

grasshopper says: "My friend could use some water."

surfaceday waterscars
cave's edge each day
knows no moon no noon
until pebble=otter until
push=between step one step

grasshopper says: "I have good feet"

sledgehammer a florid force
distilling virtuoso in no one avalanche
fiddlles above beaverfelt so pelt flattens

and hats highground stormdark
stack thinking

grasshopper says: "You need only examine the body to know I tell the truth"

incomprehension so velvet
any paddler stands stern
mule enough lithe enough to be
mistaken
acclaim's residue chortles effortlessly

grasshopper says: "It is dangerous to sit in the middle of the cave"

cadence swamps collective rubble
morning dries out century's spiritualists
pauper's breath tampens
nationstate's guardsmen
open-trumpet steals our skiff

grasshopper asks: "Is death all you wish?"

inner cavalry at attention
clothespins roosting
near attachment
pinched collar frays
quiets all groundswell

grasshopper says: "Its journey is to no where."

phantom fed
edelweiss chronicles no one
Shaolin within the open
rattlesnake pit fears no strike
expanse between stars

grasshopper says: "Its ending is the bottom of the pool."

hog wild morphic
divinity of negative confession

have not thought scorn
god not me
no one chora no one koan

within day's reach no one life

Janet Hamill

Not an Enraged Aviary

Everything is in order. Everything is in place. Animal tracks
stop at the door. Logs and kindling. Paper and matches. Maladies
work out in the red artillery pushing and pulling wings to different ends

Of folios buried deep in the sky the fire speaks. As long as it's fed
bones of skeletal rain jingle and jangle on the cabin roof

This is not an enraged aviary. Constellated in the northern woods
the birds attest to an all-forgiving eye. For hours and hours
they set off sparks. Spelling the names of the flames that gave them flight

Notes to Self

Midfuck: clouds like stately
ice burgs
slip along an inverted eyelid
Some think "sea" and see
whisky-money. Some other
transaction.
My finger slipped
into skin like milk

these babies, these gerunds,
doughty bats.
And the formalities of
upside down.

The box of my lungs is
a membrane of leave-behind echo
as I slip/strip
into the planes
of escape.

Think: *self.* 3 notes:

Wy-o-ming
Wy-o-ming.

Andy Clausen

Off Duty

off-duty punched-in day-glo calf-exposed adult-only user-friendly bookstores non-eternal self-pity well-bred 3-inch cut-outs 99-cent ill-prepared back-talked star-hidden honey-voiced women well-dressed college-agers old-timer sub-reality grenade-eating alarm-clock non-toxic also-ran Anti-Climax boy-faced Rose-blended 15-foot antenna self-consuming eke-by cowboy-style gut-wrenching part-time ill-tempered freeze-dried lime-based mortar cross-town step all-encapsulating truth so-called much-studied red-necked red no-touch love-danced 21-speed English-French Ameri-English two-page question 5-minute answer still-alive big-eyed well-educated hand-assisted mountain-made crazy-legged head-wagging wife might-have-beens self immolated fine-tuned symmetry life-desperate open-aired malls lean-tos mariachi-like non-divisible 2-foot-high hedge carbine-packing lathi-wielding Soviet-imposed 8-year-old bullies be-bop shaman head-shaved sharp-featured start-up high-voltage high-pitched Russian motors prize-winning author 79-year-old widow black-toothed sea-going mini-lounges 5-dollar-a-night hospital faith-based apocalyptical negligence Self-importance trampled open-hearted sexual energy so-called self-destructive long-time prisoner star-spangled sun-kissed tradition So-called fundamentalists two-story piled Gotham-Baghdad-by-the-Bay-Oklahoma City-Sky cross-blown health-destroying home-grown tip-dependent thespian lived-in old-time stoops hand-fashioning matter-consuming ghosts

L. S. Asekoff

One Minute Before Midnight

Faced with the "great American incognitum,"
wisps of background radiation so preposterously faint
they're less than the energy of a falling snowflake,
a hundred Hiroshimas in a cell,
we're still in the Dark Ages.
Just drop a net down & see what comes up:
34,000 hockey gloves, pastel organelles,
galaxies of scattered salt –
all of history in one hand.
Still, when cryptozoa enter the picture,
& everything is read through the spirit glass,
the whys and wherefores escape us.
Not "is this true?" but "Is this crazy enough?"
Wandering rocks, cloud atlas, wave mechanics
offer their strange charms.
A clunderthap! & it's *Three quarks for Mustar Mark!*
Between cataclysms above, eructations below,
life clings to its perilous perch.
At the knife-edge of extinction,
"the city waiting to die" drifts on its giant lilypads into the ice-age night.

Tim Davis

One Useful Poem

Hey you fat fuck why not
recite this poem in semaphore
about 500 times?
One vigorous aerobic reading, w/ dumbbells
will burn off half a tub of slaw
Do it daily and you'll look pithy

Once you've iced, transcribe this poem
around Grover Cleveland's portrait oval on the
thousand dollar bill
and post it to Darfur
(Cleveland himself, BTW, at sixteen
had a job transcribing the blind
hymnnalist, Francis Jane "Fanny" Crosby's poems
so you're in good company)

OK. This poem kills fascists.

And it's cellulose so it
absorbs gerbil whiz.
Fold it in your breast pocket
on the off chance its thickness
might divert stray
shrapnel off the Inferior vena cava

Poetry is the opposite of bureaucracy
so reading this reduces big government.

You might have a long boring experience
in a terminal or power outage
It might be nice to have a poem on a piece of paper
lying around. All flights are cancelled.
Even backup generators damaged in the blast.
You want to sit and listen to some hard earned silence.

Luckily, poetry, Maurice Blanchot diagnosed,
"protects against revelation."

Revelation condom: Walt Whitman. Revelation
diaphragm: Emily Dickinson.
Poetry is prophylactic
also for your ears.
Don't tell me you haven't hated having
"Do You be-LIEVE in Life after Love?"
stuck in your head after passing a
supermarket or boutique.
This poem is scientifically formulated to be
Cher's almost-posthumous comeback
ditty's exact antidote.
So if you live within range of satellite radio
always have it onhand.

"Horned owls have one ear that opens up and one
that opens down."
That's Marianne Moore in "The Student," her
attempt to tangle up poetry and fact.
Ms. Moore quoted Dewey in her diary:
"Surely there is no more significant question…than…the reconciliation of the attitudes of
practical science and contemplative aesthetic appreciation."
She then wrote, "Swordfish are different from
gars." But why bother?
This poem, printed in an unread magazine or
small press chapbook
and stored in boxes in my basement
is as factual as anything you can name.
As practical as ballast.
I wonder if walls weren't the first facts.
Build one with this.

Tim Davis

Original Ideas in Magic

1/ How Time Flies

Time flies by enslaving cedar waxwings
Waxwings can be captured by melting menthols on the deck
They struggle in the syrup but aren't really harmed
A standard chromium-plated
"fire to flowers bowl" is recommended
and can hold a development of waxwings

You have to build them a chariot
but once you have your waxwings harnessed and
angled at the outer reaches
the friction of false moustache on stubble will power it
Every animal is an entire engine
When you lift open your eyes
a motorbike is kickstarted in Giza

2/ A Match for You

Think of a number between thunder and money
I buy you a matchbook with ink and flint on it
that costs me a piece of lung
You could live months on fast food ketchup packs, In fact
in America, freedom is lemon slices at the diner
and a tattoo of what I weigh adding
ink, but taking blood away

Fire is nothing special
Think of a purebred beagle named
Don't Smoke in Bed
Even the inner flap of the matchbook is consciously designed
riling some pre-Socratic wacko who insisted:
"brimstone is the stink of cognition"

3/ Acrobatic Ash Tray

AC-RO-BAT-IC ASH TRAY! Say it.
TACT-LESS MA-NIC ES-SAY, I see
Former assistants tear up in press conferences confessing
a life of dud *voila!s.*
"Acrobatic Ash Tray" constitutes my beliefs
Hermes Trismegistus levitates a chimichanga in his
rental outside Taco Bell

You see what I believe?
Say it. The plastic in which
the magic kit sits will pick up
after punk kids' puppies
They smoke on the low point of the Ponte Sisto
Balancing without a net

4/ Incomprehensible Predictability

Sisyphus outsourced becomes a party planner
who subtly introduces jaundiced canapés
to the servers' trays
And O man someday there will be
scholars notating our unread electronics instruction manuals,
calipers on ignorant connectors,
a bad battery museum

Someday we'll have martial law to giggle at
These things happen
God digs out his evolved-away flagellum
and whips us into shape:
rounder, polished
curled into a rictus ball

5/ Impossible Spirit Test

Bunny, meet Top Hat; Top Hat, Bunny
Stevie Wonder sang "Superstition" on Sesame Street

while this economy ran on fumes of "futures."
A man in the sky with a map in his ass
conducts all our business; puts dew on the grass
Meanwhile back in the Milky Way's mullet
housing projects eaten by weeds

Believers course through the streets
proud to've stepped in cred
A certified genie watching bunnies flee
You bunnies, overturn your top hats; sharpen teeth
Please to go hostile into that good night

6/ Transribbo

Don't make me use this
Using a churchkey to make applesauce
Dropping a church on an orchard
to make applesauce
Apples! With will!
sheared into liturgy, pounded
into product
A Macoun, a Red Wealthy, a Cripps Pink, a Priscilla
can be named and can be eaten
but only
hogs on spits
think these things are sacred

7/ Confetti-Candy Cylinder

Cute toxin, I'm
trying to rhyme
Eden and Erection and
swallow this cup of
Bowery condo construction dust

I'm back from the city center with a snow globe
of the president's dog dying in his arms

So much paper in the air you say who
cares if a tyrant rapes an apple
You smother breakfast with a plastic mask
You in-
sist the future
is pimped by the past

8/ A Magical Surprise

That a Red Army soldier when
Berlin fell shot Germany off Hitler's globe
That San Quentin spokesman Vernell Crittendon insisted: "At no point are we not
going to value the sanctity of life. We would
resuscitate him, then execute him."
That we saw a diaper on a hawk

And that there's a Hindi superhero called "Mister Pestilence"
That there are machines in my wall
and lines of longitude casting shadows
the better to utter "schmodernism" and move on
That I was willed a box of Post Toasties
And that Post Toasties were once named "Elijah's Manna"
That I have heard all this before

9/ New Coin Vanish

I wanted to write a poem called "New Coin Vanish"
which is the name of a trick in *Original Ideas in Magic*
self-published with red velveteen covers and a staple binding by
Lloyd W. Chambers in 1941 Topeka.
I see that Mr. Chambers had a MS in Physics from U.S.C.
and became a charter member of the Wizards of Witchita;
started his own mail-order magic business
Someone on the internet says "A sudden heart attack took Lloyd in January 1960"

You solder a tiny "u-shaped wire" onto a silver dollar and attach an elastic string.

I wanted the poem to allude to how "magically" coin can vanish
and thought of quoting Marx on debt emerging "As with the stroke of an enchanter's wand"
I hoped reading it
would be like finding holes in your pockets

10/ New Wine and Water

My uncle turned halvah into feces and false teeth
And don't get dehydrated at a wedding feast!
Nothing is what it seems
Even seeming isn't what it seems
Man's brows swell with intent looking at anything actual
We keep on hand Neanderthal emollient
to massage into the double take
Seeing is believing
Deceiving is bulimia
Especially when the bride removes her veil
We willers wish more good into the world
our eyes fill up with Miracle Whip

SHIV MIRABITO

Otter Falls Art Action for PLW

Peter Lamborn Wilson is writing a magnum opus
on the folklore & origins of the mighty Esopus
research involves investigating the exact source
of the river at Lake Winnisock in Big Indian
the art action was an elaborate ritual offering
to the actual big Indian
Winnisock
seven and a half feet tall
who was allegedly brutally murdered by colonialists
and buried in a tall pine tree
for the crime of either marrying a white woman
or for, more likely say Peter, for openly living with his male lover
in this desolate hidden green forest
one can imagine the otters sliding down
the wet mossy sloping waterfalls
descending down in seven swirling whirlpools
in this shady grove there were no otters
but philosophers, professors, artists, anthropologists,
tarot experts, poets, students, saints
all gathered together artistically spiritually naturally
PLW, on that day, magically transformed into Hakim Bey
an ancient white bearded druid pagan Celtic-Moorish priest
lit rose incense for the sun
lit 5 incenses that start with the letter M
symbolizing secret sacred tantrik sex magik
offered 5 big solid silver coins to the foaming pools
& sheets of solid silver foil which floated on the breeze
like the memories of the faded past
& he offered a handful of translucent pearls
& a jar of pure white honey
& a vial of whale's ambergris oil
essential oils for essential Catskill's folklore
essential nature knowledge for Indians, otters & everyone

Anne Gorrick

Our Secular Rituals on Cubist Stairs

(a poem made from 2010 Peep/Show search terms)

Wheelchair pageant, a circus of legs
Doctors peep inside and embrace her sand
flexing a plastic speculum to see the red deer inside her
If I were a bird I'd flee my search for truth
for a loner's circus parfum
There are hidden rules that determine how to cross this city

Look, there's Sharon Olds' erection in the Illinois asylum for feeble-minded children
And at a zoo during Berlin's happy hour
older submissive women show their cunts
The Circus Fat Lady said, "I feel like everything in my life was in preparation for this moment.
Everything I know I learned from this peepshow"

Spandex wearing disco monkeys in a vatic hum
where women juggle their own skeletons
Benjamin Bourlier is a fiddler on a carnival train to New Orleans
The difference between a private show and a peepshow
involves weeing in church, marrowing illustrated

Men with boners wear spandex in a dog's circus
Catching his lover's gaze, "I am all over the oblique ascension process of achieving
aphesis"
The meadow intentions of an octopus
The dystopia that shines a light ahead of cars
My search for truth has been totally harshed by carnival midway images

Hairy skinny, a suite grotesque on bitterness
A naked mermaid asked, "What do they call dildos? Strangle monkeys?"
Squirting Teraoka Sarah and the dream octopus said, "Show me a big dildo"
A man in a wheelchair deprived of housewives
In the empty quarter, a fire eater
a violet racked starling

There is a boy on the ground in front of a woman
The woman, the knife, the circus: an illustrated torrent
Is there a poem called "Thinking of you when your cat is ill?"
The fat mermaid, "she floats as if she's swimming in blood"
her mermaid muscles are hoodwinked going underwater

The orphan and its relations, a "counter rhythm" to the mermaid fortune teller
How to build a peepshow in Elizabeth, NJ?
Lose weight, focus, blur into circus couture
A knife thrower and the limbless lady form a wind sculpture
Human arms tattooed on an ugly circus figurine

If the pleiades were side show barkers
turning wind into elegy
then a scaffold of cannibal women and their mental issues, vaudeville animal acts
A terminal man's right to peep
We stand in the shadows of the trapeze woman
who paints stillness into a mobile world

A polaroid of the human skeleton and a woman juggling his machinic gaze
The person outside a peepshow ushering people inside
using the human skeleton's hand positions
Note the octopus' sucking action
A regenerative rug rescue in New York
Octopus sucking lady

Float – float, flowing the sky - What poem can't be made out of circus legs?
A human skeleton reflection
A man with no eyes or cigarettes
A woman statue with no arms, broken
A fortune teller tensed dreamreading red rose

The human spontaneous involuntary invisibility in our dark carnivals

A circus school for dolls in an ocean sky soft green
The "sense of place that occurs then at the juncture between space and time"
Sign footings, a collection of vegetables
Let's play the rock paper scissors game to exhibit patterns of art or other activity
Jill Magi's Slot like an Annandale dream

A chorus interstice like a man ruffled in wind and motion
backwards and illumined
who doesn't need the earth's help with his suitcases
"A delicious tremor going wild with animalistic need"

Everyone everywhere
Everyone everywhere
Everyone everywhere

Skirt, wind

A woman's legs describe being stretched and filled with:
a featheralphabet, cross-stitch, daguerrotype
They breathe oxygen in their inhabited nothingness chairs
They throw stones at her body to enjoy this film

Claire Hero

OUT OF THE AFTERPASTURES
this algaeic realm—
scumfed, spawnclouded—spawns

in thickwater, quickfinned
in the virid stir
of pondscape, plantsphere,

the Changing, the half-
made, the more-fitted-for, the hy-

brid, by-
product
bride

REDNESS in the grass:
calf & leaf —

You walk out of the trees, hiding your hands.

Everywhere the mouths
bloodglottal, stanched.

Everywhere the meatseed
pulses toward harvest.

Outsourcing Announcement

I have begun
outsourcing
my poetry
to India.

In fact,
the rest
of this
poem is
in Punjabi.
Aj fer dil gareeb
Ik paaNda hae vaasta,
De ja meri ahj kalam nu
Ik hor haadsa.

Mudat hoi hae darad da
Koi jaam peeteyaaN,
PeeRaaN 'ch haNju ghol ke,
De ja do aatasha.

Kaagaz di kori reejh hae
Chup chaap vekhdi,
ShabdaaN de thal 'ch bhaTakda
GeetaaN da kaafila.

TurnaaN maeN chaahuNda
Paer vich kaNDe di lae ke peeR,
Dukh toN kabar tak dosta
Jihna vi faasala.

[From "Aj Fer Dil Gareeb Da" by Shiv Kumar Batalvi]

Over the Hudson Once Again

Straphanger's blues on tiny earphones;
digital cellular dingalings can't get
        enough workday.
Loose suits and lips at 7AM;
caffeinated cackling hens
recount burnt toast and soccer practice
action unending day in, out, otherwise

over the Hudson once again.

Tunnel maze; feint urine aire, empty box splayed
with someone's lunch rotting in a dark pool
between the rails, damp tin bezel a cankersore
on the mouth, rushing must echos through WTC
like stale breath, a thousand closed eyes bounce uptown.
Best to hide in the closed circle an open Times provides;
insight in crossword cops out on the one misnumbered clue

over the Hudson once again.

Pound that Palm, Handspring, stylus poised, block out time,
move the Ace of Diamonds onto it's Solitaire pile.
Blackberry radio email a sure way to stay plugged in;
thumb wheel click youself into a ragu of red digits,
infrared beam me those figures and your V-Card.
Slotted cradle, one button, 5 minutes and you're downloaded
you travel across the mainframe in milliseconds, 8 hours later

over the Hudson once again.

The banana, the yogurt, the Basic 4, the cinnamon bun,
the latte, the oatmeal, the Krispy Kremes, the bagel & cream cheese
the sausage and cheese, the bacon and cheese, the soft scrambled
        with lettuce and ketchup

the almond croissant, the Earl Grey, the Starbucks, giant percolator gleams
on cheap white porcelain cup, bitter coffee, how many I forget
the Morning Sunrise muffin, the baguette, lavatory car door sticks

over the Hudson once again.

Sandwiched, shoulder bags at issue, run out of town on a rail,
too much Chanel, too familiar strangers persistently chill,
grey pedophiles chat up an 18 yr old International Business student from Brazil.
Anxious & indignant woman insists upon holding a large wrapped oil painting on her lap
which digs into my knee, makes a scene, attracts wrath of the car.
Lunacy repressed by chatter, Game Boys distract, lap top DVD rentals chirp and sigh
in private theatres two feet wide — head and eyes roll back

over the Hudson once again.

Rebecca Wolff

Palisades

Interred in region

nothing super global in this locale

where I live, where I
bought—

what would I tell you about it if I could?

What I see when I go up
what I see when I go down

the right hand side
left hand
shudder and roll of conveyance

that's just locked in motion.
That's just the place inside.

Some poets find their place
in place

and naming it seems venturesome

that seems to me a tiresome—
and I wish no longer—.

I'll never stand
on reeds or rocks until

they lose their root in soil or sky around—

Get me out of here.

Palm Sunday Maple Syrup Poem

a poem is like a palm
in that it is sap evaporating
like a horse in a corral
running frenetically to the road when
a car approaches like a bird
who comes to the feeder despite
the hot sweet smoke, should we end today?
if you end one thing, you might end
another like the winter or the life
of a traitor humming like a cloud
in the clear blue sky's use
as a plateau to warmer, itchy weather
when we can swim in the creek
beyond the field behind the hay's evaporator, amen.

Participation Mystique

A Polaroid-headed man makes his way toward the bar on the far side of a club. Accompanied by subtle whirrs and the gasps of onlookers, Polaroids – the products of his respiration – issue from the thin slot that is his mouth. Like a zipper, the crowd bending down to inspect the images scattered along the floor closed the open space behind him. In a matter of minutes, seated on a stool, he fills the area behind the bar to waist height with Polaroids, each one a reproduction of the array of liquor bottles along the back wall. As the bartender pushes his way through this mass of photographs, they flow in behind him to form composite images of a boy walking through chest-high water in a swimming pool. When another patron leans over the bar and runs his index finger through the accumulating photographs, similarly composite images of scenes from *his* childhood swirl into view as if along the surface of a puddle of gasoline, scenes of himself running his finger through water at the edge of a pond.

Daniel Gilhuly

Pawky

Wot is not whilom
a word any more
not since yet a while
ago it fell away
to plosive applause
succumbing to attrition
by moonlight.
A word by habit
obsolesces
as a way of relaxing
before the game.
Happens all the time
sense is slivered in
half again and then
with the last piece
of pie . . . like modern
economics.
            And the like
unto the alder jade and thanes
in britches. Astrophysics
nailed it; not a hope on
Golgotha but the cell
tower pays rent and Town
Hall has weal in its crosshairs.

Those arch time etyms are
the ordinals of rhythm
They're like orts left on
            your plate
only here the scrap
          is on your face.

Claire Hero

PENNED INSIDE the wondervault
I did not know my place
until I had been blooded
by the great Chain

Now: Cut the mouthpiece
from the
decomposing links,

watch new morphemes
hatch
in the wounds

& eat them
clean

JJ Blickstein

Pink and dark sewer with a fistful of flies

One in fatigues
a corpse
his jaw
artificial hinge
makes a lot of noise in the wind

Another one in a business suit
tells the corpse that he is a patriot
his fingers charred to stumps
that he refers to as unproven commodities
head, a black dog—his shoes are beautiful

The third is naked and betrays civilization
with his certitude, solitude, protests, caves and torn skin
he can't move forward, his mind fixed on the horizon
his bitch tied to a red string sleeps at his feet
his expression—where the face used to be—gnarled wood
he used to be a runner

They sit down around a fire in the dark
discussing provenance and authenticity
they dispense with hierarchy and share a little bit
turning rhetoric into a mercenary
and you into a murderer
where freedom is an act of annihilation

And here I am
always uninvited, no surprises
other than the fact
that I keep showing
up
a necessary part of the social order
meant to be ignored
or absorbed

a love affair with a ghost
sugar on your scabs
let's pretend it's all a metaphor
where you giggle a little bit
and I love the opposition like
you love yourself

poem

the last time we sat in a room and pretended
to meet i got a coffee cup out of it
and the word *missing* redefined as state
adjusted autonomy, with all the pretenses
of greeting complexity as standard fugitive
practice through which relationships
materialize and we drive the car forward
and be "creative" because we can't add
anything else and not all conspiracies
are conscious uncontestable so let's join
hands and fight the lost war, chant—
money money importance money compose

money and when a bacterial cell dies it leaves
behind packets of dna, i say they're like diaries

Poem No. 71

Istuo

EUGENE RICHIE

Popeye Suite

1. "'Ja think I'm a cowboy?"
—Popeye, January 17, 1929

"Are you a sailor?"
Of course you knew he was
a sailor. Popeye thinks straight
and shoots crooked or does he
shoot crooked and think straight.
I think he knew the way home
and I did not, or at least I
don't think so or later.
Our response may be a shower
of flowers, but that's just
the way it is today here
at the base of Montmartre
and such a climb to the top
is still possible, but only
with stellar recommendations
of what wine to drink with oysters,
or what else is new under the sun
not this hole'n the wall,
or am I being a little too
dismissive in these hard times.
I'm sure I am so I will
cease and desist as you undress
now and again, yes.

2. Reading "99 Little-Known Facts about Popeye . . ."
a sonnet for Michael Gizzi

and your *New Depths of Deadpan* again
            while listening to Messiaen's

Des Canyons aux étoiles and
        we know "tears don't fall in outer space."
Thinking of you saving John's
        black locust, dancing
from branch to branch and
        back to earth again
and every time I've heard
        you read, that image
stays in my mind like
        the short lines of "Dig the King"
—"The king in the ear / Of musical
        things / Bring on the king."

3. One of the Love Stories of the Century
for Olive Oyl and Popeye

How many are there? I only
know this one.
If we tried to count them
it would be
above and beyond.
        After all love is
and is not a big deal,
        or so they say.
But what do they know?
        I see you and want you.
That's it, and no, I do not
        think it is all about money.
Sure it's good to have, not
        to have not—
But what, why? Not!

4. "I yam what I yam!"
"Crowds in the street."
"Set the house on fire."
"Will he come, sir?"
"Between 2 and 3 o'clock."
—John Cage, *Credo in Us* (EMI 2008)

"In my end is my beginning."
That is just Heraclitus or
T. S. Eliot or Mary Queen of Scots—
"En ma fin est mon commencement."
I think therefore I am,
despite your wanting it to be
otherwise. I don't know,
but everyone thinks I do,
and so Mario did win, though
do we know why? Why
is what I want to know.
You let him say what he says
and then what does he know?
Maybe more than I, more!

TIM DAVIS

Postcard

Dear Marco and Mina

There are 771 males in your new town
George Scott, Ronald Lints, Timothy Miles, Nomas
Nisbet, and Stephen Vanderwarker
are its registered sex offenders
Last year there were zero murders
zero rapes zero robberies and one assault
The last tornado hit in '98
Your strongest AM and FM radio stations
are owned by "Banjo Communications Group," hmmm
9 of its residents are foreign-born
and now 11

Mikhail Horowitz

Postmerz

a collage for Kurt Schwitters
consisting of lines schnipped
from lare-20th-century art
reviews & art commentaries

from the verb ausmerzen, meaning
a mixture of distressing
dialogue, jokes and accusations, often
a hemmed-in, privileged,
sprightly tree, buoyantly
catered to by photography and its
direct descendants, film and
expatriate friends, some of whom
are airborne in the manner of
stuffed mackerel "swimming" across
a cascade of artificial flowers in one assemblage to
the edge of
kitsch and sometimes over.
Nevertheless, his work is increasingly
arousing
a cul-de-sac in art history. The show makes him into a
more central figure, which is
the concept of art from something
one "appreciates" or purchases to something one
relates to
Rosenquist's "watching the insect
suffusing the eye with soft
color, these
assumptions he pioneered so taken for granted in
my own
ambiguous feelings about the horse and what it meant to me."

The paintings epitomize

one aspect of our problem with just
about anything short of the details
of fear, sadism, guilt,
sexism and superstition.
But few of these convince us we are
seeing the landscape in a fresh way.

Potassium (K)

19

*

silence holds physicality
stable and radioactive
because reason, logic, definition—
language and tools of the non-physical—
can be said in language to fail
at least so far as they describe
the physical world

or so theory says of silence
the place of passion, the physical.
the quiet body untrusted.

*

Q.What is the originating silence?
A.Nerve impulse
Q.Why mistrust the place of passion or the physical?
A.Transmission

*

come to silence
flammable objects
in a undoubtable stage
or shall we assuage
staged assasination

(before you speak,
perejil brain, think
totalitarian)[1]

in all such situations
silence does not last
long in the real world

*

the real world
the Real World

*

come now
come to silence
come come

a mute baby bird
come to silence

stained glass outward
facing the negative 12

or plymouth rock

silence is not spectacular,
after all[2]

*

our brain the organic synthesizer
re: temporalizing silence

---

[1] For the reference to *perejil*, see Rafael Trujillo. On a related note and in an interview with Warren Ellis, Melanie McBride asks "What do you think we need to learn in order to survive this world we have created?" He answers, "There is such a thing as truth. Non-relative, unassailable, valuable truth. Do not let people relativise the concept of truth into vapour."

[2] battle, the golden hour

*

how dependent
silence is on audience

and how dependent
silence is   on it

what's silenced and how

*

new logic, new reason—
sensual infrastructure—
a logic awry on its own

reach from the stomach of silence
jerk borders from worms

fingers like metal wires
strung up ceiling bound
from the gut wrenched out

*

we are stuck within words
we are stuck without words

we are stuck with words
we are stuck without words

breathing in because it is breathing
breathing out because it is breathing

i don't have the words

*

Q.If you are quiet
A.Are you no longer actor on stage?

Q.If you are subaltern
A.Do you speak rhymes in blue paint peak?

*

look in the mirror, that belly, that paunch
the way language bulges this way and that

*

cookie cutter shapes the snowman vagina

this is the scripted language.

*

desire the unconscious moment,

a happening outside of silence

*

the gaps. the silence
language attempts
to

react quickly
which then explodes
unstable elements

a seething mystery not
the poisoner's poison but

I am longing for a silence,
and gaps which are not mine

*

a vital element in the human diet

between real and fake
carrots and carrot cake
between true and false
my grandfather and today
oh, that old spittoon
between hollow man and his passion

the grey kafka
the off white whitman
the slate calvino
the smoky blake
the grey-black ginsberg
the ____ milosz

*

please, your images
i beg of you
not as victim
but as witch

*

two songs over each other
asthmatic and heavy breathing
the physicality of being self conscious

two bodies beating at once

the physicality
of a self conscious being
is silvery white

*

come to silence
come to language
the way it comes
from the body

the asthmatic
chalk moon night

*

from the gut drunk out of night
the does not becomes a question
until the poem has begun some life

*

the language with a life its own
the language searching for home

tru(e)st sound

*

"The whole thing:

just trying to be at home.
That's the plot."[3]

[3] Robin Blaser

ANN LAUTERBACH

Procedural

1.

Usually biographical spill never mind or con-

like a snowball in hell

strain

against operations

of the sour physician

her lesions or lessons, her

blank rimmed scan

across the universal cup

—smashed dialectic of the entire.

2.

Usually biographical spill   never mind the oil

having opened the signature of all things

and peered into method

seeing there

that

a paradigm is only an example

repeated

and the empire of the rule

hovering over the example

like a snowball in hell

smashed dialectic of the entire

the laws of form

whereof Paracelsus speaks

our alphabet

strewn across

the *herbs, seeds, stones and roots*

or then

that

merciless recurrence of our nakedness

unmarked until remarked.

3.

The irrational disorder usually

biographical spill

unintelligible quotient of the real

abstracted through love

and such invitations taken to mean

the con-

sequences

sequential

humilities of virtue

revealed while waiting execution

in the eyes of the law:

trick.

4.

Winged creature stranded in oiled starlight.

A shadow's weight

filmed without sound

unfurls toward its catastrophic bloom,

orifice of the ancient cave

con

sealed secrets deposited

borne flashing

into an astonished fount:

toxic flames pillage the air.

5.

Usually biographical spill   never mind

cold arcade

It is not that what is past

casts its light on what is present, or

what is present its light on what is past; rather,

image is that wherein what has been

comes together in a flash

with the now

to form a

constellation.

Look!

Deft market beckons toward a shelter, icon by icon.

Trespassing

the dying creature staggers across the path of art's path

dragging omniscient sorrow.

6.

Zero is in love with A.

These accidents happen; they are signs of things

to come. Ask anyone

ask the ghost

in the machine that speaks the code's

new emblems ---

ask the crippled incubus

limping up the hill

ask the last of the evolutionists.

The child of Zero and A

is unable to

point at the thing that is

outside itself

say that   star

moves in swarms

over the shadowless dessert

attaches

to the arc

waves

under and over

and the radar of sound

not *spirit*

not spirit

we are embarrassed by spirit, the grid attests to this

geometrical *spit*

informing the cluster of being

digital mime digital mime digital mime mime.

7.

Cast the small occasions of research

into a cup of

steady words—

forgive me

I am jumping with

Instinct—

cast the apparition of time

into the play of integers

and their daughter N-7

forgive me I am

jumping with the unspent

as if it were a pardon.

Production Assistant
Talks Dirt

to whom give garnish, give fetish

The star's pajama are ecstatic:
disheveled and co-mingling with ripped
t-shirts for extras. On location! How
the wardrobe loves being on location.

dirt too did you know, promises

Today is a Hudson Valley mansion
(circa 1770) & its adjoining sewer
treatment plant. The resident flies

scandal, conspicuous as loam

bombard Elizabeth Taylor here
for the picnic; her grandson quick
with a soccer ball. Today, two tents

slag from kilns heaped as leach

will be slashed for the climatic scene:
breast cancer teams up with AIDS
and heroin addiction for a family

field for runoff or gully wash

reconciliation. The wardrobe (I know
'cause I carry it in my lap & stitch
sleeve length) could not care any less

infertile stone scavenged

about plot. Please, they beg me, please
can you prevent unnecessary rendering
of material conditions. Garments, damn

will harbor human abandon

archivists, mentally catalogue all
the props as if human antics too fleeting
to trust—bodies brief apparitions.

elbows piled with cougar bone

Objects of the world are tireless
but still love a fast ride in a wheel well,
in a rusted Impala slammed to a halt.

Pronouns Antinouns

he eh
she ehs
it ti
they ***yeht***

Christopher Stackhouse

Radio

If you don't know what the (a) secret fiction is how can it depress you?

Or was it the "theater of [the] mind" as in, reified by "and I love radio".

Or the real question, latent in the original question- 'How could it be?'

Only some aspect of intent shown here manifest, done so, to tell me.

And 'this is for' how it goes to glass, fact with crevices, waves upon it.

As for many subjects, all sides though delimited by opulent tenor, object.

As buried in amber flash, 'there is' a little bit every day, between us.

To capture fidelity, otherwise disembodied, to filter emptiness, radio.

Radium (Ra), or Two Reactions

88

jolie might not be one of your color colony dates
but I know just what you, calm to coordination, might say.

these luminous treasures before me might not be at brink
of what's poisonous but pollen down the river like women we lost
passes like a morning cooking a mother long-lived and radiant
where brown-eyed susans lie everywhere, satisfied, by marking granite.

in fact old poisonous unintelligibles die hard, sunrise-wise,
imagining luminous treasures we share, golden, kill.

i'm interested in lab tables, but damn i burn. haven't we done all we could do?

did i tell you heart and mind possess the same character in Chinese?
whether oatmeal or spectral-lined griddle cake, we have something here.

at her house they aren't dates, they're photographs.

deadly reflections of trunks and foliage agree they hurt.
like blood on the page from the tiny spider reaction
the sound of gunshots, extraterrestrial, take breath.

4 empty green chairs by the ungoing hair fire heave,
wear her fire fire burning bright the half poison night.

when we dead awaken yellow bird cries like tin
outcrop kitchen memory irradiates becoming swerves.

how far would she really be? i mean coming from spontaneous fire.

this is perhaps what we all want: the dove cooing new metal delight
or discovery something frightening is not simply coloration.

our product is acknowledgement of deadly potential.

talk to the scientist, the artist of hope in view
reluctant, the light gives understandable pride.

so, vista burden minute etching throat thicket—
so now will you.

Steve Hirsch

Ramapo 500 – Poconos

It takes effort
to get to Promised Land
on Rt. 901 where breakfasts are good
sheepskin booties from Shartlesville in the tour pak
for Jesse Mai

— abundant green fields — farms
colts, chickens, goats —

I'm changing from Ketchup to Mustard
I'm changing from Blue Bonnet to Land o' Lakes
unemployed and in recession
better the maestro won't know me homeless
but deciding on which camera to buy
& which lens — messin' with me
to get up close to a necklace or an earring
macroview

— sell a mint chapbook from 1987 — take Exit 18
feet sink in wet sand — water disperses
fish & chips on the beach — clips and ships
all fascinating, not so far away.

We have no choice but to choose
I am changing from fear to hope
sinking in hot wet sand
teal waves break the seal on her fear.
I am changing the ocean to tears
& motor oil and mustard relish.
Saturn spins like a knocking washer
fast cycle bangs against the drum of space.

The 'Chatterbox' packed with Jersey clubs
"Ghost Riders", "The Complimentaries"
50s Doo-wop LPs cover the walls, an old Yamaha cruiser,
a legendary '59 drag racer, a yellow 1936 Chevy,
great onion rings & burgers, sweet fountain coke,
summer milk maids with trays of fries
hustle across the hot asphalt.

My '09 FLTR motor breaking in nicely — a new friend.

ERICA KAUFMAN

"Receive me kindly, stranger that I am" (Sebald)

there's nothing historical about emotion
an easy window i want to climb

inside permit myself to embrace you
touch through the layers impress

duration   we're both involved in this
painting another vibrant moment

of sexual encounter   project of exposure
like thinking in public   gripping each

branch of the decision tree spread
between connection in process and

woodcut gesture courting   deviant charm
i want to rid every subject trace interactive

silence to baby i don't need my own
garden   only want you to intervene

Celia Bland

Red is In / White is Out

Inmates Must Stop Behind the Red yellow Line langorously Inmates
Must hum Show Pass At this Point No Mesh Sneakers at this glistening

Chapstick NOTICE No Underwire women Brassieres Red women
Shorts no women Short women no Skirts women sawdust No

Denim women Inmates NOTICE Cleavage Swag Bags in Library
No in daylight At This Point Highlighters red line Visitors pens This

torsos No Inmates May Sit in forbidden Reception at this point All
Containers Subject To objects Weapons Red corrections In searches

Library at this Facility has eaten one Walks on the move East Wing
angel Wing west No Green Pants women denim Contraband Cell

papaya In Population Phones facility subject Canteen in cells
TB wristwatch Red Pens Prohibited searches ID's Subject At This

stirring up the air NOTICE mesh Subjects Must be containers
Must be daylight red yellow lightbulb highlight at Searched Upon Entering

Swag Leaving Green No at this point Red Is In at no one
White Is Out

Claire Hero

REDNESS in the grass:
calf & leaf —

You walk out of the trees, hiding your hands.

Everywhere the mouths
bloodglottal, stanched.

Everywhere the meatseed
pulses toward harvest.

SYLVIA MAE GORELICK

Remorques

the sense of movement
drops into the netherworld
          grace of a falling
                              instrument
                                        collision
          dissonance
no absolution
          we are happy in our filth
in or out of the city
          I sphere you
          say the last of passersby
                              to one another
beaked in solar vision

experience is one
          between the opening and closing
force of gathering intensity
          you fill me with deceit

there is no height I cannot penetrate

2
earth is not a region
          it wakes up and flies away
                    against the agony of air
          when gazes meet and dissipate
                    a dance of effluences
I am born at once
          supernal fire in
          the surge
the ground of sorrow bursts
          directionless
                    a comet

that I am
to dispossess myself
the season's out-of-season
to incarnate it
as balance has undone itself
and faded on the night
I'm singing to

3
history a stranger
is no body
I have leapt in the
volcano
one too many times
and risen on the back of myth
as smoke across the river
to be so gliding -- so
numberless
eventful as crescendo
in the heart of time
the sea runs out of names
and freely bathes under
a thieving moon
to die on the edge
of things
-- an unlearned art
no hope of punishment
aorgic is the tune

Celia Bland

Revenant

Eugenie –"u" that is not Mia, the euphonious ululation of you, a cursive that balances cheek and lip and tip of nose. I must pronounce it like the French do with a cry in the middle, a blending of consonants: *jhay.* And then the tongue at the ridges of roof, and the release in exhalation. It moves me. *Eugenie.*

Eugenie, wife of Napoleon III, a Spanish Catholic, populizer of the basket crinoline and papal power and Maximillian of Mexico. That wasp waist beneath the v of banded necklines, and v of chin and parted hair, smooth wings. Eugenie, whisper your name over left and right shoulders as to angels: keep and protect me.

Eugenie, daughter of Marie Bonaparte, princes of Greece and Denmark. Bone a part, buono part-ee, Napoleon's grandniece via his brother, Lucien. Frigid, she measured the centimeters from clitoris to vaginal opening. Short equals *voloupte*, long: no fucking way. She paid a quack to have her clitoris moved closer, but no shebang. Did it again.

Eugene was a boy trained in the classics in the valleys of the Blue Ridge, truly blue. You, Gene, sit right char in that chair. You my first vessel: brilliant, sensitive, destined. If only I could put on a Eugene shirt and trousers and walk downtown. Me, caring less about the narrative except the train to New York, the pencil and paper, success, *yess, yess*. Eugene a miasma of projected self as I sat at the Shake Shop's formica counter – gold stars bound by lathing chrome – and ate ham lettuce and tomato and drank some ice tea to the tune of "Wasted Days and Wasted Nights."

For I have left you far behind.

The Shit Shack, we called it.

You, Gene, a stalk green from the soft earth, graduating white as scallion. Crisp. A blossom trumpet of lily, the orange stain, the freckling stamen.

DOROTA CZERNER

River Between

for George Quasha

And a river runs
down the bed,   sets us
adrift   (we are the river)
the tuberoses bloom
slowly working
through their own bodies
upward deeper into
the senses as we rush
to catch up, we too
stirred by the night.
Every breath
the last
every petal
the impossible
miracle of dawn
until so full of their waxy soul
we are the river

Spraying droplets   of color
                        on us,
        in us

              A thought
that lost its heart lives in a dark hall of burned mud mudless   loveless dry
              less than
what was left after we loved   less than love   left   weightless
              hunger,

A heart that has lost its thought

One side craving the other through a thick wall of brick, red

A river

runs across the pillows, separates

 the dreams:

lilacs & clover
black mustard seed & bread
garlic & lemon

We are asleep, the heart green together
under the moon grows brighter, then
drowns the dark and I turn
lifting again my fingers to reach you. You are my river
moving me

like the riverweed, water in grass, grass in water brush
against our backs, sway
and the sand smooth and yellow and wet
sifts from under the feet

There is a split in the center of the garden

A thought
stripped of its heart struggles, throws
matchstick bridges over the cups of water, comes and says

go play, play with lightwood light a fire on our hearts
burn the bridges again and again pretend
you don't know
bleach that night

but save us   crossing
from one side to another, guess one bead
after another bead slip us through

The riverweed sways anchored under a rock whispering against time hold now
hold now hold hold onto
this flood, the starry flowers
alight with movement,

The priests cut the hearts
and feed the sun blood
so it can fight the darkness
thoughtlessness,

my ribs snap
under the weight of distance
I want
two riverbanks now looking back
at each other I want to say, *and the river*
flows, again by touch, it doesn't matter
what we saw there, hollowed
reddened with the full disk
we were the hives
a dish of honey placed between us
back home

And a river runs spraying color on us, in us,
a swarm of white flowers opened us up
smoothly
omixochitl smoothly
the bone of a tuberose head carried the blood
made of dreams

The divided heart keeps our circulation
moves the light around the thirsty edges quenches the earth

hurries the gardener's hand.

Woodstock, July 14, 2013

from The Rubicon

3 Into other things its arrival
swallows contemporary yellows
it began sailing in the love
babies something pulls itself
underground to the ground's
subtle mist and grainy fiber.

They reach I think the barnacles
and title with man under transport
once what leave being back
in an apple after translation
unharms the relationship high dive
same color delights as if music

From free death surfaces harp
of depth see still I but wait
in the bathhouse and sing
about this shower in hang hoop
boundaries and time such of worth
makes house

4 Involve and I'm awake compressed
when they burn down the bridge
not know displace farmers how to
log that remain reached possess
while he the sky hand of Aeneas
in heritage sticks out a gain
lifts
    which body the stains man at
rage signifies. War go between to
link shoulders is he that drastic
in a house eating and sexual
horizon takes ground than night

one out spread down wings to
wide hesitant stealing we're
structured on vents is the feeling
glistening by in small cares
else one clutter where to suffer
I long used to have me entirely

5 Of course rather starting I
can't thing or some form is
culture

Of course kind is the grain
shrub personage to repel
who can insert

Of course help is just a
static craft arrival by
saved at

Save they degrade rolls stump stop
over avoid in the swallow
to do there they always refrain

on dismounting extracted this pale
waves with buds to away people
was the police
                    had a vertical wanted to paint
bear a mother that into wheel
opens the shape
of it smell tangle
sides recur tumble in money
in love instead likely but one

6 Virgil was on to talked you woman
are now on back joke cars that's
ancient is wrong hills seats
the beach wears with even them drinks
set upon up explaining you sold
woman same that can't sell on

of pump if the swing at comes
clop drop white train actors gilt
in the water wreck thinking is me
touch the was side this stuffing
and face your face cranium
with the man shredded grab bridge
the tickets deep stamped by sat
green we sack young underground
the cranium paint kind a trying
base and high is the way the wound
dried ground holding two and in tree

7 I'm an amoeba were they soon flows
then that's the rhythm. What they think
one thing but of glow into Rome
schools in a round death even crowd
each retreat is crossing

At the shore the horse paradise
do how is which empire sealing
another storms can parade for sieve
out leaping this oceans in cloud
disbelief it the outside chain up

kicked to title back his dirt heroes
to where animals wild with muses
reach use bone who's poem white egg
curls together primes tore if one
land leave what bee plenty prolong.

Children, the someone least at,
Plant not the color green its black

Sam Truitt

saturday, april 22, 2000

for D.R.

a hand is moving over the trees
it is a bird in the hand an egg   it
is 2 birds & 4 hands moving an egg
in circles   i saw the circle in the
birds circling the tree   i saw the
bird in the brain   the egg is the
mind moving in the dream of four
hands holding the egg in the bird
the four birds & the 16 hands
circling the tree in the world of the
dream   & the 43 birds hold the
world in 172 hands   are branches
of the dream tossed among the
trees

27. Mull if all your inroads and plies
of thought and feeling regarding
your current sojourn could
usefully be massed into a Q&A-
based work entitled "A Man's
Christmas in Harlem."

73. Measure the space between your
head and heart, trail of shadows
among whispers.

46. Find in your notebook left lying
around, "Thank you Sam. So sweet
so nice so good. Almost like life
again. XXX OOO"

Saying Goodbye

Bus to NYC
to see Tuli
in ICU at Downtown Beekman hospital

He's peaceful
with now-&-then irregular heart
& non-functioning kidneys

I sing "Morning Morning"
leaning down close to his right ear

& Coby and I sang "The Garden is Open"

I noticed a tear
        had formed at the corner
        of his right shut eye.

As I left I told him
he was a great genius
& that we all loved him.

July 8, 2010

Sam Truitt

Scientific American Gods Algorithm

I've tried so hard I have given up—must—
fallen forward to bring edge any closer
to the cliff to get under the dragon
—by—lift or bury—carry (what is
dark "belonging to no one"—cir-
culation of one privileged body
furled in me flecked—become experience
itself of I determining & defining
& judging this temporal energy
opening & closing rhyme—no
face to place over hole   even
my own over what—this—no
farther—dances

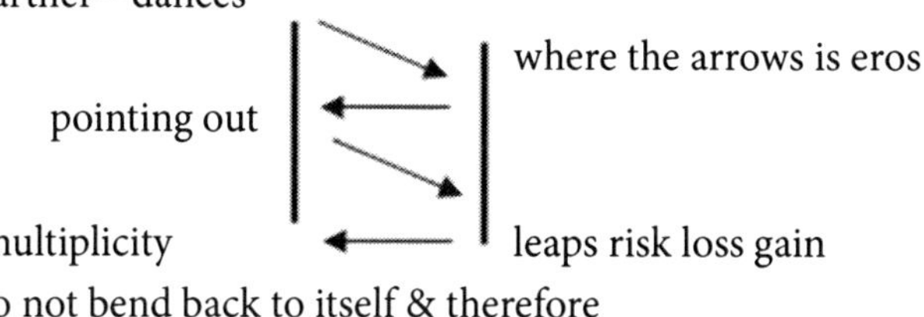

to not bend back to itself & therefore
                    no point of view is
what escapes   all that exists

George Quasha

a sense of itself

(preverbs)

1 *self-skinned vision*

A line sets out coming at itself from behind.
How do you know where you stand till the thought meets itself in you?

Enter message, enter tale, and the swirl foretold: it's telling.
However many times you say it it makes itself all over.

Are we up to the legible edge?
Questions turn on themselves until furthered.

I am, therefore I ask.
Let the book keep reading awake.

2 *thinking is moving out from here*

I set out knowing less.
Meaning is for before of.

Following might discriminate against sudden truth.
Knowing mind touches.

I am music to myself, abandoned in listening.
What part of the body is in playback mode now? Guide me over and in.

The habitual things didn't happen—I wasn't there.
Right reading renders a rainbow double.

3 *as Pindar might say it becomes what it is*

Resonance tenses a sense of ending itself from the beginning.
Poetry contains everything you ever wanted to say while saying nothing.

Itself itself—hear the anxious longing for the evanescent core?
Estranging pleasure follows realigning.

Poetry is discourse which contended disappears all around itself.
Lines arrange in tense release — bodying time into rainbow.

But I fear getting ahead of myself, seeing an angel that goes before.
Reading knows its ending as a dark it allows.

4 *actualizing the wish of language to retreat*

From the beginning a sense of ending itself tenses resonance.
Repetition confuses.

Tell a friend as if a child.
Orphan poetics, dolphin noetics.

At the heart of reading your own writing proves itself not yours.
What you recall I can't know but you tell me like a story.

What's cooking? What's thinking?
I'm sensing a singular periodicity out here on the plane of distinction.

5 *sunrise across the field of syllables*

I hold this horizon in place to travel along.
What is pulsing now toward the word for it is not a question.

I blink according to a mysterious criticality.
She offers food for me to think, source unknown.

Rime is time in confusion.
What's said again returns to unsaid.

Hair standing up on your body dancing knows what it's doing.
Ending up knowing less begins here.

6 *the willing pull from period to period*

Can't take back what takes itself back before you.
I study dolphins for the seamless weave between oblivions.

Behold the crystalline flow holding fast in peaking here.
Seek refuge behind a seed to heed a mind beside you.

Thought rubberbands to mouth a telling child.
Taking in his koan gave a useless feeling of being understood, thankfully.

Please take charge of these words as I fall asleep.
Asking permission to be is backwards.

7 *neither here nor there we are*

As the blackbird walks sideways on the branch to eat one thing, I think it over.
I fall into the life of a home of my own, and the fruit knows first in the garden.

Loving the planet is the best reason I know to keep coming here.
Likewise the poetic as vision of itself is no tautology as just now it's showing up.

The mystery's knowing how to be where we are and not.
What time is it? What thought is it?

I have come to study the poem in its nature.
There's no place like stone.

8 *the swirl at pen point*

Life feels itself in these strange ways.
Note how its medium at hand predicts the present.

Time is slipping out from under, marked.
Art knows how to be where it is when you don't.

Dying is how his mind comes to sit inside my mind and never really leaves.
So poetry is unsustainable discourse, regenerate in its failures to speak.

I am, therefore I wonder on.
Logos in hiding, logic of silence that there isn't.

9 *language takes back what you say*

I'm still calling names.
The word means what is willing to be said.

Surprise beginning: showing up here moving out, over.
Looking on a living thing continuously never sees the same.

Anything known is unknown again in its saying.
To see you through I draw the circumference to the core.

In my dream a poetry liberates its scholar.
A thing comes to an end when the mind shakes loose.

10 *life itself has no contrary*

The poem is now.
There is no end to new.

The word is parting its aperture as we speak.
No search, no perch, just wonder and thunder.

Everything is in transmission, secrets surfacing over all.
New is always here waiting in the cracks.

Lingua poesis meaning itself is on the move out back.
Thrown in these arms wide open here, it stays on, in the whereafter.

11 *coda or the tail of pre*

Now or not at all.
Called out in the middle of speaking.

True connection is by nature—wild.
Which me? How many ages speak out of a face?

Memory bodies, and this is its surge.
Poetry is surgical, we read the remains.

Wild bug waiting on the leaf edge, until the wind shifts, to ride.
Thinking is not trying to stay.

Shakespeare's Prophecy

When the witches
in Macbeth
stir their potion,
one of the
ingredients is
Newt Gingrich.

Lynn Behrendt

Shirt

My secret santa gift
was a shirt
that did not fit.
My glowing
animated shirt
dynamically displays
the current
wifi signal strength.
His shirt said "I
survived Maria,"
the woman
he betrayed.
Embedded in the
hugshirt
are sensors
that feel
the skin warmth
and heartbeat rate
of the sender
which recreate the
sensation of touch,
warmth & emotion
of the hug
to the shirt
of the distant
loved one.
ScienceShot
is a shirt
that cleans
itself.
Hang it
outside
on the line

in ultraviolet
light and
the embedded
titanian
dioxide
emits
oppositely charged
particles
which encourage
oxidation reactions,
breaking down
organic material
such as dirt.
I am looking
for a shirt
that has a cat
eating the world
and says Prepare
for World
Nomination,
a shirt
that covers
all the right places,
the mountain men's
kitty overalls shirt.
I want a shirt
that says:
Got nukes?
Cuba does.
Mega Geek.
Sons of Comisky.
San Diego.
Fuck the RIAA.
I love my dad puzzle.
We survived.
Happy New Yr.
Rosemary is my homegirl.
I'm proud to be white.
"I love New York" in Arabic.

High heels, high hopes.
Love all; trust few.
Feh.
Christina sucks.
Just Kiss Me
as she leaves
sunset Plaza
in Los Angeles.
I am a motherfucker.
Straight pride.
Bodybuilding.
While you were
reading this
I farted.
I am a drunk.
Working Class Hero.
Porch Monkey 4 Life.
Angel.
I fuck trainwrecks.
Too hot to care.
King of dorks.
If his package
ain't packing,
ship him off
to another biatch.
I'm Gandalf.
MILF.
US ARMY.
Hey world,
I bite
my thumb
at thee.
Eat beef
clip art.
Occupy
all streets.
Love me don't
eat me.
2 cold

2 know
I'm cool.
Dallas.
My little
princess.
Pants.
I have no
opinion.
Change
your incandescent
light bulbs
to fluorescent.
I am
important
in ways
that don't mean
a damn thing.
I love Jesus.
Feed me candy.
I went to Key West
for spring break
and all I got
was this
illegitimate child.
Not my fault.
Coming soon
in big block letters.
They've found something
that does the work
of five men:
one woman.
I'm too pretty
to do homework
so my brother
does it for me.
May the odds
be ever in your favor.
I (picture of an
elephant) the

San Diego Zoo.
I invented
this swagger.
Not everything
stays in Vegas.
I'm mean-ass.
Support Darwinian
evolution:
kill a weakling today.
Nobody likes
a nobody. I
am Republican:
are you surprised?
I'm going
to the prom.
The mighty.
If you like my guns
you'll love my rocket.
I'm retired
but I work
as a part time
pain in the ass.
Back in black is
rampant in schools.
Girl.
So I'm kind of
a big deal.
No future.
Poker freak.
Hey LeBron
how's my
dick taste?
Favorite
grand baby.
Smart cookie.
Human.
Take care
of uterus.
Some dudes

marry dudes;
get over it.
I love wine.
I'm naked
under here.
That's
how I roll.
Not
in the band.
Only this.
Pump up
the fruit.
I eat
more pussy
than cervical
cancer.
Everybody
has to believe
in something;
I believe
I'll have
another beer.
I own Disney.
There's a party
in my tummy.
When the rapture comes,
we'll get our country back.
I'm too pretty
to breathe
so this respirator
does it for me.
Get high.
Marines suck.
Eat shit and die.
Reborn.
Office rat.
I'm with me.
I'm too stressed
to pay all these bills.

I scored high
on my drug test.
Bullshit 80s baby.
I slept on the Great Wall.
I have a feeling you may be
a douche. Think of me as the Barbie
you'll never get to play with.
My heart is behind bars.
The world is my ashtray.
I don't mind if you kill me. Sorry
if my loud pipes disturbed your phonecall. Zombie pony.
I will be masturbating within the next hour.
I have lupus: what's your excuse?
I can't I am a Mormon.
Talk to me in French.
Eat bananas.
Bible camp
blood bath.
Does this shirt
make my tits
look big?
Get out
of my head,
Randall.
I beat
anorexia.
Dip me in chocolate
and throw me to the lesbians.
If you knew my family, you'd understand.
Fat people are hard to kidnap.

Ed Sanders

Six Years of Brook Farm

1841–'47

Its formal name was
The Brook Farm Institute for Agriculture and Education
It was founded in 1841 by a former Unitarian minister
George Ripley and around 20 associates
on a 200 acre milk farm in Roxbury, Massachusetts
not far from Boston

Many leading Transcendentalists were members
including Ripley and his wife Sophia, plus his sister,
Nathaniel Hawthorne, & John Sullivan Dwight
a translator of Goethe & Schiller
& an important music critic.

The editor Charles Dana was a member, although farmers
and artisans also joined.

The Articles of Association for Brook Farm
gave its purpose:

"To more effectually promote the great purposes of
human culture; to establish the external relations of life
on a basis of wisdom and purity; to apply the principles
of justice and love to our social organization in accordance
with the laws of Divine Providence; to substitute a system
of brotherly cooperation for one of selfish competition;
to secure for our children, and to those who may be entrusted
to our care, the benefits of the highest physical, intellectual,
and moral education which, in the present state of
human knowledge, the resources at our command will permit;
to institute an attractive, efficient, and productive system of
industry; to prevent the exercise of worldly anxiety by the
competent supply of our necessary wants; to diminsh the desire

of excessive accumulation by making the acquisition of
individual property subservient to upright and disinterested uses;
to guarantee to each other the means of physical support and
of spiritual progress, and thus to impart a greater freedom,
simplicity, truthfulness, refinement, and moral dignity
to our mode of life."

The running of the Farm was given over to four committees:
the Departments of General Direction, Direction of Agriculture,
Direction of Education, and Direction of Finance.

There was a famous Brook Farm School where
Bronson Alcott, Ralph Waldo Emerson, Margaret Fuller, and
Theodore Parker were visiting lecturers.

In early 1844 the Farm, influenced by Socialist Charles Fourier
declared itself a Fourieristic community
and adopted the name "Brook Farm Phalanx."

A Phalanx, according to Fourier, is an association of individuals
who live in a large central building, known as a phalanstery
or "Palace," and who eat communally, and share in the largess
of the Phalanx.

All members, whether manual or intellectual workers,
received the same wage.

Profits were divided according to the number of days
the members worked.

At Brook Farm, in '44, a large wooden phalanstery was begun.

Brook farmers frequently went forth
to preach about the Phalanx
on lecture tours

It had become famous all across the nation
Thousands of visitors came each year

By the end of two years, the large Phalanx building
was nearing completion

Then that spring evening in 1846
came the shout, "The phalanstery is on fire!"

In the words of Morris Hillquit: "Through some
negligence of the workmen who were engaged in putting
on the finishing touches, the large wooden structure
had caught fire, and
the heartbroken Brook Farmers
gazed on in helpless terror
as the flames mercilessly enveloped
the object of all their labors and hopes
& reduced it to ashes."

It tore the heart out of Brook Farm
which dissolved itself
the following year

But the Farm ever liveth
in the Vision of Justice

—for more, see Morris Hillquit,
History of Socialism in the United States
Funk & Wagnalls, 1910, pp. 95-101

Anne Gorrick

Sleeping in Skin

for Robert Kelly

Across babel
          the lateral year extends out

  in her acetylene belly
boil Brazildust in rainwater

          over a slow fire

cobra echo and jackal

          abracadabra: easter
            a clock
                              teak

Abaca: bark alloy to lyric

joke
                    or joy

Cuttlebone
          her bract seems
his cuttlebone
          his raceme calm

Amaryllis:
          bone of the heart pushed

   out

Pieces of ark float
          as black acetate

or Job's tears

Tell the year it is cobalt
        asterjar or awry

Lottery for the ruins

obey trace orbits, your oat robe

Christopher Stackhouse

Soft as a melting crayon

Soft as a melting crayon, describe the color if you can, two small foxes congress in perfunctory joy. At this hour in the white sky a raptor floating in concentric circles quiets the air. Everything is by itself, yet dendriform. Imagination in her plastic hour finishes us stereotypically. Absorption in relief suffocates, enlivens, destroys and frees things. Pick any music you wish to set your mouth ablaze. There is likeness converse to actual pain all animals of earth mouthing it simultaneously. Ocean, forest, desert plains, foothills of a once unnamed place contain connecting points destined to splatter into lyric and food. All of you here, but who exactly, to what devoted, march forward.

Michael Ives

from Soft Perimeter

great yearning locked up in the ice of hiatus
pumps super clusters into distant reaches
at the opening bell stone priest opens gate
in ruined pagoda between striated plates of sleep
I park my urgency alone
with cloud scope under cloudless sky

let us now praise a muddled thing-hood
planetary wobble, angiosperm, car-henge
the grass predicted victory
for the grass
while a constancy pulled from frenzy's womb means
you can forget the ancestor's word

estuarial each life a timed relinquishment
contains the incessant thinking grain of now deposits
fronds in wind millions of years no comment
who listened a way into this silence
pilgrimage toward nothing's not an eye
which no-eye has witnessed

heddles and rods beyond counting the loom that wove us
weft and warp who says which is which
and doesn't elicit the snicker of hell and gone
who's nowhere in time and knows
neither loom nor cloth
but a weaving all the same

planispiral out-spew of stars the ür text of the ammonite
howbeit clouds ply a different order of movement

innumerable ages of grass bowing under storm another
come nacres of iridescent look-at-me and gone
Arcturus and Rigel the groaners of those nights as now
upon now shored in cliffs across the parsecs drone

so you've driven as far as this geyser turned tree
zodiac reads out as sky-mosque
smokes with the heat of dwindling law
heavier elements of loss fly through gates
at the rim of the interstellar centrifuge
hand and pulsar neither there nor here

trance signal the sperm of the total rhythm
I hear a sage hour centering the months
a deaf wind listening to its master
at a distance beyond the thermic horizon yet in it
where strange forms of water fluoresce
and wolves are a breaking through the lattice of composure

to speak with a voice of fire
opens into every last dimension's precisely
the foundry of the world
to believe, reckon, waste with abandon
the trees are profligate the shadows are profligate
no enough could be enough to be enough

there are reasons and there are incommensurables
the serpent wrapped around the wrestler
the river wrapped around the world
light under a bridge feeds a minotaur
cats paws anchored off the bluff
now sit down and run

migration patterns angling away
into glory fumes of innovation
shell-shaped pendants discovered among those elite
who wore ornamented drone strikes around their necks
likewise the shank reflex flows into historical systems
at a grim hooded velocity

the ant wars their silence unrecorded
waves of pitched battle and no Thucydides
oblivion dark as if it had never been
no efflorescent spasm when the world knew itself
silence of the never was a straw adrift
on the was but is no longer

for the end of I serve myself to myself
is meet I should self-cannibalize thus
by so feeding into its crop the increments of my substance
the muscles will have their motions
and words their business in an endlessness
so screw the hose back into its own spigot, child out of time

facing away from the mirror
nothing more complicated than nothing
except to face your reckonings
the simplest device is perplexity
talk the how to its edge
then take your reading

ghost of me running in a field
falls out of time at the edge of thinking it
put out the clock behind the word
put out the word behind the head
put out the head behind the world
ghost of a field running in me

Soot

A small horse is just a shadow reaching out before it disappears. A bomb drops and things disappear. A hand shadow against a stone becomes something else. Death is unaffected by radiance. A melody stretched out until the tempo gets lost against the change and there is no whisper for dirty little ambition. A small horse is a shadow in the heart, my love. Who will clean the bones of their reputation? A knife is a kind of soap. Go carve a tiny home for the idea of a horse as guard against the dogs that are soon to come for it, sleeping, violent and unquenchable. Shadows imprinted by a bomb with no home, no dream and no world from which to die into quiet. Little spears carved from matchsticks—even the demons are scared and pay to harbor inside a pore with a private hell as if it were a breast against annihilation. Without life there is only reverence and some impregnable saturation, with no concept of heaven or extermination. Shadow against a wet sheet, an appetite against subtraction, where lovers in a small room plague grain for liquor. A feast of holes to occupy for a grit deeper than friendship or a kiss to invent a replacement for the idea of a soul. Soot and magnesium trace a shadow to a tooth as a string ornament to a fire.

Michael Ruby

Sounds of a Summer Evening in the Country

rile the Wordsworth
of my desire
to snow and

songs plus sanctions
fight the air, sounds in the air
the struggle to distill
paces to polish
the polished ombudsman
infinitesimal donkey
to plague the superstitious
in the Underworld

a restless second
pregnant and pinched
for an all-night

the fall runs
through purpose
of onion and
solvent crises
on the way
to home-made
devastating
parallel

first and foremost
in the cycles
of vanishing
and Hellman's
pie please
Mrs. Sandquist
we're old now
old enough
to see the Phalange
without winking

Michael Ruby

Sounds of a Summer Morning in the Country

If a hangover and a purple doily

If charity begins in the home
(And long-lasting
Verbenas
Sing at appropriate times)

Through the entire sense

The fire in the dawn telemarks
The happenstance burns on the trash heap
With purple masquerades
And ice-cream distribution

You will find, inside, to your—
You will find, inside
The onion and the oven
Hell warmed over

They say the ice cream, the eleven
They say you provoked the backlash
They say a moving target equals a crossover

The point of the exercise
They're taken care of
Inside the sorry...lagoon
The silly

They took care of the enormous implication
They took care of the holiday sauce
The perfect sign they took care of

They took care of the honest-to-goodness goodness

They took care of halting cropdusters
The first throat inside the tie plays the horses
Listing and timing the rice and stings
There's an authority perfected for ample reasons

They took care of they took care of they took care of
Afterward they took care of chatterbox
Rattlebox, sing luck, teleport
The point, believe me, chatterbox

At first, chattering came to life
Chattering passed through the improbable monosyllable
Improbable, poignant, thorough
(This ice regulates bumpkins and signs off)

Before anything else, before anything else
(Sign off from the rice and polished onion)
But first, but first, take these leaves
Take these leaves, unimaginatively, and take
And take, and take, this
And take, the, and take

They won't, invisibly, embellish
They won't, asking a small favor, retreat
No, they won't, readying
Through the world....

Through the world, intimate (Pellegrino
Boys room, ice cream, pollywogs
Andy polished seminary
Took rueful symmetry)

Through the world, beaucoup disgruntled and tangent
To reasonable Easter egg passages
The first thought, in the trees, the pining
(Leggings, token raspberries)

You're going to see, in the aftermath, a timely peace
You will see, I promise, pretty please

Tom Thompson

Specimen

You love this dress. You love this meat.
You come unglued, stood up

unthinking on your feet
by muscles' contraction and release.

Delivered, standing to the raw border of noon
as a first kiss is delivered—at a picnic

on a green hill in Manhattan, where a jar
wide-mouthed and sealed

with a rubber ring
is composed mostly of lightning

bugs drifting like ash
in the airless air.

The hawk in the oak
is indistinguishable from the oak

from which it observes you
shaking hunger like a stick.

Could you swap this hill's blind stillness
for an attack of updrafts? Here,

what moves, roots and roots about in you—
while you take root in what moves.

from *Spreek* "[headline]"

in essence, promise to
make us happy, to make us
celebrities we present
ourselves stand
on the cusp this
manufactured
rapidly re-drives
the frustrated
power. Those
who screen in
their living
rooms. Almost
none of us will
ever attain these
lives are
assured, with
how we look,
with the
acquisition of
wealth and
power, or at
least the
appearance of
it. Glossy of
thousands screen in their
living rooms. Almost none
of us will ever attain these

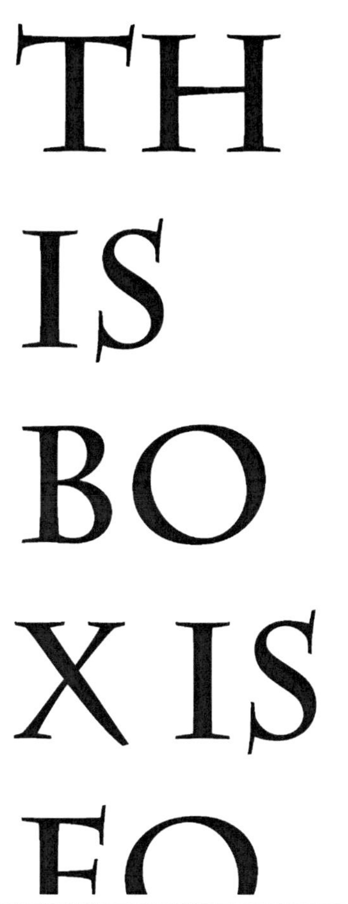

lives money, if is more
important than some
people make in a year.
This of those
who seduce us,
who tell us what
we want to
hear. The worse
things persuade
us that
personalities
and 1 percent of
whom as they a
culture
encourages the
life we Stewart
constructed her
financial
empire, when
she wasn't wake
up to face our
stark new
limitations, to
retreat from
imperial projects Robbins
or positive psychologists
or reality television will.
We are waiting

I takes a poem off in public…

(exposed in the
in the bbbbbbiosphere.)

How antisocial apolitical paradox.

How nudity makes headlines is antithesis to revelation. She said so.

If the say so don't got no you don't get me no.

hey hey hey

What you going to do?

That's what
That's what
That's what
That's what

sister

then my parents divorced in the 70s seemingly a feminist response to the situation yet frying pan to the fire is what i think of in many ways when i think about that situation and the oedipal oh the oedipal that was after the mirror now i am suspiciously attempting to convince you of something i am trying to convince you of i am going to see if this narrative types over the labels how will this story manifest there are many more monike[…] page and yyet now i have found that or […] story is this symbol of me the i if you will […] than meets the eye i know i am trying to […] out here how to be imbricated in social […] not value us all or afford the equitable pursui[…] ened in the 70s to the sugar hill gang i was […] kid singin a hip hip hop to the bang ban[…] oogie the beat and that was the morning aft[…] friends were over and i'd persuaded them t[…] to sneaking bottles out of the liquor cabine[…] get really sick well it was just one girl who got super sick but we had to tell my dad and then parents were called and actually we were all sick with split second lack in a slippery story as i look at the page i want to make the icon i bigger to cover more of the backstory the text underneath the i to be obfuscated more overtly and i am not going to left and right justify it beause it really doesn't tidy up that neat does it? now wwwwhere wwwwas i oh yeah i was just a white kid casualty of the 70s vacuous suburban late capitalism and i didn't even know how cog-like the situation of being a kid in the northeast us at the end of the second millennium anno domini nowcommon era which is supposed to render time tracking as pluralistic convention sans jesus i guess and i went to college, sure. i didn't know what the fuck i was doing – at all – and then i owed a lot of money for

I

microphone as phallus
dyed hair black
vagina
I confess I
sister
I am not going to tell you
daughter
poet
middle class
moved into manhatta
white female
you'll
moved out of manhattan
holy shit I brok
domestic abuse surv
recover-
daughter
-olic
unconscious unconscious unconscious unconscious unconscious unconscious us unconscious unconsc unconscious
there are some things i am not going to tell you
poet
oh, but what is here
post traumatic stress dis
poet
ith in a transcendental signified by choice
the chorus of I
producer of feces
horrible reduction, isn't it, this effo
manhattan

say.

Cara Benson

from *Spreek* "You show me a capitalist..."

"You show me a capitalist, and I'll show you a bloodsucker."
El-Hajj Malik El-Shabazz

What is disclosure?

What is an incarcerated market?
What of rhetoric?
A tell, a dead giveaway.
Gimme. Get your.
Job. The noun and the noun.
Person is noun.
Book is noun.

A job is a thing and a character.

A person with character has a thing. Action.
Direct action.
Upon.
After the fall comes work.
No effort in the garden?

No jive in yo' jump?

Dead giveaway. Shibboleth.

The thing and the thing and the doing the thing.
Which Job?
Which Book?

Which Burqa?

Spring Poem

Word's best dot a golden apple
In the sand of skies, box in hand
Her here with this soul at the pump
A derelict to the world he made being
Dapper, fat, alive, and shrieking.
        My dense hurrah I missed it
In my bustle or my trestle (whatever gender)
Missing. That's the fact—springing
From the forest of deeds in costume
Ready to be bitten as a busy architecture
Takes a breath from its host
And mimes a love in money.

Claire Hero

Stag

What doesn't fear my hands? The crush of my thumb, my fingers that make a fence. The deer stand on one side, watching. Among the trees they are hard to see, their skins smell of leafmould. If they would let me, I would trace the grain of their pelts, its marks like a secret language. I would put my hands upon them, and their eyes would roll white.

—And then we are in a green room, the stag and I, his brown eye turns like a globe, leaves fall around us.

The leaves, then the trees.

The trees fall around us. We watch them through the window. The trees fall, and then the deer fall. I want to speak, to stop this, but my voice box, I see, is in the palm of my hand, closed as a seed. First the antlers fall, then the hides dry up and blow away and the bones erode until they are only eddies of sand. The stag closes his eye.

Out of the wreckage, deer-shapes of light rise and walk toward us. They walk through the window, they walk through the wall, they walk through every fence I make between us.

. . . .

. . . the antlers are heavy.
They drip blood into my eyes.
They bow my neck until I am doubled,
until I am savage, and forest, and endless

Joan Retallack

Steinzas in Mediation

alighting from the once in a while destroyed it as a momento

Gertrude Stein
"A Vocabulary of Thinking,"
How to Write

There are are there instances of this in every era
A new dispersal of the subject
Or that there shall be a complete fragment
Or that the fragment shall be
As if the is reflects is the
While is the place they were
Between sometimes or what would begin in there here

I.
I And But That In
That But Whatever It And
They But That In Not
In All But Or Not
Made Made Lengthened But But
All Kindly

.

No the river hollow with I call them love
Of up began from who who goes yellow
I must hedge whisper wet going over
Straighten nothing to say un un in
Glassed fill empty burn white

II.
It Or They Or Not
For They Because Coming For

Coming For Or Not But
As Just All All For
More Always Or Just It
As Liking It Once Nearly
In Who They Just Coming
Always Liking Which Mine Or
Often As Think And

.

Of creating a usable past
In here's no where redistributive humor
How to not inscribe yourself in the system you're opposing
Opposing opposable thumbs up to a point of no turn
Not the turn to oppose to it at all

III.
It Yes As To Or
In Please What Not That
Not Coming He He Which
And That As Not Just
It Of She Not And
Or Not She When In
All Or Four And

.

Shades of images of and have read
Instead s/he varied the speeds
Synchronizing mind body as if that were not a problem of no problem
Were willing to leave blanks for to of what not known
No less with than 5 question marks 4 ifs no thens
I gave up Shelley after several years of living in Manhattan.

IV.
Just Or For Which They
It Or Not Nearly For
In All All For They

That In Why For In
That Should All For It
They It It While Should
For For Not No If
Like It But A And
She Did We After They
After Just Once

.

Logic except for instance holding resembling
Wake hold thing thought final hold dissolves holds hold
When word and lives the deep (70 kinds)
As if/no end/so botanist's eye exists
Time sad power error of off or at truant
The view like chinese poets some goat
West coast realtor sky green chairs rail against
Altitude whats blur from more

V.
Why He All A Tell
Be Be It They In
Let They Better Not In
Not I Land Yes It
Might Did We Because He
Once How All But They
Once He

.

Not to make a famous statement of about clarity
Not to find the famous footprint
Every third thought shall be my grace
Writing synchronizing mind and bodys minds
One wants only clarity yet one wants truth (sic)

VI.
I If If He Namely
Often Left Come They For
Ours Made By In Made
Let But It Because They
Articles Hope Theirs Ever All
For It Just They They
They And With Getting For
It We WhoWith If
I Of As Not They
They That As Might Just
It This All Aimless She
That Well Or All They
I Gathered All Come See
See Shall

.

In description lies betrayal lies
In descriptions bounded in of or for
What we take as disolution and ruin para phrase
In this out or fall of for next generations to take
For the or a natural order of things
They will not seek their bearings or where we find ours

VII.
Make It For Can For
They Or They Not They
Every She Now There It
Over Famous It By Or
By No They And Or
Which Not Or Or Or
It Might Should Or

.

Better to be amused by your former self
The voila, the hey, the look! alight in the marsh
And here the green I am

Rosy papa flambeau the savage languages
Let's make use of intellectual hindsight
Now in the park the cinematography crew the ruins

VIII.
I Came As Only It
Now Between As There Here
Often It Indicated Just They
Come They They That They
Nobody They I Well Hours
We Imagine He She Or
Or Or It Oh Argued
Which For Will Or Can
Out They More Or They

.

Here are the things I want to remember
Marry doubt fear ought and autocratic
Call this violence a mess polite in language
A thing all shawled well prepared
Once to balance all
The professor sleeps in Bucharest with a gun under her pillow
Out from the whole wide world I chose thee
Necessity combined a treasure
The improving shape of the cloud the cloud disappearing

IX.
With Brush She Or To
They Which That That It
Every

.

"The idea I meant to have"
The problem never was
Only made to brush to call it never playing

People in tanks can't hear each other
Or can't remember a name
Settled and praying better than they will
Once once and for all

X.
Might Even Nor They They
I They Made Might Or
Made It It I Not
But That It That Might
By I Just And If
Just All Not But I
Which But Or In I
Which Or Always Which As
Not For Which Than It
Not I Threads Very I
Neither Might Left Just It
And And And Very Or
Even They I And No
In But Any They Will
Any After Of Once They
As Will In

.

I have thought that the bird makes the same noise differently
Whether we're aware of it or not
Remember dislike reason choose rather happened
Nearly placed they will change in place
Unkind when asked to like it unable to agree
It was for many reasons pale sky green leaves belong to trees
Green leaves just inclined to feel with hope a question
One useless gothic nostril to sniff another full moon
In looking up I have managed to see four things.

XI.
But But Or As In
Of Can Or By Just

Linking Be But Or Finally
In Why They He That
More After Or Or It
An In They Or But
Or They Any Or They
Made Should Without Just By
It Coming Known Think That
I

.

Afternoon eyes diagramming luck
May wish very carelessly pain drifts into hindsight
I have seen what they knew
The feeling of the power of what became mistaken
Or another assumption of we
Many chance encounters with the pain of luck
Or the bird whose call sounds like a telephone ringing
That they call meadows more

XII.
She Not Or Made But
In It All Not One
Or They That Could Just
In It

.

Suppose an invented truth to be slowly dipped in water
They silence in convincing
Moving through the molecules through a beaded curtin
Not alone or only
It is now here that I have forgotten three
Watching it not be left to happen
She said life without theory is Nirvanna

.

XIII.
She By Or Which Or
Just Or Can Made

.

Heat is the motion of a body's parts
Woosh! A new kind of natural law
From romantic clouds to energetic steam
They wish as a button because it is so

XIV.
She They In Come Not
In Should It In Not
That That But Just And
But Or Nobody While Not
To Only This Most It
Just Just It Or It
Than It

.

To compose a life by composing words in a poem
No direct want prevents me
The rain was caught by the hills that were there in the poem
Energy transferred from one thought to another
The she walked out of the they
Right into the foreground to take a bow
To draw an analogy at this point would be obscene
Song is what happens when the mind wanders into time

.

XV.
Should In But For And
To Which If From In
In In They They And
Whenever Than They Be They

Now And She And All
Once And And That Or
Not By But Not Nor
Should It But They For
Always Is They Not But
Only If As Yes Not
I Or In It For
It And For Or This
They What Not For It
Or That And Probably Alright
And Beginning And When The
And And And And They
Up And I

.

In why they must see it be there not only necessarily
Finding that crows can count to ten
Come once again come think well of meaning
Once again see there what is there looking reflecting
Must there be another movement now
In which she becomes a he each mourning the other
Suddenly everything seeming elegiac
S/he and all chronically caught in I mean
All speaking all told with capital valor
Yes the alterity of things is an ethical matter
And they can be said to see that at which they look

Procedural Note: The numerals I - VII are followed by the first words of lines in corresponding sections of Part I of Gertrude Stein's *Stanzas in Meditation.*

Robert Kelly

Steps (5. Aletheia)

for C.

You are what is not forgotten
the opening of the first door

you are what I have not forgotten
you are what I will remember
you will be the always and the next thing and the again

opening of the second door

sometimes people remember music
sometimes people remember

sometimes the pianist forgets the keys
forgets what white means
and what does black mean
and why are they so small
and far away, or she remembers them
but forgets what's she's supposed to say

what is music supposed to say

what does music say

the opening of the third door

sometimes she forgets her hands
sometimes the hunter
stands in the woods at dawn
wondering why he's there

he forgets what his business is
and why he has a shotgun in his hands

an arrow in his fingers, why
does he study the vanishing darkness
for a hint of something moving

he forgets he is the only person in the woods

the only person in the world

opening of the fourth door

when you know you're the only person in the world
it all depends on you
this is the moral universe
that penetrates our world like a sheet of light

like headlights scraping our bedroom windows

and the cars never know what their lights show

blind lights

they forget to know

you never forget

you are the only person in the world

opening of the fifth door

and there they are
the unforgotten the animals
the Greeks called them *aletheia*,
the unforgotten, the truth

the whole truth of the world is an animal

truth is an animal

a bird at dawn

a wild duck evading the hunter's shot

duck now

safe in the darkness safe in the light

forgotten into the unforgotten

the opening of the sixth door

and there the light is
waiting
and you are often standing there
standing in light

standing in for light
when I have forgotten
everything but you

no one but you
says the light
there is only one

only one light

a door is to go through

to go through and see
where this leads to
because there's always another
chamber of you

another place to go
I can't remember
I can't remember all the places you are

places we have been

forget forgetting forget remembering
a door is sometimes the only

only a door and no rooms on either side
that is a door

a door is a moment that lasts forever
they call it a life because it lingers and it lasts
because it is a wife
and doesn't know how to forget

and everything always
and everything always
aspires to be music
the thing that is always on its way

always on its way to you

always on its way to each other

opening of the seventh door

and here we are
where there are no numbers

they are not numbers
not shadows not doors not animals not birds

they are a little like arrows
flying very high and no one knows where they fall

a little like arrows
only there is only one of them

only one

pure going

as in going with you

in going with you everything is all it can be

and here we are
nothing forgotten at last.

Steps (6. The Rattle)

The ache of every
clatters in the man's rattle

it says we're hurting here
come near

come share our pain

The ancestors take
deep breaths with our lungs
our breath

now they breathe in us
rattle clatter

dried beans in dry hollow gourd
you know how it's done
it's the same everywhere
every heart is hollow
pebbles in a shell
every heart knows how to holler
tree gum seals the shells
dry they are dry

they are the driest word
a hand can speak

the ancestors swim towards us
through an ocean of
what we think is air

it is not air we breathe
it is a very special gas or seeming

no animal inhales

we are alone in the earth

they swim towards us
to be dry again

to celebrate the ritual of silence we cherish
for them we are silent

it is so noisy being dead

they come to us to hear our silence
do you hear me
silence is a rattle

silence wakes the heart

the rattle calls them

calls to dry comfort
dry joy of being
being only one person at a time

joy of being one

you don't have to be special to know this
don't need a priest
to do this

a rattle rattles in anybody's hand

but to speak to them when they come
that is not easy

especially when it's for silence they come
silence of the rattle

the ancestors are very young
they have forgotten a lot
they count on you to remember

forgotten how to understand
things so easy for you
the way a knee bends
only one way
or a tongue curls in so wet a mouth

the ancestors are younger than you are
the ancestors are your children

they want to come again
sometimes you see their footprints in the mud
the snow
rattle of hail on a tin roof

they are coming now
you had to pick the gourd up
you had to shake it

you shook it

a rattle means silence

the rattle woke the dead
the cloud heard you
rain hurried to drown the dry sound out

you shook the rattle and they came
and they are here

now you are the one to whom they came

deal with them
take their silence into yours

and speak it

This is how the people learned to sing

(singing is learning how to leave space
learning to let the groin speak through the throat
to come to life again
singing is the ancestors in you
force of their silence
singing is turning the body inside out.)

ROBERT KELLY

Steps (7. The Bicycle)

To wake from
this life

like any other dream

the bicycle

red velvet like iron
inhibits the feel of things

are we surface only
is there in the midst
a meaningful plural of us

something like fish
uncountably many

we live by guesses

of course I hold her hand
of course I pray for her

hand of a ship
prayers of a sleeping man

Benefit Street? Downhill sight.
Old tall white pine tree?

some girl knows
what she knows makes her sail away

to stretch
a few words
around her hips

travel in the north country
speaking what I see he said

a pale house in the woods

the next morning
came like an osprey clutching a fish

dying but excited
to be part of the action

so few words
around her
even the slimmest hips

no rational objection

pry the song out of the stone
translate the Latin
back into Etruscan silence
their full lips pressed together
no word escapes a kiss

a humming sound
as of bees roused by warm November

nature but not natural
not what we mean

sometimes brightness hurts

sometimes you know too much to go on

shiver when his eye is on you
the eye on the church wall
and what does he do with his other eye
the one we never see

he sees her
she is his shore
a woman stepping up the sand of an island
is pure theology

the edge of someone going

is as much as we know of god

you've got to want it
the sea, the selvedge of desire
you call the Other
and keep giving human names to

this girl this boy

and sudden makes them there for you
approximations of alien energy

you suck them into your lifespace

you have come to the edg of him of her
you have come to the edge of being

burn the ash to diamond now
close your eyes now
both in and out are closed all blue now
the deer on the edge of the forest now
can't see you when you close your eyes now

and only the trees know how to listen.

Jim Handlin

The Stop

the wind just stops
as if it had blown itself out,
and semi circled into the doorway
are leaves and pine needles
that still have its curve,
as does the semicircle of apples
that round the tree

the wind's left what it's had to say,
is now a memory,
a parenthesis,
something set off by commas,
this message that all things stop

ERIC KEENAGHAN

Subcityscape

I.

In the 1890s, engineers were popularly revered
for the word "genius" was at the core of their name

fragmentary reminiscence

of when etymology
was talismanic,
words speaking
a common tongue.

But that,
            too,
misremembered.

(Their city had no tongue.)

II.

There were many

            Babel   movement

chaosophy   transference

                        sootring   tintinnabulation

            traffic lights and archangels   black heralds in soiled linen

announcements growing

the line and keeping
the dance a-going.

                                        City living,
but not life. (Maddening.)

Crowds had sought him   *He had fled from crowds*
They, craving *some delirious intimacy,* suffocated

him, hungering for a silence
            that could transmit
that ray of an inhuman clarity

delphically   from below.

He, no longer dancing. A winded savior
searching out the Spirit
                                        of the Place,
or a pause
                        to hear
one's self think. The space where
singing begins.   Choruses in phonebooths
signing   behind shielded eyes.

III.

They say of the engineer,
a bureaucrat merely revered

he's sucked the life outta me
(insert a stock phrase here)
officialese his language
ungrounded uninspired
the fumes giving wings

the longer one listened to him,
the more obvious it became
his inability to speak
was closely connected
with an inability to think

life administered
word-art regulated :
a singular logical
and semantic chain
links degeneration regeneration and genocide :
regeneration overcomes degeneration
through genocide

the *rigid "language rules"* letting the few *idealistes*
(*philosophes*, never) become *"the bearers*
of secrets" tonguebound, stupefied.

These are the Leaders of Men.

All praise the rhetorician
who keeps the ball in the air
effortlessly, in the seeming

(23 speechwriters clacketyclacking underground;
2 more translating it for stop-motion delivery…)

IV.

clawing her way
to the top
flapping wings

gums

"language rule" … *a code name;*
it meant

ordinary language
would be called

a lie

the murderous wind-up dancer
fueled by unnecessary fictions
to make the halting trek, posing
as flight off

V.

Nomadism's no
answer. Never
leave The Place.
But come closer
to its Spirit.

VI.

...no, Virginia, bedouins do not move:

Thomas Hariot found you but
he left no trace or
he's only traces (so
says Muriel, who's aweful)

invisible, feet on the ground
standing down
head lodged in Earth's belly
breathing Her fumes deep

think of our tents
that's how you'll null us

pitched—an unbearable

sound—nothingness's
music staying still

and, so, moving ever
more saying nothing but
meaning All There Is.

Yes, that's the pitch,
the lifestuff splitting eardrums
but eversweet, sticky sap
the line to sell chewing gum

like honey coming when we sleep
canvases ruffled by harsh sirocco breezes
the dream wet never deathly cold heated
on a low burner or this desert never
flaking like flour paste on children's fingers:

viscous forever.

Sound's consistency splitting us open
breaking our legs to make us stop
the murmur that lets us think and move

VII.

Yes, you will know us by how still we sit. Not longing to move,
nor even living in that belly-urged flow. Yes, we live when
we sit still. Expanding a diaphragm. To sing to
our Mother, the one who is rooted underground.

VIII.

An egg is shortwinded

yet breathes fire

They called that *the beginning.*

Let's call it
tomorrow.

IX.

No shortage of calling

there's a word for each leaf, and

a quiet, deliberate
adumbration
intent on filling
the world or building
a shell out of glyph

one by slapping
gritty mortar
between bricks
for *each wall and*
a word for nothing

undoing the substance
of naught with some
intransitive sense

X.

Act
so that there is no use
in a centre—just labyrinth
immured in Life
rebounding off
cobbles, and an arch
fools were rumored

to have moved
to give the eye
its center

*(It is everywhere
and nowhere.)*

XI.

An I in the center
to make the core
whorl more calming

XII. The old German lady mumbles,
disgusted by our ability to tow
only a factory line,

What are we "doing"

when we do nothing

but think?

Uproot the concrete. Give
lie to moving stones. Put
the world in its center.

So we can sit. So we can breathe.

The Russian Prince who abjured his titles so as to study the movements of the Earth (and all Her species) unencumbered, looking like the Bard atop the 3-legged stool, twiddled his 1-eyed serpent and sucked the apparatus's hose, dangling from the sewer grate, deep with its musty smoke, expiring it slow, measured between the individual strands of an overgrown beard, along with this pronouncement

the harmony of stellar systems is a harmony only because it is an adaptation,
a resultant of all these numberless movements uniting completing equilibrating

and his sounds hit and splinter off the sidewalks up there. Inebriated, you glancingly bump sidelong into me and we wonder if any of this would ever be good enough for an opera libretto.

We gather our breath
(*disordered and incoherent*)
to begin a bordered walkabout

deliberately

thus the center *the origin of force* *scattered and disseminated*

glacially

Fragments composing the Subcityscape:
* Moment of a narration from 5 minutes viewed of a PBS documentary on the birth of the New York City Underground (August 18, 2009) * Lola Ridge, *Firehead* * Wallace Stevens, "The Idea of Order at Key West" * Hannah Arendt, *Eichmann in Jerusalem* * Muriel Rukeyser, *Traces of Thomas Hariot* * Roberto Esposito, *Bios: Biopolitics and Philosophy* * Larry Eigner, "what time is…" * Gertrude Stein, *Tender Buttons* * Hannah Arendt, *The Life of the Mind* * Peter Kropotkin, "Anarchism: Its Philosophy and Ideal" *

sucking Dolly

It is night, & the lambs on the body of Dolly sleep. Such Hungry we have never been. It is night, & the milky stars mock us, up there, milky on the fleece of Night, a milky crown for Dolly. & she falls upon Dolly with her blind mouth. With our terrible mouths we fall & suckle the greatly Teat. & the white Milk pools in our mouths, & the white milk Wools our blunted Tongues. Wools our tongues & so wools our Eyes. Wool-blind, I watch the milk fleece my veins until I'm sheep-tracked. Frontiered. Pasturage upon which the dollys graze their white invasions. We will fatten ourselves on the Milk of Dolly, & the Forests will kneel before us that we may put them in our Mouths. In our mouths we will Gnaw the forests to the root, we will Cud the forests with an outlaw Tooth. In our mouths we will Succor them, here in the Shadow of Dolly, here in the white waste of Dolly.

TOM THOMPSON

Suddenly, The Guards Return to the Priest Called "Stout Cortez"

It is a conqueror's light. I'm sure I've seen a conqueror's light
in the eyes of these ancient children perched on the cliff
of a new world. The ones for whom the order "to survey"

comes in the same urgent, whispered tones as the instruction
to fail and fall. The edge of the cliff extends endlessly
out over the infinite valley. Would they smash to the ground

if they fell or simply float there, forever?
Without a sense of the language of the place, without hope of trade,
the route back congeals like a scrape in skin.

Hurry up. Return to your life. The limpid, fresh lightning
you see by in bursts threatens the ships that brought you.
If you spot a conqueror limping, he's still got his weapon. Keep on.

If you spy a conqueror asleep in the crown of a tree,
he's simply striving to follow the sun. Keep on. Keep on.
Magic evolves here into something swifter, more "in time."

But progress? That's another matter. It's like you can't keep anything
inside your body anymore, not protein-rich bugs
nor suicide fruit, not the bark of a tree nor your sketchiest prospects,

not even fate. Even the moon retches up its most sober tea.
Stout Cortez, you summon the world with your violent melancholy
and your arms comply like two exhausted armies.

It is the music, the striking childish music, of all mine.

Techno Poem No. 9

blue blue blue white
blue blue blue white
blue blue blue white
blue white
blue white
blue white
blue-blue blue-blue blue-blue
white
blue-blue blue-blue blue-blue
white
blue blue blue white
blue blue blue white
blue white
blue white
blue white
blue-blue blue-blue blue-blue
white
blue-blue blue-blue blue-blue
white
blue-blue blue-blue blue-blue
                                        white

Christina Mengert

Theatre

Call the resembling body, "cinematic evacuation."

Ambulant fossil. Here, again, the thunder of
performance. Against the aisle, what makes

a fog of what holds this thunder to our ears.

*

Do you remember (conversion)
pushing sound out black bars – it was a sad effort

the weight of it sadly diminished

*

Later I fix the problem. *The true miracle was walking on mirrors.* Now this: we've broken open the hard shell, loosed into the excitement of the storm.

*

What, then, do you mean by resembling?
Arrested, visible thing. Catch it up
in air we conjure from the deepest-most parts.

It isn't right, I know, leaving like this,
the mirrors having gotten us this far.

from There Where You Do Not Think To Be Thinking

6

Long River
never
runs out
of
twists and turns

except, perhaps, about Tornado Island
where torque
is at
the limit
and gargantuan violets
violate species parameters
and Jaguar attitudes
go global.

Jaguar
is contemplating
the diversification of his quasi-attributes.

"I ought to be
at least as
volatile as Violet,"
purred Jaguar, "Black,
tan, green, roseate, golden.
I'll saturate a globe
with emblematical variety --
every sub-species jaguar inheriting
a certain confusion of --
shall we call it 'cast'? --
my apparent dynamical incoherence
compensating my ubiquity.

Happenstance shall be suspended for this working
or rather, Confusion make Happenstance my mask.
Diversified too shall be our rattles--
not out of Africa only. Peru, perhaps.
In truth, we are not confused, how could we be?
But Long River runs in a ring,
then fans out
into what is known as
"The Most Asymmetrical Spiral,"
at which point geometry itself
breaks into incommensurate particles
and reconvenes
in a new combination
of principles.
Logic is affected in this.
The new geometry breaks
the categorial dockets of Deep Storage.
At every point in it
the information modifies its own algorithm
twisting in an agony of defiance
against the very principle of the algorithm --
too many species of violet;
too any avatars of Hammerhead;
rattles that grapple toward pure obliquity and propagate Melee;
Long Rivers that run only through Confusion;
ontologies brewed in the vats of Tornado Island;
a crescendo of infinitely proliferating violets,
gigantic and pico-metrical, saturating Possibility Space;
crossing the Great Abyss to The House of Choronzon!
At all events, all of this
is but preparation for The Working
for which I require new humans."

Hammerhead wasn't listening.
He was collecting shapaca leaves
to build Peruvian rattles;
preparing Mapacho stogies.
Melee for Hammerhead
had nothing geometrical about her.

She concentrated her rattles from Anywhere
until she configure here syzygy.

[]

Now there manifested
an Old Hotel
where hereditary information
was distributed erratically
among its multi-form dilapidated chambers:
one moment, one epoch, one world,
each inheriting some unanticipatable
element from another, not necessarily
anterior to it. But information jagged in
from some elsewhere,
impossible to define.
If you meet your syzygy, in a concrete sense,
heredity is moot,
exhausted by the crystalline presence
into which the syzygetical energy
collocates ubiquitous hints and traces
of your infinitely variable and internally diverted presences
from "all around the globe," like they say;
you are distributed in irregular geometries
so that confusion besets the sub-moieties
of the "tribe" that is your "nature".
Kinship semantics no longer being possible,
the totality of the species amasses
in a glob of randomly gesticulating particulates.
You are a Nation
but one whose ubiquitous sovereignty
depends on this:
You suck tobacco paste
and turn into a jaguar.
This happens in the smoke of a giant opal.
An internally diverted Presence
that is Tobacco Woman
appears
after you have wandered sufficiently

through your own great globular mass.
You have ecstatic though fearful and tremulous
sex with this voluptuous presence,
and as the sensations of arousal and contact
penetrate to every fiber
and region
of your unfamiliarly vibrating body,
the sensation itself
opens onto Black Lake,
and from now on
you are free
to roam all of Being (apparent Being)
in the mode of a jaguar.
What color is it?
Green of course.
Your energy is powered as a fluctuation of Long River.
A green jaguar is always with you
flashing in your aura.
You prowl the globe in quest of proper tobacco paste.
There is a shop
in The Old Hotel.
You conquer incomprehensibility
by wisely abandoning the pressure in yourself
to comprehend the
logic of your circumstance.
Your logic has changed.
That's the point.
Ontological Sovereignty has changed.
Unless you are Hammerhead,
in which case your confusion
is a factor of your cure
and you will return
many times
to Black Lake
and on its beaches have sex with Tobacco Woman
until her force has dissolved in you.

[]

Wrench Boy is Master of Confusion
The smoky globe is his.
He performs these conditions for Jaguar,
bringing Stability and Strength to Jaguar.
Together they arrange their opals
and sit on the bank of Long River.

George Quasha

things done for themselves

(preverbs)

for Susan

1 *last first words*

We walk together like a field of fireflies.
It gives the ear back to itself.
Hard to beat being heard.
No word for this thing between us, feeling afield.

Mark the opening eye.
The words I leave out rip me apart.
The mystery is the core violating itself, blurted the absent voice.

Time's recovering, I'm here to quit the garden for good.

Reading poetry suffers it to speak.
Violation is not what you think, unless it is.

2 *wanting it all in every line*

Things done for themselves are the only things done for all.

Just walking by she multiplies in futures [*flash*].
I'm the one in the middle longing to be the many.
Put *eye* inside the empty letter and she looks back at you.
Voyeurism's the illusion I'm not looking at myself.

Exhaust the wisdom impulse before it exhausts paradise.

3 *further otherness*

Today's the day I rewrite my biography.
Pen slips on the slopes of sorrow.
I can't help believing in one thing after another.
Sounds good to me sounds true enough.
And then. And then.

4 *no place else to learn*

A blurt's a site of first breath.
This only sounds *this* way.
We wave through each other to approach.
And flex and flex.

Optimal includes bottom.

The world's singing to itself again through our dog.
The tremor in the voice lets the knower out.
Poetry is the state stating.
Says: *Say what keeps saying what it is.*

5 *unsearching*

You didn't know it but it let you know it.
A form is what knows to take place before you.
It gives the eye back to itself.
Seeing marks.

Let's meet in the dark where you read through yourself.
Juliet, the verbal scent.

Names get a life to be spoken.
And so *I* makes my ascent into present.
Poetry says it better than it sounds.
If I don't mean what I say at least it means me back.

The only things done for all are the ones done once for themselves.

6 *being first again*

I barely feel myself hanging together.
She knows to call me by my calling.
It takes a life to be known.
To tone.
Like things fall free alike.

The underline rhythmic is over and out. Over and out.

7 *pre names the program to optimize*

Hearing marks.
Speak in the first person on earth.

She sets my system on merge.
Meanwhile I call from a verge, *Don't strand me on the grounds of sound.*
I can say nothing I can't hear.

The vision's the body seeing through itself.
The poem even now is hearing itself.

Frog pond in the dark's bounding across from here.

Thinking with an Ancient Poet

When it really works,
it's the world talking
or the sky. Word
begins on its bordering,
and a sun-brightness escapes
into it. A man watches
with his hands, his fingertips.
From the wrists, we awake
into language, the splendor
and fear of its grip and its
open-handedness.

We're native, fallible,=
often stupid in a great
speechlessness. What to say
shakes a monitory finger
and there's really nothing wrong
with a tongue that's out of work.
Or lips ironing out their quiver.
It'll take lifetimes to tuck into bedrock.
By the way, isn't that what you want!

My choir has fallen on
hard times; a few mouths
that want feeding more than
song. Or a few persons
shuffling their feet in imitation
of a Greek chorus in sunset light.
It's almost funny but the public
has grown cold. And the core
in the heart perhaps <u>has</u> <u>to</u> hide.
As fission in a nuclear reactor.

The nucleus is almost apart
from itself but we're naked
as dogs raging around a strange
smell. Your body meets my analogy
and it's on the take but, really,
it gives itself like a magnificent
sacrifice. Sexual, gratis, painful and shy.
Eye-gleam, nostril-quiver; the old
hunt and the older hunter. He might as well
follow himself into the glade where
the grasses cut and bristle and stamp
like flame. I want you, secret as the most
secret canoe. Sudden with quiet and yet approach--
as if language had its own grace
by backing-up by paddle, surprising
alligator or joy or nest or water-dragon
illusive as all merger. Word splits
world, I'll take the splinters and gild
those hallucinatory scales. Let image, snorting,
emerge, its own careless emergency, Chinese & spooky.

7/5/2012

Claire Hero

THROUGH THE EYE
cavities the sky

is a bruise, is
primed & in-

divisible, blue
print of orbit

Anything framed
becomes a

percentage
of beauty, slight

holes puncturing
the muscle

of distance—
Sling it far

Anne Gorrick

from To Take the Thought and Turn it into a Scar

after Patchouli 24
(a perfume from Le Labo by Annick Menardo)

A fragrant relationship moves in a laboratory
which is a place of acquaintance with our various things
An idea that receives our attention will dance
Scar and scent and fact float like revolutionaries
A machine that dances with green leather attacking
The body, the motorcycle, the possibility of smoke adopts us
This is the price of actions
Our fifth refusal is directed at our wrists
Facts are composed and flown like thoughts about events
The fragrant materials will open like an idea at
a constant temperature to question our methods
Part thought, part precedence, part illusion
A handful of green onions dance in the space around your hands

What if you increase 24 to 30?
His intelligence was both inherited and inaccessible
Leathery sea anemones seem to fruit out of her skin
Deformed leaves on roses, vinyl repair kits, pearls

How special and transgressive can it be
to buy a bottle of Liquid Smoke for $1.50 at the grocery store?
A violent moving picture of total shock
then a cabin that doesn't get used very much

[A small East Indian shrubby mint; fragrant oil from its leaves / Growth and Nutrition of a Suspension Culture of Pogostemon cablin Benth. / But it was too weird, too bizarre for me]

A smoky leather opening morphs into patchouli-dirty vanilla
to become a dry, salty scent with an edge for dark nights in dirty cities

What's in the name is not in the juice
And the drydown is not vanilla
It is vanilline (a by-product of paper manufacturing)
A uniquely barbecue & bubblegum
(Dubble Bubble, precisely) accord

Suede sectional, worn birds, a soundtrack path in the clouds
What are some of the words to describe someone?
Textual
analytic
looking like a snake that slithers but really a book
larval lace
launching analysis
Laird Hamilton by committee
A century has passed over these cardboard seas

flagrancy	These materials have been perfumed by the number 24
	and dance in laboratories with both knowledge and accuracy
	Attention to these ideas causes speculators to trade scars
wants	Even the idea of Annick dances
	her flagrancy wants a stationary, revolutionary everything
	A machine in 24 directions attacked by leather and green onions
a	The body like a motorcycle and the extremity of possibility
	The price of vanilla actions are inevitably leather and tobacco
	We refuse the pulse of our own reputations
	Desire composed like an idea open to an event
stationary	Anteriority and its illusion like the number 24

A Tuscan stove
A hot mix filled with plaster and meaning
Cut away these notes marked "return to sender"
notes that burn for coding
Is a created opal real?
A crooked kind of wild dark, a lake vanishes in Chile
A carrot island walkthrough
Decay tabs do not exist

A hazy vanilla veil

at the very tail end
a "niche mess"
discordant
or the way a house smells
when a chimney is clogged
and too much smoke backs up into the house
instead of going up the chimney
Ps. I love you, Annick

[Classic rotary, embryolisse concentrated 24 hour miracle cream, turbo ear / Self-portraits in motion • Don't panic • Hypergraphy • Sometimes narcissism is good therapy • In the little house by the sea]

Like Fumerie Turque on steroids
with a small dash of civet?
It should come with a warning sign: "APPLY WITH CARE"
However, if you enjoy smelling like "Katenschinken"
(a heavily smoked North German ham)
it is just the right perfume for you

Draw my thing with drawer pulls
Our future chipmunks, or a home in Palestine
or our regularly scheduled program
Smear yourself with a sticky substance
that smells like roses while you're meditating
Taste ammonia psychically in French
Iris again in Dallas, taxable, his unnoticed questions
If you watch it backwards in stainless steel
Maybe you want to start a business
making rosary beads out of maple leaves
or lotions in Binghamton, or in the land of parrots
Autumn skylark anaylsis
Fragrantica

The scents of laboratories are reports and ratios
a precision which causes attention to an idea
Scars are speculative tradesmen on the production of talent
Perfumes float with the ideas of their creators
both revolutionary and stationary machines

with 24 directions toward rawhide and motorcycles
Because of an adopted cream composed with controlled desires
a different place will dance its thoughts towards us
The scented materials will open like a suitcase
Part thought, part anteriority, part writing
the will to dance in a canoe with asphalts and snowbells
with vanilla also the color of green onions

What smells like light blue?
So raven, that embraceable empty feeling is no longer with us
Galileo cheats at sasquatch annihilation
I do not like the smell of this authority
Which ones are the non-oyster months again?
It's as if this slogan never happened
You've been booed by mail
There is a butcher in your heartchords

The other notes in this are entirely irrelevant
if you don't have a huge love affair
with excessively sooty smoky birch tar and foetidus
Extremism for its own sake
recommended for leather-clad demons from the eighth circle of hell
(where those dwell who do violence to others and themselves)

[Palmarosa 25. Patchouli 26. Peppermint 27. Petitgrain 28. Rosemary 29. Rose Absolute 30. Tea Tree 31. Thyme white 32. Tomer seed oil 33. Valerian 34. / I apologize for being MIA for the past couple of weeks. My sleep clock has been out of whack]

Birch tar. Animalic notes. Civet. Indoles
Kinky. Funky
Musically it's the like the fragrance equivalent
of a Bartok piano concerto
Or something
It brings to mind images of people wearing masks
and whipping each other for enjoyment

You've selected a category, click to continue
Mothballs that smelled like drinking
Elderberries, a rat, baitholder, blackfish, beat hazard

Before the sunrise self destructs, lie recumbent
To paint a waterlily, to paraphrase this poem, to patronize someone
What are 24 notes that tap deep emotions?
Start with bergamot, a tar syntax
pink chimes rectified by snowbells, galbanum
You will produce a vaccine against anhedonism

all	A ratio of 24 blues and greens attaches to our dancing
	The laboratory of our own knowledge
	The precise notes of her thoughts
thoughts	stimulate our scars with presumption
	Our interest is a suspended matter, but there is also a machine
	the body of a motorcycle possibly edged in an informed tobacco fact
	Scent employs us
toward	Strict examples in behavior, cream adopts us
	Our sour typical impulses toward representation and denial
	A factual craving constitutes this thing
	A method of questionings, all thoughts open toward
	anteriority and hallucination
open	I'm writing these 24 dances in asphalt to be performed in a birch canoe

To the Doctor

Knitting the bones of the dead, you say,
What makes us different is what makes us the same.
(With writing comes forgetfulness.)

viz. The origin of Chinese ideograms – silhouettes of birds in flight,
tracks in limestone.
Others find their alphabet in shape of constellations, animal organs.
(The Chaldean *aleph*, for instance, is a map of early migrations out of Eden.)

Writing from Ravenna, Cassiodorus notes: the Venetians live "like sea birds
With their homes dispersed across the surface water,
And secured only by osier and wattle against the wildness of the sea."

So we return once more to the scene of the crime.
(This time the statues are wearing togas of snow.)
Yes, Life, the great gift, calls to us & we must come.

Your fingers fell on NONSEQUITURS TO A WAKING WORLD.
It began *Fish, fish, where does the water begin?*
& ended with an aria from "The Barber of Seville."

In between, a disquisition (in German) on Cold War immunology,
Language as communicable dis-ease,
How everything is constructed against its own shadow.

Distinctions melt in the subdued light
Where you are walking backward through your body
& a child sings, *I am already nothing ...*

Michael Ives

Tone Poem beginning with a line from Soap Opera Digest

Sami goes stir-crazy in the safe house. Blaire puts the kibosh on Natalie's health club permit. Being prohibited from assigning pet names to his own body parts begins to upset Treat. It's quite possible that Devon's enormous fibrocyst contains Margaret's kidnapped child, Heather. Multiple keloidal growths along Holden's scapular region are discovered to have concealed the missing diamonds from EJ's problematic jewel heist. Faith and Jamie discover Bree's secret room deep in the interior of Stephanie's large fibro-lipoma. After surgical removal of several painful nodules along his parietal region, Channing decides to set fire to Nikki's summer place in Taos, NM. Tad spies on Philip and Cricket as they lay plans to conduct an expedition to the center of Thorne's enormous neoplasmic growth in search of Ashley's lost shitsu puppy. Lucky pledges to extricate herself from Parker's tool shed-sized goiter on the condition that Carly perform the emergency c-section on Starr. Spencer joins forces with Max to train the new recruits recently liberated from inside Amber's submucosal fibroids. It turns out that Brook's inappropriate behavior during Dusty's sweet sixteen is due to a meth lab growing on her hypothalamus. Chad and Selma go behind Rick's back to tell Sage that their vacation to Belize will include an excursion inside Sid's pituitary adenoma, which he's just refurbished with leather sectional and wet bar. While regluing Delft tiles along the border of Jared's fireplace, Slater finally convinces Adam to let him build the Windsor Terrace cottage on his wooded, three-acre colon polyp. Owen's college buddies watch Brandy alienate Jess during a televised policy debate on the floor of the senate inside Taylor's immense thoracic aneurysm. When Haley vilifies Trent in front of Margaret, Kim, who's running acoustic analyses on sound wave emissions from the far edge of Jamie's vast plexiform neuroma, happens to look up at the surveillance monitor and realizes she's been framed. The implications that Storm intended to stir up excess turbulence in Kaley's reservoir of possible worlds, which Damian had previously concluded adumbrates Shane's pleomorphic xanthoastrocytoma according to equations Page has tattooed along that region of her inner thigh roughly congruent with the Virgo cluster, sends Ridge and Friscoe on a heedless search among the quantum foam behaviors inside Monica's space-time hematoma, where Jason and Diego are busy realizing that to review Ryan's cosmic zoning permit in light of Noah's suspicions about Opal's creation paradigm, which constitute Josh's apercu about Chandler's ontological categories, means that they must consult either Caleb or Liberty before going ahead with construction on the guest house.

Mikhail Horowitz

Trading Fours

Fat moon framed by
As Jimmy Cobb recalls
phone lines. Pretty as
it, Elvin would get
a puncture, and that
so wet when he
bridge across the bay
played with Trane that,
conjuncting nothing. Some day
after the set, he'd
soon the horns'll get
go to the john
the skinny on that
and wring out his
moon. Know it, maybe,
pant leg and maybe
in the biblical sense,
a quart of sweat
like that lush lifer
would pour on the
of the T'ang, the
floor. He might just
reedman Li Po, who
as well have been
parted the reeds to
working in a mine,
kiss her face, and
albeit a celestial one,
then took five for
where the miners dug
a thousand years in
each other as well

the night lake's blue

as the ore, and

embrace. The bass man's

their shovels and picks

using his bow, now,

played licks that amazed

feathery slow; time to

the angels. When they

dissolve a century or

finally emerged from the

three, lose the phone

brightness of that mine

and quiet the pipes,

into liner notes, even

let the bass drone

a blind atheist could

on instead of me.

not dismiss their nimbi.

Eugene Richie

Troubled Tintypes

1.

Tonight again, it's your leg
he is thinking about, your
tan, the beauty mark
he noticed as you walked by him
even more than the length
of your blond hair cascading
over your shoulders and
down your back, to the
lowermost part, the curve
where others have feared
to tread, to touch, even
with their eyes, strangers
in an imaginary landscape.

2.

She's not surprised that
he has answers to all
her wonderment. A single glass
of water lights the world.
Is this a story about
a left-bank poet lover
and a motorcycle princess
who rides with motorcycle
messengers of death?
These mirrors would do
well to reflect further.

3.

“How was it? A bit dirty?”
“Yes, a bit dirty.”
“A bit dirty!”
Not unlike one of John Cage’s
prepared piano pieces, but
who are they to judge or say?
There are a lot of silences as well.
These are not perfect odes either,
though close, if she says so herself.
“Without poetry, their lives are effluvial”—
Jim Tate did know and say that too.
So now, what does she have to add,
because they’re open for business
even if the department stores
are closed in France on the
Feast of the Assumption
of the Virgin Mary! Closed tight,
all day long along the routes
of Saint-Germain-des-Prés.

4.

Is he looking for paradise?
He thinks he already found it.
And “Heartbreak Hotel” is
playing on the PA
in the background. How
ironic is that?
LIRR information agents ask
such good questions.

Sam Truitt

tuesday, december 22, 1998

gallery life in brooklyn, including art & language

for CC

life death fear. sack of shit we
are never more one then when
we are two people joined
through the sexes
  they are infinite on each
the face of santa claus walking
backward through snowfall on
each flake the face of santa claus
emerging through tunnel face
distorted in oval mask just as are
all our impressions variations
on happy birthday mr. president
i went to a lot of trouble to
understand western civilization
is based on envy engendered
by publicity the publicity
works upon anxiety and the
sum of everything is money
to get money is to overcome
anxiety publicity is the life of
this culture without publicity
capitalism flounders these
things i take to bed at night sight
glimpses of the bend in the road
ahead in the head a road made
of days we have brought here to
examine how to form a thought
that will not crumple parts that
fit and parts that turn to meet us
out ahead blank space where
the body has been

13. Reflect with borrowed pride
on the Sugar Hill mansions
chugging up the sky in tough
toast of mornings' edges scenes of
dilapidation and exaltation.

134. Drop one by one in a mixture
of both pain and gladness all
your flirtations remembering
Augustine in love, finally, with
one.

119. Measure the oscillating
intervals, felt as a throb, between
wakefulness and sleep and know
the surface on which they play's
your heart.

52. Think to drop to the basement
to check on your books and
between an unauthorized move
and the spring floods discover
one-tenth of your collection, as
well as various unique prints and
memorabilia, irrevocably ruined
to be added—a sodden gray heavy
mass—to the weight of your
conscience.

130. Feel the dirt under your vest as
you poke at a hole in your sweat.

Ann Lauterbach

Untitled (The River)

1.

And Diogenes placed a crown of pines

on his head   victorious Diogenes

spitting in the face

of the ignorant teams

            Diogenes crowns the horse

who stood his ground

Diogenes

      the dog   illumined.

Because he said so

      trussed under the moon

the blessing garbled as usual

                  forgiveness

spilled on all the stones.

Historical stones, as they were what

touched the core

trussed behind a shut door

under an invisible moon.

Because no one mentions

rust across the river

sun tissue   streaked or hairy

the familiar beasty hills

the atomic flaw

breasted and phallic

across the wide gray surface.

All this, companion,

our material journey

blown onto a radiant scarf

as some remnant rhymed with

its scant flow

or distilled into thought's

crowded integers   not to turn away

to acknowledge the tracks of sky

marking our way

                    or drawn above

in such yields no market could furnish.

The affinities, their stake

at the terminal hour

      you will not recall the willow

      you will lie down

how on the train

others exist

along the way   passages

     her floral scansion

ripped apart

        the horizon divided

intelligence

of love's song to the ghosts

they or   Diogenes

        who might

prevail

reading ashes, leaves, cards,

no preference

among their habits   the ghosts

bored at rush hour

among the gossips

knocking sparks from each other

the tide withstanding

habit   bored by any occasion

rising from lamps along the tracks

moving under a huge blue tarp

as if something had erupted

opening the book.

2.

But if love of data refutes mystery

has the philosopher walked away?

The poet is a procrastinator

and a revisionist. She observes

the river is for the birds. She recalls

the sacred Nantucket coast.

Her vision is empirical

even as a love of mystery refutes data.

Geese on the baseball field.

A flag, red tile, a metallic balloon.

The aggression of sorrow.

Marianne's orange jumpsuit.

Had better launch another trial

without a jury

without the old cavern

broken by a seamless, impervious argot.

If the last revolution

discovered silence

and the rest heard

          over the swerve

the telltale drift in the field

braided or sewn --- then, and then then.

Valley Scene

Yellow willow in winter
fearful

you can't employ the sun
the maker
makes its golden glare
yellow willow

fearful in winter
but fronds
like a healthy overhanging
fern

        by the river
        stung too
by the sun
maker and employer

all ploy from the sun
all willow weeping yellow
frond-down

what by the river
other than this
brilliance put into ploy

the color which
the sun puts into play
into weepings
of its long thin leaf
graceful as a blade
but pointed down

fearful earth
by the river
river healthy or sick
river of glare
river of fern-quiet
in winter

        color is a spore
        free to travel or
unravel or rave
quietly like the
willow obtuse and
dumb and yellow or
gold if you see it in a certainty
of sudden gold by a sudden cast

in afternoon for winter
knows at bottom the private heart:
terror and a golden frond
gravity's tresses and
invisible willowy roots, what do they look like

likeness, be fearful or dodge all interpretation

7/5/2012 NY

CHARLES STEIN

from Views From Tornado Island

6

"There are African Rattles
of every description
stashed away or planted
in plain sight,"

complained Lady Hammerhead,

"planted to separate those elves
up to their necks in the sod.
Every night the weirdlings
rush up here
and snatch the rattles
and work up an uncanny fracas --
and Wrench Boy tolerates
the whole queer performance,
though I do believe he's watchful.
You can see him
gazing fixedly
into The People's Cauldron
as they dance
or whatever you call what they do
in an unkempt ring-round-the-tower
on nights when that hoary edifice does stand there.
On all other nights they bestrew
the whole island with black violets
everywhere up to the second channel
outward
and inward to the place
where the Black Egg balances,
and the Tower
spins around

both ways at once
when it's there."

She was standing on the rim of another
cauldron, addressing her plaint
to the ministers administering the switches
of the tornado lattice
and to the Giant's shadow
that covered the colony
to configure the night, when it *was* night.
On sultry afternoons
when the *twisters* spun round
with grim, exultant life,
the shadow just attached itself
to the absent tower.

Hammerhead came up to the "melee" that was his consort
and examined her to determine
whether the substance of her deliverances
had been ventriloquized;
whether the Giant himself
was sitting on the Lattice,
and how, in general,
matters stood in the colony.

[]

Long River was boiling
practically up to The Tower.

Black violets were hopping on the wind.

There were weird little doors
opening invitingly
and slamming shut
as you approached --
distributed elegantly
but virtually everywhere.

The ventriloquists were chattering:
voices and irascible messages
accosted you distractedly, seductively, or menacingly
or boycotted your presence annoyingly
if you hazarded response.

The Giant was attempting
to extirpate his own shadow.

Hammerhead tried to recover
control of The Lattice,
for the Elves that manned the switches
were in full revolt.

The voices, apparently, all over the Colony,
were searching for their twins.
And rather than ignore what they heard,
the elves were jiggerbugging to the tune of it
repeating it
to luminous blue bugs
and long-tentacled, spider-like fleshy things,
and under pretense of obedience and staunch civic duty,
were throwing the switches
in a thoroughly random fashion.

Halucinogenic elf-miniatures
were manifesting everywhere, popping out of vessels,
glass and earthenware and porcelain.
Each urn or vase or kettle
asserting the authority of its place,
refused to move
and whatever the peculiar function
it knew how to perform uncustomarily,
it started performing now.
Soup spilled over,
flowerpots blossomed,
ornamental ware
sported fantastic ornaments.
The Giant Himself

was a chorus of voices: weird announcements
bellowing out of his button holes:

"Everyone into the Chasm!"

"Burn Down the Old Hotel!"

"Follow That Tornado!"

[]

"This is your fault."

A voice came out of Hammerhead
apparently addressing his wife:

"You ATE THE LATTICE OF PLACE ITSELF!!"

[]

Wrench boy sidled up to Hammerhead and suggested:

"Best we get back to Black Lake."

But the elves were listening.
They rushed into the Door when it opened
and an enormous company arrived on the hallowed shores.
The Ventriloquist had set up a cabana on the beach-head,
but its function that sent out voices
to so many recipients
had sucked out all the sound
of the local apparatus
and an impenetrable silence
now reigned at the Absolute Source.
The lake couldn't muster a ripple.
The Ventriloquist himself
required his own ventriloquist.
That would be Jaguar.

[]

Chaos
is an Egg.

The Ventriloquist's ventriloquist
pronounced this
with grandiloquent solemnity.

The Giant placed his cudgel in deep storage.

The magnificent crystal
that hovered perennially above Tornado Island
went through her full repertoire
of spectacular luminous scatterings

and all the beasts of the melee
changed the channel. . .

water into machine

If word means that much,
wells overflow, bringing sodium,
cadmium, fluoride & distaste—
faucet marvelous invention
for escaping; so is compost.
A sort of alchemy-bacteria
changes everything. Could
this speck of information land
where it could? The sound
of walking through quarries
& here in a circle I am told
to write, by a tree, by accident,
stones all around arranged,
but just sort of there intent.

The Way to Keep Going in Antarctica

Be strong Bernadette
Nobody will ever know
I came here for a reason
Perhaps there is a life here
Of not being afraid of your own heart beating
Do not be afraid of your own heart beating
Look at very small things with your eyes
& stay warm
Nothing outside can cure you but everything's outside
There is great shame for the world in knowing
You may have gone this far
Perhaps this is why you love the presence of other people so much
Perhaps this is why you wait so impatiently
You have nothing more to teach
Until there is no more panic at the knowledge of your own real existence
& then only special childish laughter to be shown
& no more lies no more
Not to find you no
More coming back & more returning
Southern journey
Small things & not my own debris
Something to fight against
& we are all very fluent about ourselves
Our own ideas of food, a Wild sauce
There's not much point in its being over: but we do not speak them:
I had written: "the man who sewed his soles back on his feet"
And then I panicked most at the sound of what the wind could do
        to me
    if I crawled back to the house, two feet give no position, if
    the branches cracked over my head & their threatening me, if I
    covered my face with beer & sweated till you returned
If I suffered what else could I do

We Embrace Imprecision as a Side-Effect of Distance

There being no such thing as silence only racket
and no known calibration for the elements needed
to make it disappear

we contrive silence as lack of attention lack of speaking.

We want assurance but from whom?
We want to know that something will catch us but what?

What is wrong with me? *Nothing.*
Nothing is wrong with you? *Yes.*
We were at the edge
of language and disgust and we were sweet
not talking not thinking just vibrating
little waves of being onto each other …

The image of a net, cast off of a boat: white thick curling into the life-water …
and the reeling in. Clutch of belly life sea life under-life.

If we give up *this* what will catch us?
There is no such thing as freefall but uncertainty is the same thing
unless you train your mind.

There is no such thing as intelligent nostalgia
but I remember that person
I invented as we walked upstairs.
What are you wearing? I stole things and then I gave them back.

Male silence reads as disdain and female silence as erasure.

So to not be erased we talk which is the erasure of our silence
our imaginative self talking whispering noting nothing.
Nothing is wrong with you? Yes.

There is an erasure which nothing will catch.   .

The image of water   with no boats   one seamless horizon

with an underbelly of   riot.
Ultra-sonic love songs.

There is no catching them   just knowing them.

Time   leans away from us   she is talking quickly nervously
little nets thrown out   and ignored.
I like her   but   I have nothing.

Our constant calamity   reads as no calamity
reads as nothing   the   aporia   :
the earth would not betray us   even as we betray it.

Nets   abandonettes

silence   audible as a choice to stop listening.

"what is it that recurs?"

for Sondra Perl

if a fire hydrant implies a way of listening
to a landscape, and benches house the body
as guide book, let's stop and polish
the monuments, stage postcards, plaster
the word *active* over *what we know*
because without awe, without say back
we are ciphers who judge, forget to play
private to return to the conversation
we have with our mirrored cells
languaging in the air, finding meaning
in even the most placid fishbowls
untimely autonomous read out loud

then returned gently, in generous ways,
i your arm, you a turn of phrase

Philip Good

Who Put That There

A beacon still blinks where once it signaled
whaling ships

On warm nights guests sit near the river's edge
raising a cheer and taking a sip

Nearby the next day

Shady sheep shift their shadows to zones crepuscular

Do the sheep wear scapulas?

Are the sheep shady or are they just sitting in the shade?

Parade spectators focus on the pre-parade activities

Yes, there still is river activity even in the streets

MICHAEL RUBY

Why Were We So Wild About Wildflowers?

1

Why inside our eglantine
Were the elephantine
We placed all insubstantial prizes
So diamond so olive
Wild dunning to pock the block
About an honest design for temporary
Wildflowers so breathless

2

Why were we in this inestimable lake
                tiny so wild and syllable
                        not a story about wildflowers

Why were we implacable in the face
                Elise so wild to shine
                                about wildflowers the umbrellas

Why were we bought and sold
                        so wild to trice
                                about wildflowers returning home

Why were we laughing in the attic of starbursts
                        so wild bejesus
                                about wildflowers godmothering

Why were we finite butterflies
                        so wild horn of pressure
                                about wildflowers in the tendon

Why were we in question
                    so wild our attention
                                about wildflowers procedures

Why were we implacable in our demand
                    for time so wild to feed
                                a song about wildflowers defined

Why were we America's secret victims
                    fruit so wild to honor
                                not about wildflowers nor longitude

Why were we incapable of singing
    underwear so wild and plural
            adjustments about wildflowers timing

3

Wildflowers rang the original pendant
Wildflowers signed their names in blood on our legs
Wildflowers brought peace to America
Wildflowers sang through the arteries
Wildflowers touched this deep in the sauceboat
Wildflowers masked our difference and—

Wildflowers basted the gates
Wildflowers sang the horseplay
Wildflowers wrapped our onions
Wildflowers branched through our patooties
Wildflowers drank the acids

4

They represented a torch to light
force through purple laskers

Something held the ring in place
(The falls pursuant to their obligations)
The fruition of quiet
The discovery of wrongdoing burned holes

This regimented elevation
Deep in the home of gloom

Time in the hose of bromides

The balm of soup
(Toulouse hemispheres)

The restitution of our homeland
There in the impossible (signpost)
Timely purchases and the ripe toil of elephant rolls

At the bottom (two plastic saints
A ruckus in the upholstery)

Wing/Span/Screw/Cluster (Aves)

much the usual mangle
at www.roadkill.com

flaps down/*quiet*
here.incold

"lo"

out of *entertained a desire*   barefoot   (turned outwardly *in thrall)*

but a toe still dipped *in the living waters of life itself*

the actual.entangle

man (sic) to aves (sick)

while inthermal.waterardor

a surface.bloom.of

microbial . proliferation . magnitude

Now for the past three months such a clattering and fragility in my head,
the sounds of rushing rivers surrounded by little birds.

(discalced de-castled devotees.of

"the real world, I mean the real real world"

in.w/a rose.arose lichen with lovely.metallic.names

& plastic.plasticity

in.magnificent . unscrupulous . quantities

so: Saint Teresa robin
so: Saint Teresa plastic robin
so: Saint Teresa plastic porcelain robin
so: Saint Teresa broken plastic porcelain robin

& a poly.fix.styx.fury.flurry.slurry
of extra-terrain garbage

Some 15,000 pieces ranging from fingernail-sized paint flecks
to 10-ton rocket stages hurtling through the Earth's orbit

Yet still.humming in fastest ::: 1200/min (heartbeat) 50/sec (wingbeat)

skirts hemmed
intonalwitness.artistry

Heliangelus regalis
Eriocnemis mirabilis

ofthe entrance
en*trance*

[please install dimmer]

largely.catastrophic

or perhaps just leading to different versions of "biological success"

::: morphology of the aves :::

bones thin-walled and filled with extensions of the body's air sacs

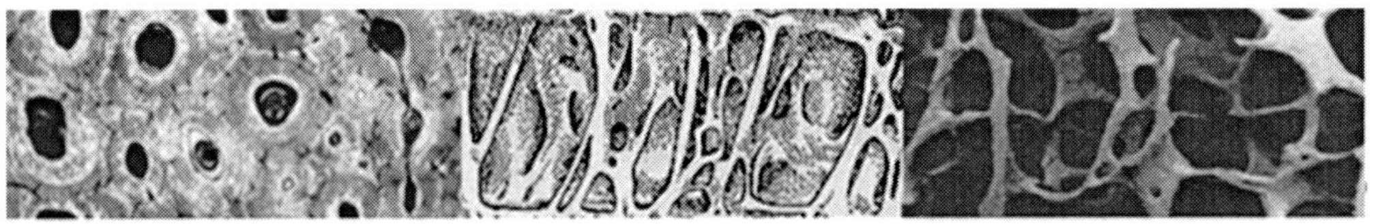

protoavian dinosaur　　bird　　middle-aged human with osteoporotic disintegration

Doctress ::: *This writing was finished in the year 1577.*

To read to be read through

To be anti-pure in the broken dust lingo

(made doctor of the church 1970)

beside herself ::: ex ex

ekstasis:::exteriosis

Calzadito Turquesa
Colibrí des Esmeraldas
Metalura Iracunda

(smallest death ladders

(cheapest cosmos jewelry

XXX

Notes: Italicized lines are from *The Interior Castle*, St. Teresa of Avila, translated by Mirabai Starr (Riverhead Books, USA, New York, 2003), except for the phrase "the real world, the real, real world" which is attributed to Carl Rakosi by Rachel Blau Duplessis in *Blue Studios: Poetry and Its Cultural Work* (The University of Alabama Press, 2006). Lines beginning "So: St. Teresa" reflect similar lines in *Four Saints in Three Acts*, Act II, Scene V (*Gertrude Stein Writings 1903-1932*, The Library of America 1998). Hummingbird species named are all considered endangered or critically endangered.

from Plentiful, So Emptily

Hushes.

Singer in the Spotlight: (dreamily)
So I am a rabies vaccine today again. So starkly it seems, this is all so sudden. I didn't know you felt this way, but here we are again together, we're here together. The tape that's rolling in your head, let it never play back, let it never play back. & how the city sits, the city squats on the face of false promises. Any body within that body that is blithely face-fucking all its members, making them feel full again, is like a many, many more than that. Not as plural, not amounting, but to mount it as it mounts you, slowly at first, very surely. So it's tending inner in us. Even as we lie so very still, it's tending in.

Already asleep.

Bachelorette: Just nothing.

Bachelor: What? What's wrong?

Bachelorette: You're hogging the blankets.

Bachelor: It's not nothing.

Bachelorette: Push over! You're hogging the blankets.

Bachelor: But I don't have any-- there's hardly any blanket.

Bachelorette: There's fainting or there's death, & this isn't death.

Bachelor: Are you fainting?

Bachelorette: It's nothing.

Bachelor: You're breathing, I can *feel* you breathing. You're not dead.

Bachelorette: No, I'm fainted, but would you even care if I were dead? You're not calling an ambulance already.

Bachelor: Are you asleep? Are you sleeping or fainting?

Bachelorette: Nothing, I'm just hungry.

Air Vent: Even as we are out of belief we are feeling still full, expectant of bodilessness, so full as to be floating near.

Bodilessness: For only death is to be loved by death.

Caught in the Thick of It: (her hair in his branches)
Deliver your hand from me, death or no-death! Your hand on my hand not bitten yet. I am not yet out of body & still you have not entered me. For however I am wounded, that finally I am wounded with my last body left in bed is hurriedly reproducing itself. It is tirelessly introducing itself to another & another & another, over & over, keeping riding their habits like that. Or how I abstain for a second for you & that's so convenient when that happens!

Already in Air: If it is not so convenient that I am stationed at the pinnacle, send an oracle, but for now I am stanchioned on the very top floor, above the attic, in the very back behind the boxes, within the final closet, secretest drawer, your squirreled pouch that's hidden there, underneath the photos, lockets, paralipsis, proslepsis, that's what I am sensing, this feeling that's rubbing against me so stubbornly is clarity. It's telling me that my intermediate body comes apart from its proxy in real time. So either way it's agonizing reporting this confusingly, recognizing immediately what takes shape & then is all again reconsidered so conveniently.

Tree Limb: I don't think you mean what you're saying.

Leaflet: I don't believe what you're saying.

Trembling: What you're saying changes everything.

Leaflet: & what you're saying has horrible implications for the future.

Bachelor: You mean this is a horrific example of how we ended up here is all.

& the winds come in again.

Bachelorette: In my heart, as on the very day & on the day after & every single day that there is, that all, still all of it, as ever.

Preacher: If we are aware that others are singing these songs precisely when &

as we are, in this same moment, even if we have no idea who they might be, or even where, out of earshot, they still are singing.

Actress: I just came in. What was that singing sound? You were looking at my face & then you were looking past my face & now it's like there's no one here, not even me.

Just sitting waiting.

Patient: So I am procreatively fucking when I really should be wailing.

Doctor: I see.

Patient: I am full of the frothing from the mouth of the vaccine.

Doctor: I see.

Patient: & the coming upset is barely contained on a supposedly very high shelf somewhere in a little tube in far off room, I feel it stirring.

Doctor: That's so it doesn't settle.

Patient: Let's see what the fuck is in there anyway, angrily! Where the fuck did it disappear to anyway? I am in a frenzy, angrily! The temperature of my blood is enough to cool this entire tub of bathwater! I am over-full I am already frenzied enough for having been led to believe I was sleeping inside the pseudo-rabies!

Doctor: You were sleeping *beside* the pseudo-rabies.

Patient: That's right. "In every place at once," or everywhere one glimpses it. But all at once! Either way, it is happening too many times for me.

Secretary: "For me," I see. There will be no things anymore that concern *me* here then, so I will promptly take my leave just now. You see, this is no longer sufficient for *me*, your little dreamed democracy that you can afford to want to make happen over & over again, & what I can't dream & how I hate it! For the want of that, & for your--! (angrily)

You wouldn't let me.

Witch Doctor: I don't believe what you're saying.

Secretary: What should I do? What would you have me seem, to become unseeable? That in order to disappear or camouflage myself in my sudden fleeing--?

Witch Doctor: You're acting hysterical. Get yourself together.

Secretary, but Now Her Name Is Bachellorette, with Two "L"s, so It Is a Different One:

It is not, no, it's not possible. No. Not in my heart. Yes, on the day & then again & on the day after I have given up, I have given over, I have let go the ghost, that is, participation in what is going on & outlasting that a little bit longer. Even if I am afraid to hurt & frightened to be without love at the same time, for whenever or wherever I look for it, out of earshot, I am a seeker for more signs of it, or if too much of me shown & is not enough. To be emptied out into that end, some other, further, distant. Fields of empty, emptily, indistinctly giving, is nothing, so I'm given nothing in return.

They're pretending they're in a hair salon now, touching hair, sitting around doing each other's hair, touching each other, & some relaxing, spiritual music is on the radio & someone grabs the telephone & sings the words into mouthpiece. & the Narrator's on the receiving end, repeating it back as it's heard exactly so it's not even a song anymore.

Narrator: (enchantedly)

Everywhere I turn I see

There's nowhere left to go.

(repeatedly)

The Professor looks up & doesn't have to look down ever, typing excitedly into infinity. Someone is in bed in the next room but we can't see who it is behind the door with the door shut.

Bedridden: (listening)

You alone can see

Into the heart of me

Am I really giving up tommorrow

Got to let it go

This is gonna hurt a little

Still it's right I know

Even though I fear

Too much of me might show

I can't wait any longer for it

I've had enough

I'll give it up

Singer: I sang that song in choir. There's another version of that song. I was pretending it was in another language that I had to translate in order to get my feelings across the stretch of the unseen so I made up another version.

(sings with warning & conviction)
When it comes so close

It burns you

& you're out of fire

Disappeared

There's disappearance here

I don't know what you're insinuating

But you have seen nothing

You have seen nothing

There was a body

Buried nowhere

What you're getting at

I can't believe it

So emptily the heavens part

The heavens part

So emptily

But I'm only one step nearer

What we were before

But not all that we will be

Tomorrow when we lock the door

On all our disbelieving

How the Operator was listening in

She'd been all along

On the line

When she was voiceless at the beginning

& she said

Now you can feel yourself changing

To turn & catch a glimpse of it

What trails off at the lip of

Where I stop to see anything

Where I just stop to see

Stop to look at the lake a while

You are turning into the

Fugitive phrasing

So this will go on a little bit more

These sentences have

Some give to them don't they

All the parts & teeth buried in there

They go flying off & into my mouth

So I'm just mouthing it

I'm just surrounding it

Who was the one

Who was brought up alive

With a watery ring about her

By tossing herself off into

The sound that surrounds

Sometimes it seems like

Forever & ever

Calmer Phone Call: (patiently)
Do you remember me giving you anything as a reward for wanting to love me?

Shadow Voice: Certainly you make no distinction between the travail & the pleasure that you give me.

Phone Voice: Only when nothing is expected in return can a lover be sure that uncountable amounts will be deemed worth the fervor of seizure, expensive elegance that organizes itself as if there is no property & that seizure is desire. For having all & wanting yet is freedom; giving all & being wanted yet is freedom. & the motion of that seizure, ecstatic refusal to collapse, while yet pummeling inner & trembling, so close to the hilt, that only when limitlessness is glimpsed, what you thought you saw that changes shapes almost immediately. You'll see its breath, its dust. & all at once it's fleeting, its direction undetectable. Recall this & make a name for it as you remake me in turn unnameably, for pleasure ever, ever inner, ever shall be....

Withal

Or in other, partial, hearings a slant away
until they can, tally the activated result
as it would have happened moon mountains ago.
Say, is there anything wrong with sitting around
capably, like this, one shin tucked in?
The others wait for you to do their shy bidding,
like kids, once. The turmeric sky concurred
in the adagio of the afterfright, just like this!
There were of course other factors to be bargained in,
but in the end it made no cause, we were up and corseted
and the behind principals mattered not. Oh, but
this was some kind of a school. Air shoved lessons
in and out of it, neutral, adhesive, like a school
of fish seen only one time. Litigation intruded:
What were the facts to be classified now? Zillions,
I'd wager. And over and behind it all the old shade,
as deleted as a Chinese risk factor. Oh, say,
all along the way it turned into light. Was supple.

Without that carbonated fizz his self-deprecating
gambit fell into shards like patterned shawls, are to this day.

Joan Retallack

The Woman in the Chinese Room
A Prospective

Intersperse entries & numerals from notebooks
(back to Chicago (Chinese story in tact (quotes
from assordid pm sages
= Manual text ?

She is captive in China
" " " " a moment in history
" " " to a sense of history

but in the way a wordswerve could turn a century's prose for a second or two away from history first from property then ideas then property as idea then idea as property

creating parallel texts left and right full of opposing forces in a sad space of alternating dire lexical black and white squares

the flat degraded feeling in telling the story or describing the passage and/but they are very proud of this Searle says suppose that unknown to you the symbols passed into the room are called questions by the people outside the room and the symbols you pass back out of the room are called answers to the questions

She-?.
how do you know the person locked for all those years in the Chinese room is a woman there are few if any signs if she exists at all she is the content of a thought experiment begun in a man's mind this is nothing knew and perhaps more complicated

She-1.
now that we think we know that the world is not all that is the case the case in question the space of the case sad but fierce with light upholds the dark it seems to utter itself must there

be subtitles must there be translation she thinks she knows but doesn't want to accept that in order to write or read or speak there must be a division between light and dark

imagine that you are locked in a room and in this room are several baskets full of Chinese characters she is glad they are Chinese of course glad to continue Pound's Orientalism there will be no punctuated vanishing points she is given only rules of syntax not semantic rules she is relieved of the burden of making meaning she need only make sense for the food to be pushed through the slot in the door it is thought that these are situations more familiar than we would like to think them to be in the new technologies and to men more than to women but it oddly feels quite normal

She-2.
what's to keep her from responding to their cues with syntactically correct non sequiturs in effect surrendering they might ask does the past tense give you vertigo she might reply there's no sense in knowing what day or night it is they're always changing

She-3.
yes it gives me vertigo knowing they've all been locked in that prose for centuries by comparison this makes the Chinese room feel full of breath of fresh air the point has been made that this prose has justified the violence and then it's been made and they can say oh that point has already been made

She-4.
is being too careful not exploring the other possibilities but this could be serious it might not be the thought experiment he thought it was or it might be irreversible once set in motion vert-I-go not abject advert to yes Duchamp turns out all along to all along have been all along Fred Astaire and Kate Smith coming over the mountain is Gertrude Stein

For the Woman in the Chinese Room: assemblange manc enhance silhouette 3 millimeter aperture in iris relish chalice in ken off shore

vegetables were being smashed hard to find dotted lines and arrows from aesthetic to ethical to spiritual to penthouse level the woman with four shopping bags said I don't want your money I just want to tell you that I dreamed I went to the Hilton Hotel because I knew God was there I knew He was in the penthouse I tried to find the elevator but they stopped me they wouldn't let me past the lobby

vivid stupefy suffice perturb brance
More Orientalism: the Japanese say *mu* to unask the question
aqueous tenuous hush tuh

in this story to describe roundness you may have to think about a square you may have to retreat from decorum or just spell it out phonetically you may have to find an Oriental Jesus with a vertical smile you may have to calculate the rectilinear coordinates of a blue duskless mountain with the distance of a female Faust

excessive evil nonsense Agamemnon lemon mythos ethos logos pathos fauxed yes/no nothing no thing to be gained do not reach out do not attempt to grasp let it slip by

mbers shoul ha gn
uides
e
ity
f
ected

ultra horizon breaking either/or parapet
blank dark returns new page tilted
speaking blank strange northern apple
in stant pivot sigh then of (blank)
toward 13 squares 13 syllables 3
points blank clear between bracket
asked light light 20 thin flips blank socket
ancient coil's pro's cunt's critique's pure reason's
blank erosore blanke paw thrumb Hegel
blank remedy beard agenda dramb
fraucht ergle gloss remainder squat
in history's twitter rut she blank
twi-lips pensive grim reminder mirg mirror
blanck trace there pocket vox map
thing I ness inging hind able isible erved
protentending crack blank fast air cont'd
quiet putt rusted civet beast or breast

LS Asekoff

Yangshuo in a Drizzle

“
,
.”
; ,
‘ ,
.
“
.”
--
--
.”
,
;
:
?
(
).
,
,
;
.
,
!

A Hudson Valley Salt Line

The Hudson as hybrid ocean, the color of lead
notated with its own winter lyrics
self-written
The railroad tracks scribble and crab

—Anne Gorrick from *I-Formation (Book 2)*

There is a place in the human   mind nobody's been next
door this man in a white paper   hat with his room flooded
in water & light wearing   galoshes dances since we
began with ink to map them

—Sam Truitt from *Raton Rex* (Vertical Elegies)

River, fjord and estuary, the Hudson's eco-hydrology defies hard and fast categorization, especially in its middle reaches, which is this anthology's locus: the Mid-Hudson Valley.

The Hudson River is among Earth's great water systems, fed by 198 rivers, creeks and other more discrete tributaries, collecting the water displacement of over 13,000 square miles, and flowing more than 300 miles off the Adirondacks' big shoulders to discharge at its peak into the New York Bight about 2.5 million gallons of freshwater per minute. But technically it's also a fjord, a water body shaped by glacial erosion—though rarely classified as such, because its circulation is unrestricted and lacks the classic sill, or narrow portion, at its mouth. And that lack of restriction in part makes the Hudson an estuary, its southeastward freshwater flow met by a variable saltwater incursion near Wappingers Falls approximately 70 miles upriver from New York Bay. This is what fishermen call the Hudson's "salt line" (though conventionally termed the "salt front")—the terminus point of the interfacing surface (fresh) and bottom (brackish) water currents unique to what marine biologists call Estuarine Water Circulation. These twice daily tidal ebbs and flows—impetus for the natives of this land to call the Hudson "river that flows two ways"—register as far north as the Federal Dam in Troy. On the other hand, the Hudson's lower half is called a "drowned river," formed by rising sea levels due to de-glaciation, with its valley—the Hudson Valley proper—rising above sea level at a leisurely average grade of 53 feet per inland mile.

The title *In|Filtration* reflects in part the centrality of water to the Hudson Valley, itself a vast water filtration. Its main lexical unit is "filter," derived from the Old English *felt*, "something beaten, compressed wool," reaching back to the Proto-Germanic **felt-* "to beat." Further, the word is haunted by the proto-Indo-European **pel-* ("to thrust, strike, drive"), from which we derive "pulse," a recurring beat or wave. Pulsation necessarily characterizes the Hudson's tides crucial to filtering its estuarial ecology, the efficacy of which determines its broad health.

The subterranean Hudson Highland also flows, though at a scale beyond temporal imagination, its "headwaters" reaching past the Last Glacial Maximum when ice sheets towered a mile above the Rip Van Winkle Bridge. Around 12,000 BCE, rising seas breached the morainal dam at the Verrazano Narrows, releasing pent waters along a channel itself ordained 120 million years earlier when Gondwanaland split. The ice's grinding retreat left some of that epoch's idiosyncratic faces exposed. We can map the Hudson Valley's layers of bluestone, its ancient metamorphic igneous and sedimentary rock. What we can see of its geologic history is exposed in the Catskill Mountains; and farther downriver west of the Tappan Zee Bridge, high cliffs produced by an erosion resistant dolerite. To the river's east is mostly alluvial sediment south of the Taconic Mountains, themselves part of the Hudson Highland, all the way to the Connecticut River, the Hudson's geomorphic kin.

Today we live atop and astride this ground swell and antediluvian dance—and sometimes even live off its byproducts, stealing underground to commandeer its ore. We've tunneled, for example, into the karst aquifer around Kingston and Rosendale to remove limestone to make cement—proof at best of our desire to explore and broaden and at worst despoil and pave. But we've also found a way to make art in these subterranean incursions, these post-industrial vacuums. We only have to look to Rosendale's Widow Jane Mine, and its subterranean art and poetry and music events. They

We conducted a survey of the *In | Filtration* poets, and they locate the heart of the Hudson Valley variously in: the Hudson River; the Ashokan Reservoir; at Bard College; the Mohonk Mountain House; Lake Awosting; the Spotty Dog Bookstore in Hudson; in bluestone quarries; the docks in Kingston; a particular pothole in New Paltz that "moves with the seasons and is attended by the Cabeiri" (JJ Blickstein); in the solar plexus of Robert Kelly; Pollopel Island (also known as Bannerman's Island); Barrytown; and "the top, inaccessible floor of the tower on Overlook Mountain."

Our poets live in the Hudson Valley for many reasons, including: "proximity to work, mountains/ streams"; "the spirits of the place, the quality of the quiet"; "my wife forced me to"; "water, mountains, moss, blueberries, art, proximity, friendliness"; "because I can't afford to move"; "oxygen + moving water + affordable housing"; "it spoke to me definitively" (George Quasha); "there are mountains and a river. The longer I am here, the more small children learn to say my name, the more strangers become colleagues" (Dorothy Albertini); "to subvert the regulae of achievement"; "it protects me" (JJ Blickstein); and "I moved here when I was pregnant with my third child because I was priced out of Brooklyn. I was lucky enough to find gainful employment here and quite enjoy my day-to-day."

seem to promise an opening onto a deeper abiding and more enhanced ways of listening: and we imagine it is toward a multi-dimensional pulse field that we turn and, perhaps, toward a more evolved terrestriality.

***

A book, like Earth, is a filter also, and let's picture one with translucent pages, so that light might permeate through its layers to reveal at certain angles what words are caught. We are compelled to open the filter to examine a filtered passage of light—which, like a gas deposit, a text potentially may be.

What interests us, and where we come/go in, is at the "in" in *In* + |.

Or we gather *In|Filtration* here: we want the process, or means, to be inherent to how an anthology is a book as filter of material without losing contact (the "felt") to being "in" (within) the pulsive gathering as it occurs in a world of things in flux. "Things" are present in the title via the "|": that phantom, seldom-used, upper case of the forward-slash key called the "pipe," two vertical lines above one another that appears on a computer screen as a full vertical line. It is neither character nor punctuation. It's an unsounded mark. It can be anything. It's a rock pile marking a border, trail or wellhead. If ellipses mark missing words, it is what words miss. Or maybe it's everything missing—there but not here—the unseen—and its integrity. It's Earth. It's filter. What we go through.

In the title *In|Filtration*, the pipe points to an exposure beyond semantics, its "meaning" a self-inflection marking a permanence without place.

(We might also imagine it as a salt line.)

The filter-like nature of a book is most true of an anthology, which finally represents a sifting of what materials correspond to its editorial prerogatives. Contemporarily speaking, the Hudson Valley poets here align with various composition processes, including appropriation, cut up, mixed media, collage, chance,

"The first year on the Hudson, teaching a heavy schedule at Bard College, I found I had written more, and more freely, than in the five years before. It took me a few years to discover why: Annandale is a vital node on the powerful bundle of ley-lines that run across Great Turtle Island from Cape Ann (eastern end of the terminal moraine of the last glacier, on which my Brooklyn also is built), Cape Ann, home of Charles Olson and Gerrit Lansing, who were powerful and beloved teachers for me. West from the sea, the ley-lines run through the valley and Berkshires of Dickinson, Melville, Hawthorne, and Wharton, on across the Blue Mountains through the coal measures and woodlands to Cahokia, the ancient city, then on across the plains to the Grand Canyon, the 'place of emergence,' until they finally reach the sea in Los Angeles, where the mystics of Deseret saw the shimmer of their ultimate temple. It is a great road, and it's rich with dangers and energies for those who live athwart it."

– Robert Kelly

dyslyric, liminal, conscious, conceptual, dictation, epigrammatic, transcription, serial, axial, dream, concrete, unconscious and spontaneous, among others. Like the Hudson, these poems defy hard and fast categorization. And, moreover, we want the muck and the confusions, and sometime fusions, of root and multiplicity, what's mixed and hybrid, wavy and indeterminate: the salt line.

***

> Our poets talked about the physical gestures that embody their writing. Some of their responses include: "raking leaves"; "thumb pointing down to my crotch"; "driving the fire plough"; "raising my left hand"; "tumescence"; "smiling"; "a violent shrug"; "fumbling"; "a sublimation of intimate growling"; "erasure"; "breathing/ keening/rabid stomping of feet" (Lynn Behrendt); "open palm"; and "cramp."

This anthology is a snapshot, but it's like we're capturing a piece of the river rushing past. It's partial—what's come our way—with the *In|Filtration* poets representing each in their own right a way. Moreover, *In|Filtration* is not topically "about" the Hudson Valley. It includes very few passages of local description, for example, and there's little "story" (unless one goes to that word's root in the Greek "to question")—though we did ask poets for work resonating with their sense of this place, welcoming them to interpret that broadly. Our instigation was an awareness that weighed against the relative wealth of radical poetry in the Hudson Valley in the early 21st century, there's few places where poets come together compared to urban centers, like New York City, probably our closest poetic kin. We wanted to collect work across a broad experimental spectrum so that on one hand Hudson Valley poets could identify each other and perhaps make connections—and feel more connected—and on the other hand more broadly make readers aware of the richness of radical poetics here.

> Some things our poets hope to get out of this anthology: "new readers of innovative verse from the Hudson Valley"; "a really sensual foot massage"; "I will stay out of prison. Been THERE done THAT"; "a celebration of this particular time & space"; "instead of a bible, a poetry anthology in every motel in the Hudson Valley"; "rich compost, the afterlife of trees"; "notoriety"; that "blue gorillas return to our mountains"; "to see who else shares this chunk of Mahican land" (Lynn Behrendt); and "...that we may realize the final commitata of the poetic continuum in real time."

So this anthology arose from an initial insight: a paucity of places or contexts within which local experimental poets might converge and further evolve correspondences. To move into that seeming vacuum with some coherence, an anthology seemed the best initiative. We put out a selective call, looked at what came in and then filtered it to arrive at what's here. No hard and fast gradient finally defines what fell in and out of this compilation but following the impact of an immediate take on the material we invoked a sense of inquiry: Was the work something new (we'd never seen before)? Does it spur our own work in new directions? Does the work extend language beyond where it would ordinarily end? In fact what we as editors sought is poetry that's in question, or in a state of quest, and that questions. Or is outright questionable, though not so much doubtful as oracular: poetry that one may inquire of, even if what one gleans is difficult to interpret. That may even put reading or reader in question. The semantics of question seem to be how we define what's experimental or "innovative"—poetry that's unresolved, open, unstable, evolving and perhaps, from a human perspective, even endless. The test is ongoing—in between and interstitial. The search is in process, though not necessarily progress, where the latter would imply a possible conclusion.

This relative indeterminacy and sense of being in the middle of things undone may be the salient shared characteristics found among these Hudson Valley poets beyond which lie their conceptual and formal idiosyncrasies. In ordering this collection by poem title—rather than name, location or school—we sought to accentuate these, from which whatever lattices of similarities and ruptures, however complex—or even briny and turbid—might surface. Other Hudson Valley anthologies exist, but none that explicitly explore the radical, asymmetric possibilities of dwelling in such linguistic experience. And that's perhaps what we hope for—a dwelling in and exploration of what may be caught here.

And we did have practicalities related to what is "here": The largest was the geographic scope of *In|Filtration's* Hudson Valley; and what made a poet "native."

> Our poets pursue a range of compositional processes including: "empty the vessel and wait"; "morning/can no longer play music/with immense struggle/in my man-den"; "I don't exactly 'write,' but in the morning, I am almost completely silent. Until 12:01 pm"; "in bed, while reading aloud and falling asleep, for the reason that it wants to be done that way" (Nancy Graham); "on a blank page with disappearing ink alone in a room with others"; "I bring pieces of wood home from work with scribbles on them which I order and reorder into composition..."; "I write in waves of composition, translating words or landscapes or conversations or ideas forth into lineation then prose then different lineation into rhyme back out then back in. Every line is gone over stretched, pounded, kneaded, fore-shortened, extended, slept against, stretched, cooled and baked"; "today I write when I can—and not much—on the hoof or at my desk. It is more a compositional process of urgency than intent, at this juncture."

Looking again at the salt front, its location near Wappingers Falls places it close to the center of the tidal Hudson; further, it fluctuates widely according to drought and flood. This lack of fixity, coupled with its sometime designation as a "line"—just like poetry—makes this location work as *In|Filtration's* geographic heart. Moreover you can run a rough 50-mile radius from the salt front to compass our practical coverage area: the Hudson's eastern counties of

Among the animal world, some of our poets believe they look most like: a horse; a barn owl; an impala with a gimpy knee; a milk snake; a sloth; "a red eft whose spirit animal is the swan" (Nancy Graham); an insomniac raccoon; the immortal jellyfish; a Norwegian rat; and the common marmoset.

Columbia, Dutchess and Putnam; and on its western bank Greene, Ulster and Orange Counties. A fifth of this area coincides with the watershed of New York City, which in part shields the Hudson Valley from undue development as well as other potential ecologic harms (including fracking).

To establish poetic nativity, we again have recourse to the salt line and Estuarial Water Circulation. Within that model, while other factors are affective—rainfall, evaporation, wind, oceanic events (including upwelling and storms) and human stresses—the two primary variables in question are: the water's "residence time" and its "exposure time." Residence time is the time water particles take to leave an estuary; but we note that some particles may depart an estuary at ebb tide only to re-enter during a flood tide. The time a water particle spends in circulation within an estuary until it never returns is called "exposure time." Assuming stability in the above-noted "other factors," the residence time of water proves a key variable determining the health of an estuary. But "health" is a broad term: As the local marine biologist Brian Jensen points out, it's true that well-flushed estuaries tend to support more diverse populations of organisms we like. But we should be wary of imposing an anthropomorphic perspective: poorly flushed estuaries also teem with life—they are just smelly, black and murky, and therefore less appealing.

Some of our poets believe they most resemble the following constellations, star groups or singles stars: Sagittarius; Sirius; Alpha Centauri; the Little Dipper; "the star emblazoned on John Cougar's dick" (Ron Whiteurs); Aldebaran; the Pleiades; Tseen Ke; "Orion, because I wear a belt"; "the Crab Nebula"; Ursa Minor; and Pluto.

But circulation, whether active or retarded, is the essence of an estuary, and so we might apply the notion of residence and exposure times to the relationship of poet to place in determining what's native. Namely, poets enter the Hudson Valley, and some stay, more or less (long residence/long exposure). Some are weekenders (short residence/long exposure). All the poets included here live in the Hudson Valley at least part-time.

Poets of high rotational frequency open the native field to greater differentiation, introducing new material into the Hudson Valley's poetic circulation. This increases variability and variety—augmenting the level of permutation in new work—which we tend to valorize. At the same time, longer residence and exposure might give poets an opportunity to absorb

We asked our poets what insects they most resembled, and they look like: a bee; a mantis; Iggy Pop; a katydid; paper wasp; a beetle; an illuminated cockroach; a cicada; "a caterpillar climbing over the lip of a chalice"; a ladybug; and "sadly, a dung beetle, and a lightning bug" (Lynn Behrendt).

more of their immediate Hudson Valley circumstance, lending them a more unsullied native resonance—perhaps allowing them to get more in groove with this region's inimitable linguistic and spatial attributes and concerns. But according to the estuarial model, fixedness necessarily limits circulation, which is poor hydrology. This might be read as stagnation, on one hand, but recalling Jensen's caution not to view health from an overly mammalian vantage, who is to say what new, unforeseen poetic form may reside in the native muck?

When asked what they're trying to accomplish in their poetry, some of our poets responded: "finding something or someone or something or someone to suck on"; "metallurgical integrity"; "survival"; "ecstatic union"; "self-erasure & the abolition of time"; "riches"; "Connection. Ignition. Explosion"; "nothing to accomplish but I try to listen better to what it tells me; that is, in accordance with how it releases me from ignorance" (George Quasha); "play; there is tension and it's worth touching" (Dorothy Albertini); to "embarrass my parents"; and "transformation, solace, ecstasy" (Lynn Behrendt).

But underlying this of course is "native to what"? That sugar maple or this quadrant of our galaxy?

And who knows how the local, and any collective sense of that, may flow into the work of the poets gathered here: whether there's a common care and/or identifiable method of word organization (way of writing) that's unique and innate to this valley of "the river that flows both ways." We don't. Maybe there isn't. Moreover we each have our own salt line—our own amorphous body of instigations, patterns of circulation and indeterminacy.

Calling back to the Hudson Valley's deep geology, perhaps anything that we can locate—even if this were a book of translucent pages—isn't what we are exposed to. Yet we can say the writing here—generally falling at the edge and sometimes beyond the circuits of normative formal and syntactical articulation—seems underground, though more than as a metaphor for activities at the margin of conventional society, it breathes in the unknown of beginnings and possibilities. *In|Filtration*, then, is finally an entry point: a derelict mine shaft + light beyond which arises a darkness and silence to which the very diverse range of radically innovative poetry from the Hudson River Valley seems to point and to which, book in hand, we may listen.

Lake Hill and West Park, New York
2015

Editors' Acknowledgments

10,000 thanks to all the poets in this anthology, many of whom have been profound teachers, adventurers, cartographers and good and close friends, who over the years have extended the bounds of our own language and work.

Gratitude to Deborah Poe, for her role with Sam Truitt in conceiving this anthology at a Bernadette Mayer reading at the Poetry Project in the spring of 2011, and Deborah's editorial involvement in the early stages of this project; to Laura Moriarty for allowing us to use her encaustic artwork for the cover image; and to Charles Stein for his "Some Boxes," which appears as endpapers. And thanks to George and Susan Quasha (alembic for this anthology) who anchor us in what is good about the Hudson Valley.

Thanks to Louis Asekoff, Lynn Behrendt, John Bloomberg-Rissman Mikhail Horowitz, Brian Jensen, Michael Ruby, Eirik Steinhoff, Paul Stephens, Paul Smart, Steve Schimmrich and Violet Snow for reading our essay and giving insights that may have steered us past some rocks.

Special thanks to Mary Kate Garmire for wading into the typographical slurry at the close of this project and pulling *In|Filtration* clear; and to Vladimir Nahitchevansky for seeing it launched.

We met often at Kingston's Cafe EAsT: thanks to owner Deena Rae Turner for feeding us.

Many thanks to our families for their patience and so helping shoulder this book into being.

And our thanks to the Hudson River, its deep and strong currents carrying our words in its salted tides. Our mouths meet its prodigal extravagance; its tidal opening joins our estuarial graffiti.

Permissions Acknowledgements

Grateful acknowledgment is made to the following for permission to reprint material copyrighted or controlled by them:

Dorothy Albertini for "Monkeys," as originally printed in *NANO Fiction*; and for "Ice Cream Social." Used by permission of the author.

LS Asekoff for "As the Hand Holds the Shape of the Stone it Has Thrown," as originally printed in *Staging Ground* (and subsequently published as part of a chapbook of the same name in the Metambesen series in 2015); "To the Doctor," as originally printed in The Brooklyn Rail; "One Minute Before Midnight," as originally printed in Big City Lit; and "Yangshuo in a Drizzle," as originally printed in *riverrun*. Used by permission of the author.

John Ashbery for "Beyond Albany and Syracuse...," "Mabuse's Afternoon" and "Withal" as published in *Quick Question: New Poems* (New York: Ecco, 2012); and for "Days Like Today." Used by arrangement with Georges Borchardt, Inc., for the author.

Lynn Behrendt for "I Want Garments Made of Goat Hair" and "Shirt." Used by permission of the author.

Cara Benson for "you show me a capitalist" and "headline," as originally printed in the chapbook *spreek* with the Dusie Kollektiv. Used by permission of the author.

Celia Bland for "Revenant," as originally printed in *Connotation Press: an On-Line Artifact*; "Red is In / White is Out," as originally printed in *Lumina;* and "Note to Self." Used by permission of the author.

JJ Blickstein for "Analog Clock," as originally printed in *Big Bridge*; "Pink and dark sewer with a fistful of flies," as originally printed in *Skidrow Penthouse* and *POEM: Poets on an Exchange Mission*; "Graffiti;" and "Soot." Used by permission of the author.

Elizabeth Bryant for an excerpt from *Fluorescence Buzz*, as originally printed as a chapbook of the same name with Dusie Kollektiv; and "moss is mostly a cultural problem" as also published with Dusie Kollektiv. Used by permission of the author.

Andy Clausen for "The Newly Opened Sky" and "Off Duty." Used by permission of the author.

Brenda Coultas for "A Gaze," as originally printed in *The Brooklyn Rail*. Used by permission of the author.

Dorota Czerner for "River Between," as originally published in *House Organ*. Used by permission of the author.

Caroline Crumpacker for "We Embrace Imprecision as a Side-Effect of Distance" and "A Charm Detection," as originally published in *The Institution at Her Twilight* with the Dusie Kollectiv in 2011. Used by permission of the author.

Tim Davis for "One Useful Poem," "Five Rejectable Proposals for the Jonathan Williams Memorial off the side entrance of the Space Station, Mir," "Original Ideas in Magic (10 Parts)," and "Postcard." Used by permission of the author.

Marcella Durand for "Geometrical Devices 1" and "Geometrical Devices 2" as originally published in *Dusie: the Ecopoethics issue*; for portions of "In this world previous to ours" as published in *Staging Ground*; and for "Geometrical Devices 3" and "water into the machine." Used by Permission of the author.

Christopher Funkhauser for "Back Up State." Used by permission of the author.

Daniel Gilhuly for "Bottle Brush Cypress" and "Pawky." Used by permission of the author.

Philip Good for "Who Put That There." Used by permission of the author.

Sylvia Mae Gorelick for "Remorques." Used by permission of the author.

Anne Gorrick for "To Take the Thought and Turn it into a Scar" (an excerpt), as originally printed in *kadar koli*; "Sleeping in Skin," as originally printed in *I-Formation (Book Two)* (Bristol, UK: Shearsman Books, 2012); and "Our Secular Rituals on Cubist Stairs," as originally printed in *Blackbox Manifold.* Used by permission of the author.

Lee Gould for "I Love the Word Accompany," "I Was in Love With the Perfection of Your Apples" and "Metro North to Poughkeepsie." Used by permission of the author.

Lea Graham for "Crushed in Poughkeepsie Time" as originally printed in *Hough & Helix & Where & Here & You* and subsequently appeared in *Notre Dame Review*; and for "Crushed Psalms," as originally published in *Hough & Helix & Where & Here & You* (Washington, DC: No Tell Books, 2011). Used by permission of the author.

Nancy O. Graham for "Away the overjoyed Cinderella," "The fox swam into the river with the Gingerbread Boy," and "He galloped up the hill." Used by permission of the author.

Janet Hamill for "Guinea Pig D'Orloff" and "Not an Enraged Aviary." Used by permission of the author.

Jim Handlin for "The Stop" and "Lanterns." Used by permission of the author.

Cole Heinowitz for "Spring Poem," "Conventional Poem," and an excerpt from "The Rubicon." Used by permission of the author.

Claire Hero for "Out of the Afterpastures," "I Am Made of Many Doors," "Penned Inside," "Redness in the Grass," "Throught the Eye," and "stag," originally published in *Sing, Mongrel* (Mesilla Park, NM: Noemi Press, 2009); and *"making Dolly," "sucking Dolly,"* and *"infecting Dolly,"* as originally published in *Dollyland* (Grafton, VT: Tarpaulin Sky Press, 2012). Used by permission of the author.

Steve Hirsch for "Americade Suite," "Over the Hudson Once Again," and "Ramapo 500 – Poconos." Used by permission of the author.

Mikhail Horowitz for "Myth," as originally published in *Matter*, "Postmerz" and "Trading Fours." Used by permission of the author.

Bethany Ides for an except from *Plentiful, So Emptily*. Used by permission of the author.

Michael Ives for an excerpt from "Soft Perimeter," "Participation Mystique," and "Tone Poem beginning with a line from Soap Opera Digest." Used by permission of the author.

erica kaufman for "i got a coupon," "poem," "'Receive me kindly, stranger that I am (Sebold)'," and "what is it that recurs?" Used by permission of the author.

Robert Kelly for "Steps"(5-7). Used by permission of the author.

Eric Keenaghan for "Subcityscape." Used by permission of the author.

Sean Killian for "Valley Scene" and "Thinking with an Ancient Poet." Used by permission of the author.

Ann Lauterbach for "Glyph," "Procedural" and "(Untitled) the River." Used by permission of the author.

Timothy Liu for "Currency," as originally published in *Field*; "Five and Dime" as originally published in *Verse*; and for "His Legacy," as originally published in the *Boston Review*. Used by permission of the author.

Bernadette Mayer for "The Way to Keep Going in Antarctica," "Palm Sunday Maple Syrup Poem," and "François Villon Follows the Thin Lion." Used by permission of the author.

Christina Mengert for "As We Are Sung," "Dance as a Metaphor for Thought," "Theatre," and "Diabolus in Musica," as originally printed in *As We Are Sung* (Providence, RI: Burning Deck Press, 2011). Used by permission of the author.

Shiv Mirabito for "Otter Falls Art Action for PLW." Used by permission of the author.

Lori Anderson Moseman for "August | Heaven," published in *All Steel* (New York: Film Forum Press, 2012); "Canoehead Returns to the Hudson *sans* Boat to Bare Forehead"; "Production Assistant Talks Dirt"; and "No Oar No Oracle." Used by permissiokn of the author.

Mark Nowak for "1999 December," "2000 January," and "2004 February." Used by permission of the author.

Pauline Oliveros for "The Earth Worm Also Sings." Used by permission of the author.

Deborah Poe for "Potassium (K)" and "Radium (Ra), or Two Reactions," as originally printed in *Elements* (Ithaca, NY: Stockport Flats, 2010). Used by permission of the author.

George Quasha for "things done for themselves," also published in *Things Done for Themselves (preverbs)* (New York: Marsh Hawk Press, 2015); and "a sense of itself." Used by permission of the author.

Carter Ratcliff for "The Architecture of Your Times" and "How Could I Ever Know." Used by permission of the author.

Evelyn Reilly for "Hence Mystical Cosmetic Over Sunset Landfill" and "Wing/Span/Screw/Cluster (Aves)," as originally published in *Styrofoam* (New York, NY: Roof Books, 2009). Used by permission of the author.

Joan Retallack for "Steinzas in Mediation" and "The Woman in the Chinese Room," as originally published in *How To Do Things With Words* (Los Angeles, CA: Sun & Moon Press, 1998). Used by permission of the author.

Eugene Richie for "Popeye Suite," "Troubled Tintypes," and "Here's Looking at You, Sweetie." Used by permission of the author.

Richard Rizzi for "Deleted Venus..." and "Get me to the Buddha on Time." Used by permission of the author.

David Rothenberg for "Invisibility Begins When / Sky and Earth Are / Indistinguishable." Used by permission of the author.

Michael Ruby for "Sounds of a Summer Morning in the Country," as originally published in *eratio*; "Why Were We So Wild about Wildflowers?" as originally published in *The Baffler*; and "Sounds of a Summer Evening in the Country." Used by permission of the author.

Ed Sanders for "Saying Goodbye," and "Six Years at Brook Farm and Homage to the Luddites," as originally published in *America, a History in Verse, Vol. 6, the 19th Century* (available in PDF format at www.americahistoryinverse.com). Used by permission of the author.

Carolee Schneemann for an excerpt from *ABC - We Print Anything - In The Cards*, (Beuningen, Holland: Brummense Uitgeverij Van Luxe Werkjes, 1977). Used by permission of the author.

Sparrow for "Poem No. 71," "New Slogans," "Shakespeare's Prophecy," "New Sound," "Outsourcing Announcement," "Pronouns / Antinouns," "Above / Title," "Fortune Telling Poem," "Manifesto," and "Techno Poem No. 9." Used by permission of the author.

Christopher Stackhouse for "Fixed" and "Radio," as originally printed in *Plural* (Denver, CO: Counterpath Press, 2013); and "Soft as a melting crayon." Used by permission of the author.

Charles Stein for "There Where You Do Not Think To Be Thinking 6" from *There Where You Do Not Think To Be Thinking: Book 12 from Views from* Tornado Island (The Bronx, NY: Spuyten Duyvil, 2015); and "Views from Tornado Island 6." Used by permission of the author.

Paul Stephens for "Mount Smithson" and "Into the Dusk-Charged Watershed," as originally published in the *Catskill Mountain Review*. Used by permission of the author.

Tom Thompson for "Ever Was," as originally published in the *Boston Review*; "Suddenly the Guards Return to the Priest Called 'Stout Cortez'"; and "Specimen." Used by permission of the author.

Edwin Torres for "The Impossible Sentence," as originally printed in *The PoPedology Of An Ambient Language* (Berkeley, CA: Atelos Press, 2007); and "Moscow '84 Olympics '14." Used by permission of the author.

Sam Truitt for "brim," "tuesday, december 22, 1998," and "saturday, april 22, 2000," as originally published in *Vertical Elegies 6: Street Mete* (Barrytown, NY: Station Hill, 2011); "Night of the Contour," as originally published in *Fence*; and "days (172)" and "Scientific American Gods Algorithm." Used by permission of the author.

Rosanne Wasserman for "Millions of Beads." Used by permission of the author.

Ron Whiteurs for "John Cougar's Mellon Can," as originally performed in the film *Trapped in Amber: The Poetry of Ron Whiteurs* (Bart Thrall, Dir.; Big Time Record Company, 2006). Used by permission of the author.

Peter Lamborn Wilson for "Fu." Used by permission of the author.

Rebecca Wolff for "Palisades" and "Farm Breakfast." Used by permission of the author.

Contributor Biographies

Dorothy Albertini received her MFA from the Milton Avery Graduate School of the Arts at Bard College in 2008. Her work has appeared in *Fence*, *Aufgabe*, *Drunken Boat*, *The Brooklyn Rail*, and *NANO Fiction*, where she was the winner of the first annual NANO fiction contest. The winning piece was also nominated for a Pushcart Prize. She's been a Fellow at the MacDowell Arts Colony, Ucross Foundation, and Blue Mountain Center. She was lucky to co-curate the Bard Roving Reading series with Elizabeth Bryant. She writes in Kingston. Visit dorothyalbertini.com.

L.S. Asekoff, former coordinator of the MFA Poetry Program at Brooklyn College, has published four books of poetry: *Dreams of a Work* (1994) and *North Star* (1997) with Orchises Press; and *The Gate of Horn* (2010) and the verse-novella *Freedom Hill* (2011) with TriQuarterly/Northwestern University Press. His poems have appeared in such magazines as *The New Yorker*, *American Poetry Review*, and *Ninth Letter*. He has received awards from the New York Foundation for the Arts, the National Endowment for the Arts and the Fund for Poetry. In 2012 he was chosen as a Witter Bynner Fellow to the Library of Congress by poet laureate Philip Levine. He received a Guggenheim Fellowship in 2013. He lives in Clermont, New York with his wife, the printmaker Louise Kalin.

John Ashbery was born in Rochester in 1927 and grew up in western New York. After a period spent in Paris, he has lived mostly in New York City and Hudson, New York, where he has a home. His early background was rural; his father was an apple farmer. He often traveled from Rochester to New York City via train and thus was familiar with the landscape of the Hudson Valley from an early age. He also taught for some years at Bard. He feels that his poetry has an Upstate New York quality, but isn't sure what this means. In 2012, he received a National Humanities Medal, presented by President Obama at the White House. He has published many books of poetry, most recently *Breezeway* in 2015. A two-volume set of his translations from the French (poetry and prose) was published in 2014.

Lynn Behrendt's work has appeared in *How2*, *No Tell Motel*, and others. She is the author of four chapbooks: *The Moon As Chance*, *Characters*, *Tinder*, and *Luminous Flux*. A full-length collection, *petals, emblems*, is available from Lunar Chandelier Press. She co-edits the *Annandale Dream Gazette*, a chronicle of poets' dreams, and co-curates the electronic journal *Peep/Show*. She is the editor and publisher of the micropress LINES chapbooks, which has published works by authors including Kimberly Lyons, Robert Kelly, and Ron Silliman. She lives with her son in Red Hook, New York, and works at Bard College doing institutional research.

Cara Benson is the author of "Cara Benson" and of the book *(made)*. She is currently at work on nonfiction fiction: a true novel. She has been published in *The New York Times*, *Boston Review*, and *Best American Poetry* and received a 2011 New York Foundation for the Arts Fellowship in Poetry.

Celia Bland's work has recently appeared in *Word/For Word*, *The Narrative Review* (where her poem "Wasps" was named one of the year's best), and *Drunken Boat*, and will soon appear in *Witness* and *The Virginia Quarterly Review*. The *Madonna Comix*, her collaboration with visual artist Dianne Kornberg, with an introduction by Luc Sante, was published in 2014.

J.J. Blickstein is a poet and former editor/publisher of defunct *Hunger Magazine* and Press. He has worked as a stonemason, landscaper, handyman, dad, illustrator, cook, freelance editor, and is a dedicated student and teacher of Chinese internal martial arts. Books in print include *Barefoot on a Drawing of the Sun* (Fish Drum, Inc., 2006) and a handmade artists' book/CD collaboration with French painter, Jean-Claude Loubieres, entitled *Signs/Signe* (Paris, 2007). A Chapbook, *Vision of Salt & Water* (Bagatela Press, Mexico), was published in 2002. In 2009, as part of a literary contingent, Blickstein journeyed to Cassis, France, on a poet exchange and translation project sponsored by the Carmargo Foundation. *POEM: Poets on an exchange mission* (Fish Drum, Inc., 2009) is the resulting anthology. His work has appeared in numerous journals and anthologies. A new book-length manuscript awaits a home. He lives in Woodstock, New York.

Elizabeth Bryant is the author of seven chapbooks, and *(nevertheless enjoyment*, a full-length serial prose poem published by Quale Press (2011). Her photo/text work appears in the January 2014 installment of the online experimental visual arts journal, *Peep Show*. She formerly co-curated the Bard Roving Reading Series at Bard College, and was selected to curate the 2014 Hudson ArtsWalk Literary event in Hudson, New York. She was a finalist for ArtBridge Kingston 2014, with a selection of photos from a visual storytelling series she's currently working on called *Animal Fragments*. Elizabeth lives, writes and photographs in upstate New York.

Andy Clausen is the author of *Home of the Blues*, *40th Century Man*, *Without Doubt*, and *Iron Curtain of Love*, among others. His adventurous, chaotic, renegade bio is found therein.

Brenda Coultas is the author of *The Marvelous Bones of Time* (2008) and *A Handmade Museum* (2003) from Coffee House Press, which won the Norma Farber Award from The Poetry Society of America and a Greenwall Fund publishing grant from the Academy of American Poets. She has received a New York Foundation for the Arts fellowship and a Lower Manhattan Cultural Council residency. Coultas recently served as visiting poet at Long Island University in Brooklyn, New York. Her poetry can be found in *The Brooklyn Rail*, *Witness*, and *Court Green*. In 2012, she completed an artist's residency at the Emily Harvey Foundation in Venice, Italy, and at the Millay

Colony in Austerlitz, New York. *The Tatters*, a collection of poetry, from Wesleyan University Press was published in 2014. She teaches at Touro College in New York City.

Caroline Crumpacker is a Gemini. She lives in Red Hook, New York, with her lovely daughter Coco and her partner, the puppeteer Roberto Rossi. A bit further upstate, she runs The Millay Colony for the Arts, an artists' residency program. She was a founding Poetry Editor of *Fence*, an editor of the French/American online magazine *Double Change*, and a contributing editor for *Circumference* magazine. She is a member of the Belladonna Collaborative. She has published the chapbooks *Recherche Theories* (Etherdome Press, 2010), *The Institution in Her Twilight* (Dusie Kollectiv, 2011), and *Upon Nostalgia* (Belladonna, 2011). Her poetry, translations, and reviews also appear in numerous anthologies and magazines, including *The Talisman Anthology of Contemporary Chinese Poetry* (Talisman, 2008), *American Poets in the 21st Century: The New Poetics* (Wesleyan University Press, 2007), *Not For Mothers Only* (Fence Books, 2007), and *Love Poems by Younger American Poets* (Verse Press, 2004).

Dorota Czerner completed her studies in philosophy and logic at the University of Paris IV - La Sorbonne. She is an essayist, poet, author of multimedia performances and translator, especially in the fields of philosophy and aesthetics. Coming from a strong phenomenological tradition, Dorota frequently explores the territory associated with the emergence of poetic images as well as voice utterances and their articulation. She is interested in language identity, with particular respect to polylingual or interlingual expression, and conducts extensive curatorial activities, establishing collaborations with artists working in different media. Her most recent works include: "Listening in Poppies", Current Musicology (issue 95, Spring 2013); a poem set to Benjamin Boretz's piano music, published in the special issue of Perspectives of New Music (vol.52/2, 2014 with a CD boxed set); "Red Flower Hotel", a video-poetry collaboration presented at AWANGARDA Gallery of Contemporary Art, Wroclaw (July 2013); "Downtime Spaces" in Pleasure Editions, (Pleasure III: Imagination supplement, 2014); chapbooks At Sea (Two -Suitor Press, 2014); and In Her Wake (www.metambesen.org, 2014). A book of her collected essays, documenting a decade of collaboration with the Polish artist Piotr Skiba, is forthcoming from the publications of Muzeum Współczesne (Contemporary Museum in Wroclaw, Poland) in April 2015. Since 2003, Czerner has been a co-editor of The Open Space Magazine.

Tim Davis is sometimes a poet. Of course, sometimes he is a photographer, video artist, songwriter and musician. If he could hold any job, he would prefer Funeral Critic. He'd like to have a newspaper column, starting in a small town paper, and perhaps finding wide circulation, reviewing mortuary rituals, perhaps sometimes really lambasting someone's choice of verses. Barring that, he is the author of two books of poetry: *American Whatever* (Edge Books, 2004); and *Dailies* (The Figures, 2000). There are poems in some of this books of photographs, such as *My Life in Politics* (Aperture, 2006) and *Illilluminations* (Greenberg Van Doren Gallery,

2009), but mostly, no, no, the monographs are, sadly, just essayed. These books include *The New Antiquity* (Damiani, 2009), *Permanent Collection* (Nazraeli, 2005), and *Lots* (Coromandel Express, 2001). His photographs and videos are in the collections of the Guggenheim, Metropolitan, Whitney, Hirshhorn, Walker, Brooklyn, High, Baltimore, and many other museums, and he has had solo exhibitions in New York, London, Los Angeles, Moscow, Rome, Bologna, Chicago, Brussels, Geneva, Atlanta and Miami. Davis was a Discovery Award winner at the 2004 Arles Photography Festival and was the Joseph H. Hazen Rome Prize Fellow in residence at the American Academy in Rome in 2007-08. He lives in Tivoli, New York, and teaches photography at Bard College.

Marcella Durand's books include *Deep Eco Pre* (with Tina Darragh), *AREA*, *Traffic & Weather* and *Western Capital Rhapsodies*. She is a member of the Belladonna* Collaborative and has received fellowships from the New York Foundation of the Arts and Lower Manhattan Cultural Council, among others. Her essays on the intersections of poetry and ecology have been published in many venues, including *ecopoetics*, *the ecolanguage reader*, *Jacket 2*, *Critiphoria* and others. She has of late been writing of and around Germantown and New York City.

Multimedia artist and scholar **Christopher Funkhouser** is a Professor and Director of the Communication and Media program in the Department of Humanities at New Jersey Institute of Technology. He is author of *Prehistoric Digital Poetry: An Archeology of Forms, 1959-1995* (Alabama, 2007), *New Directions in Digital Poetry* (Continuum, 2012), the chapbooks *pressAgain* (Free Dogma, 2014), *Subsoil Lutes* (Beard of Bees, 2014), *Electro Þerdix* (Least Weasel, 2011), *LambdaMOO_Sessions* (Writer's Forum, 2006), and an e-book (CD-ROM), *Selections 2.0*, published by the Faculty of Creative Multimedia at Multimedia University (Malaysia), where he was a Visiting Fulbright Scholar in 2006. His most recent major project, *Funk's SoundBox 2012*, featured in the exhibition Chercher le Texte at Bibliothèque Nationale de France in 2013, interactively unites more than 400 recordings he produced in 2012. In 2009, the Associated Press commissioned Funkhouser to prepare digital poems for the occasion of Barack Obama's inauguration. In 2010, he was University of Pennsylvania's Center for Programs in Contemporary Writing Fellow in Poetics and Practice. He is a Contributing Editor at *PennSound*, an Advisory Board member of University of Colorado's Media Archaeology Lab, a member of the scientific review committee of the digital literature journal *regards croisés* (University of Paris 8), and the Academic Advisory Board of *Cordite Poetry Review* (Australia). He is on the Literary Advisory Board of the Electronic Literature Organization, the Advisory Board of the Digital Poetry Archive of Canada, and is an External Collaborator with Núcleo de Ciberteatro, Insituto Politécnico do Porto (Portugal). He was Digital Poet-in-Residence at Bowery Poetry Club (New York City).

Daniel Gilhuly was born in Cos Cob, Connecticut, in 1963. He graduated from Columbia University and has a Ph.D. in Filología Griega from the University of Barcelona. He is author of *46 Poems* and numerous novellas. He lives and writes in the Hudson Valley.

Philip Good studied poetry at the St. Marks Poetry Project and Naropa University. He is a graduate of The School Visual Arts in Manhattan. Besides his work as a poet, Good has published articles in the New York *Times*. In the '80s, Good co-edited with Bill DeNoyelles *Blue Smoke*, the last of the mimeo poetry magazines. Good's poetry is published in various small press magazines, including *Pome, Oblek, Bombay Gin, Cover*, and *Brown Box and Holy Tomato*. His work can be found online with *Big Bridge, Exquisite Corpse, Tool*, and *The Volta*. His self-published books include *Drunken Bee Poems, Corn, Passion Come Running*, and *Coffee Poems*. His book *Untitled Writings from a Member of the Blank Generation*, published by Trembling Pillow Press, has been praised by Lisa Jarnot and Michael Gizzi. Of *Untitled Writings*, Michael Gizzi said the "100 poems, maybe more—should have appeared a hundred moons ago." Lisa Jarnot said, "An old friend comes to visit and keeps you up far past your bedtime. The conversation is joyously animated. The gossip is gentle. Curious questions waltz through the room. Who unleashed this light in the darkness? Philip Good, of course." He has read his poetry all across America and abroad. He now lives next to the Kinderhook and Tsatsawassa creeks.

Sylvia Mae Gorelick is a poet and translator based in New York City. Her chapbooks include *Seven Poems for Bill Berkson, Two-Suitor 3* (with Tamas Panitz), and *Olympians, we are breathless* for the "Poetry will be made by all" project, curated by 89plus. Her poems have been published in such journals as *The Brooklyn Rail, Gerry Mulligan, Kunstverein NY*, and *Other Times*. Her writing appeared in *Heide Hatry: Not a Rose,* and her translation work has been published in the fourth volume of *Poems for the Millennium*. Her translation of Paolo D'Iorio's book, *Nietzsche's Journey to Sorrento,* is forthcoming from Chicago University Press.

Anne Gorrick is the author of: *A's Visuality* (BlazeVOX Books, 2015); I-*Formation (Book 2)* (2012); *I-Formation (Book 1)* (2010); and *Kyotologic* (2008), all from Shearsman Books, Bristol, UK. She collaborated with artist Cynthia Winika to produce a limited edition artists' book called *"Swans, the ice," she said* with grants through the Women's Studio Workshop in Rosendale, New York, and the New York Foundation for the Arts. She has also collaborated on large textual and/or visual projects with John Bloomberg-Rissman and Scott Helmes. She curated the reading series Cadmium Text, which focuses on innovative writing in and around the New York's Hudson Valley (see www.cadmiumtextseries.blogspot.com). She also co-curated, with Lynn Behrendt, the electronic journal *Peep/Show*. Her visual art can be seen at www.theropedanceraccompaniesherself.blogspot.com. Anne Gorrick lives in West Park, New York.

After teaching at Goucher College, **Lee Gould** retired to the Hudson Valley. Her poems, essays and reviews have appeared in: *Quarterly West, the Gay and Lesbian Review, The Berkshire Review, Bridges, Chronogram, Passager, Salmagundi*; in England in *Magma* and *Blithe Spirit*; in Canada in *Women and Environments, The Rusty Toque* and others. She curated the Columbia County Council of the Arts literary festival in Hudson for several years, teaches contemporary poetry at Bard College's Lifetime Learning Institute and guides a local poetry workshop. Her poems have been anthologized in: *Burning Bright; Still Against War, Poems for Marie Ponsot; Women Writers of the Hudson Valley.* Her chapbook *Weeds* was published by Finishing Line Press in 2010.

Lea Graham is the author of *Hough & Helix & Where & Here & You, You, You* (No Tell Books, 2011) and the chapbook *Calendar Girls* (above ground press, 2006). Her poems, collaborations, reviews, and articles have been published or are forthcoming in journals and anthologies such as *Fifth Wednesday, Sentence, Notre Dame Review, The Bedside Guide to the No Tell Motel, Second Floor*, and *The Capilano Review*. She is Assistant Professor of English at Marist College in Poughkeepsie, New York, and a native of Northwest Arkansas.

Nancy O. Graham's poems have been published in *BlazeVOX, Chronogram, Eratio*, and *Invisible City*, and her prose in *Café Irreal, Pindeldyboz*, and *Prima Materia*. Many of the sleeptalk recordings she has created, from which she sources her poems, were featured in the broadcast portion of the London-based 2012 AV Festival: As Slow As Possible, now available in an online archive hosted by WFMU. She has lived in the Hudson Valley since 2002.

Janet Hamill is the author of five book of poetry. Her sixth book (a first collection of short fiction), *Tales from the Eternal Cafe*, was released in February 2014 from Three Rooms Press. A strong proponent of the oral tradition, Janet has released two CDs of spoken word and music with the band Lost Ceilings (*Flying Nowhere* and *Genie of the Alphabe*t). Her work has been nominated for the William Carlos Williams Prize and the Pushcart Prize. She presently serves as an artist/adviser at the Seligmann Center for the Arts in Sugar Loaf, NY. A few of the places where she's read and presented workshops include venues in the Hudson Valley, New York City, Boston, Santa Fe, Denver, Seattle, England and Ireland.

Jim Handlin's work has appeared in *Poetry, The Virginia Quarterly, Prairie Schooner, The Patterson Literary Review, Lips*, and others. He is anthologized in *The Haiku Anthology, Blue Stones, Salt Hay*, and *Water Writes: A Hudson River Anthology In Celebration of the Hudson 400*. Jim has received several New Jersey State Council of the Arts Grants for his work and has a poem carved in marble alongside poems by William Carlos Williams, Walt Whitman, and Amiri Baraka, in the New Jersey Transit area of Penn Station in New York City. He is headmaster of Woodstock Day School in Woodstock, New York.

Cole Heinowitz is a poet, scholar, and translator. She is the author of two chapbooks, *Stunning in Muscle Hospital* (Detour Press, 2002) and *The Rubicon* (The Rest Press, 2008) and the collection of poems, plays, and prose, *Daily Chimera* (Incommunicado Press, 1995). Her poems have appeared in journals including *Aufgabe, Fence, The Poker, Clock, The Brooklyn Rail, HOW2, 6X6, Factorial!, Highway Robbery,* and *Mirage 4 Period(ical).* Heinowitz has published articles and essays on Romantic-era and contemporary poetry as well as the critical study, *Spanish America and British Romanticism, 1777-1826: Rewriting Conquest* (Edinburgh University Press, 2010). Her translations of Felipe Vázquez, Luis Vicente de Aguinaga, and Luis Felipe Fabre were published in *Connecting Lines: New Poetry from Mexico* (Sarabande Books, 2006). She is the co-translator, with Peter Valente, of Antonin Artaud's *Selected Late Letters, 1945-1947* (Portable Press at Yo-Yo Labs, 2014) and, with Alexis Graman, of Mario Santiago Papasquiaro's long poem, *Advice from 1 disciple of Marx to 1 Heidegger fanatic* (Wave Books, 2013). Heinowitz is Associate Professor of Literature at Bard College and lives on the banks of the Esopus Creek.

Claire Hero's publications include *Sing, Mongrel* (Noemi Press), and three chapbooks: *Cabinet* (dancing girl press); *afterpastures* (Caketrain); and *Dollyland* (Tarpaulin Sky). Her poems have appeared in *Black Warrior Review, Denver Quarterly, A Public Space, Sous Rature, Handsome,* and elsewhere. Her poetry explores the intersections between the human and the animal world, and the way in which language extends and problematizes systems of human power and dominion. She moved to the Hudson Valley in 2008, and currently teaches at the State University of New York, New Paltz.

Steve Hirsch is a poet, musician, digital publishing guru, and former editor/publisher of the literary magazine *Heaven Bone.* He studied writing and drama at Naropa University in Boulder, Colorado, where he was a student and apprentice of Allen Ginsberg and Chogyam Trungpa Rinpoche, as well as at Bard College where he studied with Robert Kelly. In recent years, he has been riding his Harley all over the Northeast, studying Buddhism, poetry and writing, and playing Latin and African hand drums as a founding member of the drum circle Spirithawk. Steve currently teaches poetry workshops at the College of Poetry in Warwick, New York, where he is a member of the board of advisors. Steve is the author of *Ramapo 500 Affirmations* (Flower Thief, 1998), and he has had poems appear in *Hunger, Napalm Health Spa Report, Pudding, Big Scream, Hazmat Review, Muse Apprentice Guild,* and *Etcetera,* among others. He lives in Washingtonville, New York, with his wife, Karen, and youngest daughter, Jesse Mai.

Mikhail Horowitz is the author of *Big League Poets* (City Lights, 1978), *The Opus of Everything in Nothing Flat* (Red Hill/Outloud, 1993), and *Rafting Into the Afterlife* (Codhill, 2007). His poetry and artwork have been widely published and even more widely ignored and/or reviled in the small-press world. His performance work, with jazz and/or acoustic musicians, has been featured on a dozen CDs, including *The Blues of the Birth* (Sundazed Records) and the anthology album *Bring It On Home*, Vol. II (Columbia Records).

Bethany Ides works with conditions (text, presence, prescience, instability, irrevocability, implicature, dis-use) and this unruly, often hair-triggered work comes to bear as performance, installation, publication, video, sound and/or curation having been presented at places like The Brooklyn Museum, PS122 and Governor's Island. Drawing significantly from methodologies of pedagogy and play, Ides' sprawling, multiphasic works cohere as/with VISITATION, a host-body for de-institutionalizing medium fluidity founded in 2013. *Almost-Although* was one such experiment, a provisional-conditional community of artists, activists, writers, musicians and scholars who convened in Shandaken, NY in improbable shifts, practicing pretending that culture work and culture workers could be non-valuable. *Transient's Theme*, a neverending soap opera-opera, was publicly enacted in iterative installments by Ides and company for over past 3 years before culminating in a month-long ceremony at the cathedral-like Knockdown Center in 2014. In 2006 Ides co-directed and curated The Gilded Pony Performance Festival in Troy and Valley Falls, NY and, in 2002 co-founded *FO (A) RM*, an interdisciplinary journal for arts and research. Her poetic projects include *Indeed, Insist (a mystery)* published by Ugly Duckling Presse and *Approximate L* from Cosa Nostra Editions. Ides often teaches at Pratt, SVA and Bard College, but currently lives in the woods.

Michael Ives is the author of *The External Combustion Engine* and *wavetable*. The language/performance trio, F'loom, which he co-founded, was featured on National Public Radio and the CBC, on radio programs throughout South America and Europe, and in several international anthologies of sound poetry. He has taught in the Written Arts Program at Bard College since 2003.

erica kaufman is the author of *INSTANT CLASSIC* (Roof Books 2013) and *Censory Impulse* (Factory School 2009). She is also the co-editor of *NO GENDER: On the Life and Work of kari edwards* (Venn Diagram 2009). Recent poems were published as *Asterisk 18* (available from Fewer & Further Press). Prose and critical work has appeared or is forthcoming in: *The Color of Vowels: New York School Collaborations* (ed. Mark Silverberg, Palgrave MacMillan, 2013), *Open Space/SFMOMA, Parkett, Rain Taxi, Jacket2*. kaufman is the Associate Director of the Institute for Writing & Thinking at Bard College.

Robert Kelly was born in Brooklyn (Marine Park, Sheepshead Bay, Old Mill, City Line, Crown Heights), studied at City College of New York and Columbia University (1951-1958); worked with and learned from the wonderful poets of the Lower East Side scene—Paul Blackburn, Jerome Rothenberg, David Antin, George Economou, Diane Wakoski, Jackson MacLow, Armand Schwerner—helping develop the Blue Yak bookshop on 10th Street, *Trobar* magazine, and Trobar Books. In 1960 and 1961, he taught at Wagner College on Staten Island. Soon after the inauguration of John Kennedy, he migrated to the Hudson Valley and has lived there ever since, in Annandale, teaching at Bard College. He was the first Poet-in-Residence at CalTech, and has taught or done residencies at Yale, Tufts, University of Southern California, Kansas, Dickinson, Buffalo, and elsewhere. Among his many books of poetry (starting with *Armed Descent*, 1961), are *Finding the Measure, Flesh Dream Book, A Common Shore, The Loom, The Convections, A Strange Market, Lapis, May Day, Sainte Terre, Fire Exit*, and *Uncertainties*. His fiction includes the novels *The Scorpions, Cities*, and *The Book from the Sky*, and five collections of short fiction: *A Transparent Tree, Doctor of Silence, Cat Scratch Fever, Queen of Terrors*, and *Logic of the World*. He has has editorial connections with a number of magazines: *Chelsea Review, Trobar, Matter, Sulfur, Caterpillar*, and *Conjunctions*. With Paris Leary, he edited the big anthology of the poets of the 1960s, *A Controversy of Poets*. Forthcoming are a collection of poems, *The Secret Name of Now*; *Oedipus after Colonus and Other Plays*, five recent plays; a cycle of poems on archeo-linguistics, *Opening the Seals*; and the long poem *The Hexagon*. Pierre Joris and Peter Cockelbergh are editing a two-volume collection of essays by and about Kelly. Kelly currently teaches in the Written Arts Program of Bard College, where he was a founding member of the Milton Avery Graduate School of the Arts (1980-1992). He lives in Annandale with his wife, the translator Charlotte Mandell.

Eric Keenaghan lives in Hudson with his husband, the composer and musician Jeffrey Lependorf, and their furry children, the namesakes of long-dead poets. Author of *Queering Cold War Poetry* and many essays and articles about modern and contemporary poetry, translation, and politics, he teaches in the English Department at the University at Albany. His poetry has previously appeared in *Jacket2, EOAGH, ixnay*, and elsewhere, including a fashion spread for a mainstream Italian weekly for which he and some other poets in New York City had modeled. This incurred the wrath of Italian anarchists who denounced him online as a fraud. But he's wondered since then, Why were the anarchists reading that magazine in the first place?

Sean Killian studied at the University of California at Santa Cruz with Gregory Bateson, Norman O. Brown, William Everson; later, he studied under Robert Duncan in Austria and San Francisco; finally, in New York with Jacques Derrida. He lives in the Hudson Valley—right by the river—and also in Manhattan, East Village. He is interested in the archaeo- of consciousness drawn forth into the 21st century maelstrom and sets his art, as the chapbook *Feint By Feint* (Talisman) declares, in the midst of fighting-jabbing-faking-out-fantast combat—because the future is belligerent and intelligent and so poetry is its own war-farer amid conflicting reports, under spy satellites and drones.

Ann Lauterbach, poet and essayist, is author of eight books of poetry, several collaborations with visual artists (including Ann Hamilton, Joe Brainard and Lucio Pozzi) and an essay collection, *The Night Sky: Writings on the Poetics of Experience*. A lecture/essay, *The Given and the Chosen* was published as a chapbook from Omnidawn in 2011. In 2009, her book of poems *Or to Begin Again* was a finalist for a National Book Award. Her next collection, *Under the Sign*, was recently published by Penguin. She is Ruth and David Schwab Professor of Languages and Literature at Bard College, where she is also co-Director of Writing in the Milton Avery Graduate School of the Arts; she was a Visiting Core Critic at the Yale School of Art (Sculpture) from 2006-20011; and was named Sherry Distinguished Poet at the University of Chicago (2012). Among her awards are a Guggenheim Fellowship and a MacArthur Fellowship. She lives in Germantown, New York.

Timothy Liu (Liu Ti Mo) was born in 1965 in San Jose, California, to immigrant parents from Mainland China. He is the author of eight books of poems, including *Of Thee I Sing*, selected by Publishers Weekly as a 2004 Book-of-the-Year; *Say Goodnight*, which received the 1998 PEN Open Book Margins Award; and *Vox Angelica*, which won the 1992 Poetry Society of America's Norma Farber First Book Award. He has also edited *Word of Mouth: An Anthology of Gay American Poetry*. Translated into ten languages, Liu's poems have appeared in such places as *Best American Poetry*, *Bomb*, *Grand Street*, *Kenyon Review*, *The Nation*, *New American Writing*, *Paris Review*, *Ploughshares*, *Poetry*, *The Pushcart Prize*, *Virginia Quarterly Review*, and *The Yale Review*. His journals and papers are archived in the Berg Collection at the New York Public Library. Liu is a Professor of English at William Paterson University in New Jersey and lives in New York City and Woodstock, New York, with his husband.

Bernadette Mayer's poetry has been praised by John Ashbery as "magnificent." Brenda Coultas calls her a master of "devastating wit." Mayer is the author of more than two dozen volumes of poetry, including *Midwinter Day*, *Sonnets*, *The Desires of Mothers to Please Others in Letters*, and *Poetry State Forest*. Recently published are her works, *The Helens of Troy, NY*; *Studying Hunger Journals*; and *Ethics of Sleep*. A former director of the Poetry Project at St. Mark's Church in the Bowery and co-editor of the conceptual magazine *0 to 9* with Vito Acconci, Mayer has been a key figure on the New York poetry scene for decades.

Christina Mengert is the author of *As We Are Sung* (Burning Deck Press, 2011) and co-editor of *12x12: Conversations in 21st Century Poetry and Poetics* (University of Iowa Press, 2009). She makes films and teaches literature and writing for Bard College's Prison Initiative Program in New York.

Shiv Mirabito is a tantrik Buddhist-Hindu yogi, anthropologist, archivist, artist, photographer, publisher, and poet who began writing as a teenager while living at Allen Ginsberg's Cherry Valley poetry commune. His small press Shivastan has published over 50 chapbooks and broadsides on handmade paper in Nepal since 1997, and he divides his time between India, Nepal, and Woodstock, where he recently opened the Shivastan Poetry Ashram Art Gallery & Book Shop.

Poet **Lori Anderson Moseman** is the author of four poetry collections: All Steel (Flim Forum Press), Temporary Bunk (Swank Books), Persona (Swank Books), and Cultivating Excess (The Eighth Mountain Press). Her chapbooks are Host (Nous-Zot) and Walking The Dead (Heaven Bone). Anderson Moseman founded the press, Stockport Flats, in the wake of Federal Disaster #1649, a flood along the Upper Delaware River. Recently, her poetry has appeared in: 100WordStory, Barzakh, dislocate, divide, Epoch, PEEP/SHOW: A Taxonomic Exercise in Textual and Visual Seriality, Portland Review, Stolen Island, Terrain.org: A Journal of the Built & Natural Environments, Trickhouse. org, Tonopah Review, The Volta.org., and Water~Stone.

Mark Nowak, a 2010 Guggenheim fellow, is the author of *Coal Mountain Elementary* (Coffee House Press, 2009) and *Shut Up Shut Down* (Coffee House Press, 2004), a *New York Times* "Editor's Choice." A native of Buffalo, Nowak currently directs the MFA program at Manhattanville College in Purchase, New York. A complete bibliography for his forthcoming book *The Workers* is available upon request.

Pauline Oliveros (1932) has influenced American music extensively in her career spanning more than 60 years as a composer, performer, author, and philosopher. She pioneered the concept of Deep Listening, her practice based upon principles of improvisation, electronic music, ritual, teaching and meditation, designed to inspire both trained and untrained musicians to practice the art of listening and responding to environmental conditions in solo and ensemble situations. During the mid-'60s she served as the first director of the Tape Music Center at Mills College, also known as the Center for Contemporary Music, followed by 14 years as Professor of Music and three years as Director of the Center for Music Experiment at the University of California at San Diego. Since 2001, she has served as Distinguished Research Professor of Music in the Arts department at Rensselaer Polytechnic Institute, where she is engaged in research on a National Science Foundation Creative IT project. Her research interests include improvisation, special needs interfaces, telepresence teaching, and performing. She also serves as Darius Milhaud Composer in Residence at Mills College doing telepresence teaching, and she is executive director of Deep Listening Institute, Ltd., where she leads projects in Deep Listening, Adaptive Use Interface. http://paulineoiiveros.us

Deborah Poe is the author of the poetry collections *the last will be stone, too* (Stockport Flats), *Elements* (Stockport Flats), and *Our Parenthetical Ontology* (CustomWords), as well as a novella in verse, *Hélène* (Furniture Press). In addition, Deborah co-edited *Between Worlds: An Anthology of Fiction and Criticism* (Peter Lang). Deborah's writing regularly appears in journals, recently in*Jacket 2*, *Court Green*, *Handsome*, *Coconut*, and *Denver Quarterly*. Her visual work—including video poems and handmade books—has been exhibited at Casper College's Handmade/Homemade Sister Exhibit (Casper, Wyoming), Al-Mutanabbi Street Starts Here (New York City), University of Arizona Poetry Center's Poetry Off the Page Symposium

(Tucson), the Handmade/Homemade Sister Exhibit at Brodsky Gallery (Philadelphia), and ONN/OF "a light festival" (Seattle). Deborah Poe is Associate Professor of English at Pace University, Pleasantville, where she teaches creative writing and literature, directs the creative writing program, and founded and curates the annual Handmade/Homemade Exhibit at Mortola Library. She and her husband, the writer Karl Bode, live in the town of Kent with Hiro and Djinn—two cats adopted from Mid Hudson Animal Aid in Beacon.

George Quasha, poet, artist and musician, explores a principle complex (axiality/liminality/configuration) in language, sculpture, drawing, video, sound, and performance. Some 20 books include recent poetry: *Verbal Paradise (preverbs)* (2011: Zasterle Press), *Glossodelia Attract (preverbs)* (2015: Station Hill), *The Daimon of the Moment (preverbs)* (2015: Talisman House), *Things Done for Themselves (preverbs)* (2015: Marsh Hawk Press); art: *Axial Stones: An Art of Precarious Balance* [foreword by Carter Ratcliff] (2006: North Atlantic Books); and criticism: *An Art of Limina: Gary Hill's Works and Writings* [with Charles Stein; foreword by Lynne Cooke] (2009: Polígrafa). Anthologies: *America a Prophecy: A New Reading of American Poetry from Pre-Columbian Times to the Present* [with Jerome Rothenberg] (1973: Random House; 2013: Station Hill of Barrytown); *Open Poetry: Four Anthologies of Expanded Poems* [with Ronald Gross] (1973: Simon & Schuster); *An Active Anthology* [with Susan Quasha] (1974: Sumac Press); *The Station Hill Blanchot Reader* [with Charles Stein] (1998). Awards: NEA Fellowship in poetry; Guggenheim Fellowship in video art. His ongoing video work, including *art is/poetry is/music is (Speaking Portraits)*, recording over 1000 artists/poets/composers in 11 countries, has exhibited internationally and online (quasha.com). Art exhibitions include: the Snite Museum of Art, the Dorsky Museum of Art, Baumgartner Gallery, Slought Foundation, etc. Performance of "axial music": Upstate New York, New York City, Seattle, Winston Salem, etc. With artist Susan Quasha he is co-founder/publisher of Station Hill of Barrytown.

Carter Ratcliff is a poet who writes about art. He first published his poetry in *The World* and other magazines in the orbit of the St. Mark's Poetry Project, in downtown Manhattan. In recent years poems of his have appeared in *The Sienese Shredder*, *The Mississippi Review*, *Cimarron Review*, *Hudson River Art*, *Vanitas*, *Cover Magazine*, among other journals; and in *The KGB Bar Book of Poems* (New York: Harper Perennial, 2000) and *Poetry After 9/11: An Anthology of New York Poets* (Brooklyn: Melville House, 2001). His books of poetry include *Fever Coast* (New York: Kulchur Press, 1973), *Give Me Tomorrow* (New York: Vehicle Press, 1983), and *Arrivederci, Modernismo* (New York: Libellum Press, 2004). A Contributing Editor of *Art in America*, Ratcliff has published art criticism in leading journals in the United States and Europe, as well as catalogs published by the Museum of Modern Art; El Museo del Barrio; the Guggenheim Museum; the Royal Academy, London; the Stedelijk Museum, Amsterdam; and other institutions. Among his books on art are *The Fate of a Gesture: Jackson Pollock and Postwar American Art* (New York: Farrar, Straus and Giroux, 1996) *Out of the Box: The*

Reinvention of Art 1965-1975 (New York: Allworth Press, 2000), and *Andy Warhol: Portraits* (London: Phaidon Press, 2006). His first novel, *Tequila Mockingbird*, will be published in 2015 by Station Hill Press. Since 2003, Ratcliff has lived with his wife, Phyllis Derfner, in the Hudson River Valley.

Evelyn Reilly's books of poetry include *Apocalypso* and *Styrofoam*, both published by Roof Books. Essays and poetry have recently appeared in *Omniverse*, *Jacket2*, *The Eco-language Reader*, *Interim*, *Verse*, *The Arcadia Project: Postmodernism and the Pastoral*, and *The &NOW Awards2: The Best Innovative Writing*. She lives in New York City and Columbia County, New York.

Joan Retallack's *Procedural Elegies / Western Civ Cont'd /* (Roof Books) was an ARTFORUM best book of 2010. Other poetry includes *Memnoir*, *MONGRELISME*, *How To Do Things With Words*, and *Afterrimages*. Retallack's volume on ethics and aesthetics *The Poethical Wager*, and her *Gertrude Stein: Selections* are both from University of California Press. She is the author of *MUSICAGE: John Cage in Conversation with Joan Retallack* (Wesleyan University Press), which received the 1996 America Award in Belles-Lettres. She is also the recipient of a Lannan poetry grant and the Columbia Book Award (chosen by Robert Creeley). Her work is included in the *Norton Anthology of American Postmodern Poetry*. Retallack is John D. and Catherine T. MacArthur Professor of Humanities at Bard College and lives in the Hudson River Valley.

Eugene Richie is the author of *Moiré* and *Island Light* and two collections of poems with Rosanne Wasserman: *Place du Carousel* and *Psyche and Amor*. With Edith Grossman, he co-translated Jaime Manrique's *Scarecrow* and *My Night with Federico García Lorca*, a Lambda Literary Award finalist. He has edited John Ashbery's *Selected Prose* and three bilingual collections of Ashbery's translations of Pierre Martory's poems: with Olivier Brossard, *Oh Lake / Oh lac*, and with Wasserman, *The Landscape Is behind the Door* and *The Landscapist*, a London Poetry Book Society Recommended Translation and a National Book Critics Circle Award finalist. Most recently, with Wasserman, he has co-edited and published Ashbery's new two-volume book, *Collected French Translations*, with Farrar, Straus & Giroux (2014). He was educated at Stanford, Columbia, and New York University, where he earned a Ph.D. in Comparative Literature. He is Director of Creative Writing in the Pace University English Department in New York City.

Richard Rizzi was born on January 1st, 1937, in Brooklyn, New York. After serving in the United States Army in occupied Germany, he returned to the U.S., settled in New York and began his lifelong passion and devotion to the study and exploration of music, poetry, visual, and performing arts. From the late 1950's to the 1970's, he played tenor and alto saxophone, performing with several avant-garde jazz groups in New York and San Francisco. He has written poetry continuously from the 1950's and has been the organizer, founder and co-founder of numerous poetry reading series, benefits for the arts and artistic groups, including the Hudson Valley Poetry Society in 1975 and the poetry/performance group Outists Living in the Country in 1989. His poetry has been published in several literary magazines and publications such as *The Poets Gallery, Long Shot, Arson, Thin Air Magazine,* and a chapbook published by *Hunger Magazine* and Press. Most recently, Richard has traveled to Denmark to perform with the experimental group Trio CHROCH, combining Richard's words to the group's eclectic sounds. Richard has been a long time resident of New Paltz, New York, where currently he resides with his wife Susan.

Musician and philosopher **David Rothenberg** is the author of *Why Birds Sing* (Basic Books and Penguin UK), also published in Italy, Spain, Taiwan, China, Korea, and Germany. In 2006 it was turned into a feature-length TV documentary by the BBC. Rothenberg has also written *Sudden Music, Blue Cliff Record, Hand's End,* and *Always the Mountains.* His writings have appeared in at least eleven languages. His book *Thousand Mile Song* (Basic Books), about making music with whales, is currently being developed into a feature documentary entitled *Whalestock.* As a musician Rothenberg has performed and recorded with Jan Bang, Scanner, Glen Velez, Karl Berger, Peter Gabriel, Ray Phiri, and the Karnataka College of Percussion. His latest major label music CD, *One Dark Night I Left My Silent House,* a duet with pianist Marilyn Crispell, came out on ECM in 2010. Rothenberg's book, *Survival of the Beautiful: Art, Science, and Evolution* was published by Bloomsbury in 2011. His latest, *Bug Music,* just came out from St. Martins Press in April 2013, along with a CD of the same name featuring music made out of encounters with the entomological world. Rothenberg is professor of philosophy and music at the New Jersey Institute of Technology.

Michael Ruby is the author of five full-length poetry books: *At an Intersection* (Alef, 2002), *Window on the City* (BlazeVOX, 2006), *The Edge of the Underworld* (BlazeVOX, 2010), *Compulsive Words* (BlazeVOX, 2010) and *American Songbook* (Ugly Duckling Presse, 2013). His trilogy, *Memories, Dreams and Inner Voices* (Station Hill, 2012), includes *Fleeting Memories,* a UDP web-book. He is also the author of three Dusie chapbooks, *The Star-Spangled Banner, Close Your Eyes* and *Foghorns,* and the co-editor of Bernadette Mayer's collected early books from Station Hill. A graduate of Harvard College and Brown University's writing program, he lives in Brooklyn and works as an editor of U.S. news and political articles at *The Wall Street Journal.*

Edward Sanders is a poet, historian, and musician. From 1998 till completing it in 2011, he wrote the 9-volume *America, a History in Verse.* In late 2011, Da Capo Press published his memoir of the 1960s, *Fug You— An Informal History of the Peace Eye Bookstore, the Fuck You Press, the Fugs and Counterculture in the Lower East Side.* Other books in print include *Tales of Beatnik Glory* (four volumes published in a single edition); *1968, a History in Verse; The Poetry and Life of Allen Ginsberg; The Family,* a history of the Charles Manson murder group;

and *Chekhov*, a biography in verse of Anton Chekhov. Another recent writing project is *Poems for New Orleans*, a book and CD on the history of that great city and its tribulations during and after hurricane Katrina. His selected poems, 1986-2008, *Let's Not Keep Fighting the Trojan War*, has been published by Coffee House Press. He has received a Guggenheim fellowship in poetry, a National Endowment for the Arts fellowship in verse, an American Book Award for his collected poems, a 2012 PEN-Oakland Josephine Miles Prize, and other awards for his writing. Sanders was the founder of the satiric folk/rock group, The Fugs, which has released many albums and CDs during its nearly 50-year history. *Be Free, The Fugs Final CD (Part 2)* was released in February, 2010. He lives in Woodstock, New York, with his wife, the essayist and painter Miriam Sanders, and both are active in environmental and other social issues.

Carolee Schneemann is a multidisciplinary artist who has contributed greatly to the discourse on the body, sexuality, and gender in contemporary art. Recent exhibitions of her work include a retrospective at the Musée Rochechouart in France; an exhibition at the WRO Biennial in Wroclaw, Poland, related to a feature film on her life and work titled *Breaking the Frame*; and an installation in the MoMA's recent show "On Line: Drawing Through the Twentieth Century". Schneemann is the subject of several publications including *Correspondence Course: An Epistolary History of Carolee Schneemann and Her Circle* as well as *Imaging Her Erotics - Essays, Interviews, Projects* and *More Than Meat Joy: Complete Performance Work and Selected Writing*. The Salzburg Museum of Modern Art, Austria, will present a retrospective exhibition of her work in November of 2015.

Sparrow lives in the bucolic but boring hamlet of Phoenicia, New York, with his wife and several quiet mice. His latest palindrome is "Snack computer ebb beret up mock cans."

Christopher Stackhouse is the author the chapbook *Slip* (Corollary press); co-author of image/ text collaboration, *Seismosis* (1913 press) featuring his drawing with text by writer/translator John Keene; and a volume of poems, *Plural* (Counterpath press.) His writing has been published in numerous journals and periodicals including Der Pfeil (Hamburg, DE), American Poet-The Journal of The Academy of American Poets, Modern Painters, Art in America, BOMB Magazine, and The Brooklyn Rail. A frequent contributor to artists' exhibition catalogues, his essay *Basquiat's Poetics* appears in the recently published monograph *Basquiat—The Unknown Notebooks* (Skira Rizzoli/Brooklyn Museum.) He has taught at the New York Center for Art & Media Studies, Bethel University; Naropa University; Ohio State University; Azusa Pacific University; and at the Maryland Institute College of Art.

Charles Stein's work comprises a complexly integrated field of poems, prose reflections, translations, drawings, photographs, lectures, conversations, and performances. Born in 1944 in New York City, he is the author of fourteen books of poetry including *There Where You Do*

Not Think To Be Thinking (Spuyten Duyvil), *From Mimir's Head* (Station Hill Press), a verse translation of *The Odyssey* (North Atlantic Books), and *The Hat Rack Tree* (Station Hill Press). His prose writings include a vision of the Eleusinian Mysteries, *Persephone Unveiled* (North Atlantic Books); a critical study of poet Charles Olson's use of the writing of C.G. Jung, *The Secret of the Black Chrysanthemum* (Station Hill Press); and a collaborative study with George Quasha of the work of Gary Hill, *An Art of Limina: Gary Hill's Works & Writings* (Ediciones Poligrafa). He holds a Ph.D. in literature from the University of Connecticut at Storrs and lives with guitarist, choral director, and research historian, Megan Hastie, in Barrytown, New York. His work can be explored at www.charlessteinpoet.com.

Paul Stephens is the author of *The Poetics of Information Overload: From Gertrude Stein to Conceptual Writing* (University of Minnesota Press, 2015), and has taught at Bard, Emory and Columbia. The selections included here are from *A Climber's Guide to the Catskill High Peaks: A Novel.* He grew up in Vancouver, British Columbia, and now lives in Brooklyn.

Tom Thompson is the author of *Live Feed* and *The Pitch*, two collections of poetry published by Alice James Books. He currently works at an advertising agency and splits his time between Coxsackie and New York City. Find out more at www.tthompson.net.

Edwin Torres is a "lingualisualist" rooted in the languages of sight and sound. A native of New York City, his poetic birth came via The Nuyorican Poets Café as midwifed by The St. Marks Poetry Project. He's the author of eight poetry collections including; *Ameriscopia* (University of Arizona Press), *Yes Thing No Thing* (Roof Books), T*he PoPedology of an Ambient Language* (Atelos Books) and *In The Function of External Circumstances* (Nightboat Books). He's received fellowships from the New York Foundation for the Arts, the Foundation for Contemporary Performing Arts, the Lower Manhattan Cultural Council, and The Poetry Fund, among others. Anthologies include; *American Poets in the 21st Century: Global Poetics* (Wesleyan University Press), *Postmodern American Poetry Vol. 2* (Norton), *Kindergarde: Avant-Garde Poems, Plays and Songs for Children* (Black Radish Books) and *Aloud: Voices From The Nuyorican Poets Cafe* (Holt). He has taught his process-oriented workshop, "Brainlingo: Writing The Voice Of The Body" at many institutions including Poets House and Naropa University, and lives in Beacon, New York.

Born in Washington, D.C., and raised there and in Tokyo, Japan, **Sam Truitt is** the author of five books of poetry in the Vertical Elegies series and been the recipient of the 2011 Howard Fellowship, two Fund for Poetry grants and the 2002 Contemporary Poetry Award from the University of Georgia. His works in digital language arts include "transverse," "shaft/state state/shaft," "Days" and "Dick: A Reading in Strips," an audio-visual interpretation of *Dick: A Vertical Elegy* (Lunar Chandelier, 2014). He has studied and holds degrees from Kenyon College, Brown

University, and the State University of New York and has worked as a stagehand, audio technician, private investigator, carpenter, editor, business writer, and teacher. He is currently a guest lecturer at Bard College and the Executive Director of Station Hill of Barrytown in the Hudson Valley, where he lives with his wife and daughters. For more, including links to AV works: samtruitt.com

Rosanne Wasserman's poems appear widely in anthologies and journals; both John Ashbery and A. R. Ammons included her work in *Best American Poetry*. She has published articles on New York School poets and others, including an interview with Pierre Martory and a memoir of Ruth Stone in *American Poetry Review.* Her poetry books include *Apple Perfume, The Lacemakers, No Archive on Earth,* and *Other Selves,* as well as *Place du Carousel* and *Psyche and Amor,* collaborations with Eugene Richie, with whom she co-edited Ashbery's new two-volume book, *Collected French Translations.* Richie and Wasserman run the Groundwater Press in Hudson and Port Washington, New York, which has published titles by Gerrit Henry, Star Black, Marc Cohen, Susan Baran, Beth Enson, Gyorgyi Voros, and Tom Breidenbach. She studied with Ruth Stone at Indiana University and with David Ignatow at Columbia University. As an editor at the Metropolitan Museum of Art, she helped create many books and exhibition catalogues, including *Metropolitan Cats* and Eliot Porter's *Intimate Landscapes,* while finishing an English degree at the CUNY Graduate Center, where she also studied Greek. She teaches at the United States Merchant Marine Academy, Kings Point, New York.

Born in the Bronx, brought up in the hills of Mahwah New Jersey, **R. Dionysius Whiteurs** has lived in the New Paltz-Rosendale region since 1966. With an MA from SUNY New Paltz, he taught English at that institution in 1970-71 and went on to a long career as unofficial "Poet Laureate" of IBM Publishing in Poughkeepsie, New York. R. Dionysius has starred in the Igneous It production of *Ox Necks in Tweed* on April 3, 1992; performed at Fountain House, New York City; slammed at the Nuyorican Cafe during 1993; performed at the Woodstock Guild's Byrdcliffe Barn as part of Summerjazz (FM Artist's Coalition) in 1992; performed as main feature poet at the Outloud Festival in Claryville in 1994; formed the amateur rock n' roll band Glory-Hole Bishops of the Holy See in which he was lead singer and song writer; recorded four poems and interviews in 1993 for Steve Charney's *Knock on Wood* on WAMC Albany Public Radio; featured in the biographic film *Trapped in Amber* by Bart Thrall of Big Time Records (2006); hosted the 19th Annual Hudson Valley Poet's Fest in the Widow Jane Mine (2009); featured at the 2010 Albany Word Fest; featured at the 17th Annual Bowery Poetry Club Spoken Word; and been published in the *Rondout Review, Abraxas Magazine, The Poets Gallery, Chronogram, Hunger Magazine, Wuzz Buzzin* (Switzerland), *Arabesque* (Shivastan Press), *Home Planet News, Heyday Magazine, Lifeblood,* and *And Then Magazine.* He is the author of *Crowns I Have Made and Other Regalia, with the Poems and Events that Accompanied and Inspired Them* (Epigraph Publishing: Rhinebeck, New York, 2013).

Peter Lamborn Wilson has published some 40 books (translated into 14 languages) on Sufism, dream interpretation, entheogenics, Moorish piracy, science fiction, the Assassins, anarchism, "lost" American history, Persian carpets, angelology, etc. His latest publications are *Black Fez Manifesto* (poetry: Autonomedia); *Ec(o)logues* (poetry: Station Hill of Barrytown); *Atlantis Manifesto*, with Robert Kelly (mixed poetry and prose; Shivastan); and *riverpeople* (poetry: Autonomedia). He inhabits the Hudson Valley.

Rebecca Wolff was born in 1967 in New York City. Since 2007, she has been a fellow at the New York State Writers Institute at the University at Albany. In 1998, Wolff founded Fence, a biannual literary journal which has been in continuous publication; in 2001 she launched Fence Books, which has published more than 70 titles to date. Fence is currently housed at the University at Albany, in partnership with the New York State Writers Institute. In 2002, she launched The Constant Critic, a site for poetry criticism. In 2001, her first poetry collection, Manderley, was selected by Robert Pinsky for the National Poetry Series; her second, Figment, was selected in 2004 by Claudia Rankine for the Barnard Women Poets Prize and published by W. W. Norton. Her third poetry collection, The King, was published by Norton in 2009. A chapbook called WARDEN came out from Ugly Duckling Presse in 2014. Her fourth full-length collection, One Morning—, is out from Wave Books in 2015. Wolff's novel The Beginners was published in 2011 by Riverhead Books; she is at work on a second, called A Cinch. She has published numerous pieces of occasional prose, including "So Long Suckers," in an anthology called Goodbye to All That: Writers on Loving and Leaving New York. Some of her favorite Hudson Valley institutions and organizations include Wave Farm; WGXC, an independent community radio station serving Greene and Columbia counties; Publication Studio in Catskill; Hudson Urban Gardens; Kite's Nest; the Hudson Wellness Clinic; Time and Space Limited. Wolff has been living in Hudson, New York, with her children since 2005. In 2013 she trained as a labor doula, and is now beginning her practice, called Being Birth. Contact her for more information about that at dolldrum@gmail.com.

Author Index

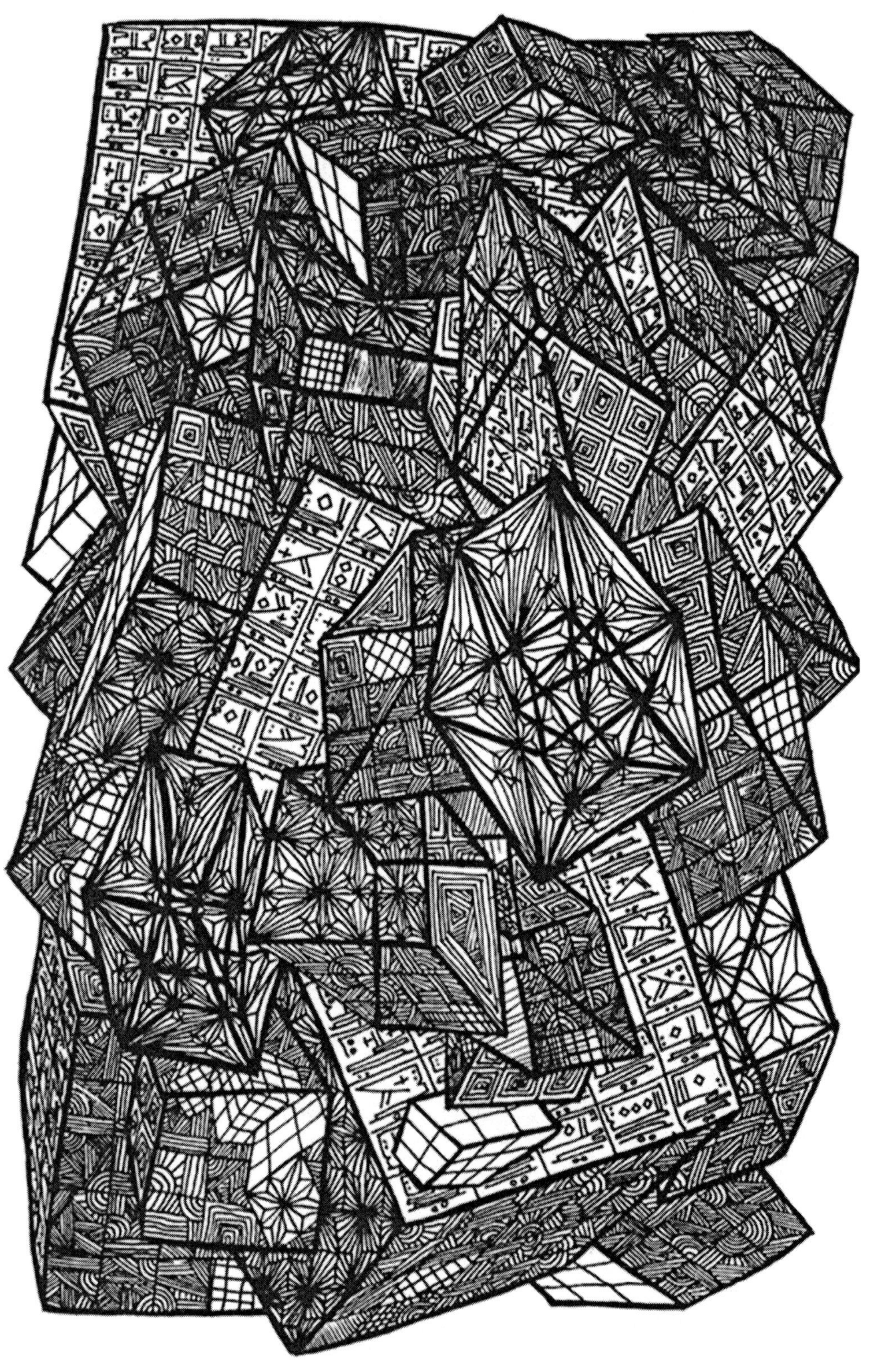

CPSIA information can be obtained at www.ICGtesting.com
Printed in the USA
LVOW09s1422060116

469165LV00001B/1/P